This book shows rut-dwellers and rat-racers how to find freedom, independence and serenity in a way so simple it gets little attention. Guys shouldn't be put off by the benign feminist slant. The observations are not gender specific. From experience I know that a few weeks meandering the byways can make a Thoreau-on-wheels. This book is about trading quiet desperation for joyful reflection on beauty in the world and reaffirming first hand that in the boonies, i.e., away from cities, the good guys far outnumber the bad guys.

— *Robert Sowell, retired chemist, Sandia Labs*
*camper & nature lover*


I recommend this book to all gypsies and wanna-be gypsies. Barb Thacker's tale brings to mind Steinbeck's TRAVELS WITH CHARLEY, except that here the usual greeting isn't about the pedigree of the dog. It is, "Aren't you afraid, a woman traveling alone?" Barb, was not afraid, and, sorry, these pages are not filled with evil road warriors or terrifying highway psychopaths. Instead you will get to know a Toyota Chinook named Tessie, several good Samaritans, roadside characters of every variety, a good dog named Ink, and a very plucky woman whose golden-age restlessness compelled her to follow her bliss — down the highway! This is the travel diary of a clear-headed, un-retirable and resourceful woman who would not be held back by our culture's increasing obsession with the kind of fear that discourages us (particularly women) from pursuing our life dreams and enjoying our own company.

— Michelle Miller, author of HUNGER IN THE FIRST PERSON SINGULAR, editor of CHRISTMAS BLUES

D1555314

Why is it that so many women at mid-age are getting the urge to hit the road in RVs? Barbara Thacker gives you one woman's answer when you join her in this delightful trip cross-country. It is also a great adventure story for those still thinking about living out their fantasies. These "travels with Ink" are part of the new literature about the RV culture — a world that shows Americans mostly at their best.

*— Joan M. Jensen, Professor Emerita of History, NMSU*
*author of ONE FOOT ON THE ROCKIES: WOMEN &*
*CREATIVITY IN THE MODERN AMERICAN WEST*

We dream of being someone extraordinary or doing something extraordinary, but we also have spouses, jobs, children, dogs, cats, houses or other accoutrements that keep us from pursuing some of our dreams. We wait until children are grown or jobs are retired from, and then we often find that we don't have the energy or money to do what we have waited for this time to do. Barb Thacker tells us to "go for it!" Any of you who are yearning for a bit of adventure, but think you don't have the time or the money or the fortitude or the nerve, READ THIS BOOK!

*— Wenda R. Trevathan, Prof of Anthropology, NMSU*
*author of HUMAN BIRTH*

I followed Barb's travels closely for over 12,000 miles and enjoyed her adventures immensely. The rapport she has with people, animals and nature tells us she is in harmony with her world. She inspires us to follow our bliss in which ever way is our way, to be true to our own nature, and thus be in touch with the source of humor and strength which will take us through any adversity. Her openness and surprising lack of fear helped her accept whatever life offered. She learned much from every experience.

*— Adela Amador, author of "Southwest Flavor,"*
*a monthly column in NEW MEXICO MAGAZINE.*

HOW

CAN

I

BE

LOST      —

WHEN

I

DON'T

KNOW

WHERE I'M GOING?

*Barbara Thacker*

Printed in The United States of America
First Printing, 1996
ISBN: 0-938513-20-6
Library of Congress Catalog # 95-83539

**AMADOR PUBLISHERS**
P. O. Box 12335
Albuquerque, NM  87195


[Special Imprint — **Inkwell Press**]

## Dedication

To my children, who said, "Go for it, Mom!"

To my Aunt Dora, who said, "Do it!"

To my Mary, who said, "You'll be okay."

To Pamie, who kept the mail flowing.

To Roland, who steered me through a writing process I found more difficult than steering for 31,000 miles.

THE EASTERN ODYSSEY

# Table of Contents

# I. Tessie Comes into My Life

On August 1, 1988, my older son Scot's thirtieth birthday, I left the small town of Las Cruces, New Mexico, and headed North. Everything for which I had to be accountable was with me, all packed into a neat little 18 foot Toyota Chinook named "Tessie." I had never been camping, had no idea of how it would be, but I knew this seemed the best way for my big black dog, Ink, and me to travel and do a trip. It developed into more of an adventure than I had ever imagined.

I had been thinking about this trip for over a year. I knew that I wanted to be East when the fall foliage was at its peak. The aspens and cottonwoods of the Southwest are gloriously golden, but nothing like the reds, oranges, and pinks of the trees in the East. I had said to my sons, "Really, the nice way to do this would be in a little camper. That way, I don't have to eat in restaurants, don't have to stay in motel rooms. Ink and I will be more comfortable with our own little home on wheels." And, I knew I wanted a Toyota Chinook. That wasn't easy since they had not been made since 1978. All the boys would say is, "Lotsa luck, Mom." However, I had one handed to me.

I have a wonderful friend in Las Cruces who, in turn, has a close friend who owns a Chinook and lives in Naco, Arizona. Lee and Liz had for many years used the Chinook to go to the Ojai Valley in California to hear Krishnamurti lecture. Half jokingly, I would say to Lee, "If Liz ever decides to sell her Chinook, for goodness sake, let me know." Well, in March Liz was in Las Cruces and called me to say that she had a neighbor in Naco who had a Toyota Chinook for sale. She told me that it looked in great shape and gave me John Mitchell's phone number. I called him and it did sound good. So over spring

9

break at New Mexico State University, Samantha and I drove over to Naco to take a look at this little camper.

John had purchased the Chinook from a local car dealer. His understanding was that it had been owned by a couple and he believed that the odometer reading of 36,000 miles was accurate. He loaded me into the camper the minute we arrived and said, "Drive her, Barb." That was quite an experience. I had never driven a camper in my life, but drive her I did — up hills, down dales, through the town of Sierra Vista. And she certainly did seem to run well. John had never used the Chinook for camping. Consequently he knew nothing about the workings of the refrigerator, the stove, or any of the equipment. He had, however, had a new set of extra wide radial tires put on and a new radio with a tape deck installed.

Samantha and I had reservations at the Copper Queen in Bisbee and left John with the promise that we'd see him the next day. It was a fun evening there, although Sam and I were awake more than asleep that night. I had never bought a toy of this magnitude before and I'm afraid my agonizing kept both of us walking the floor. I remember about three in the morning I said to Sam, "My God, it's just what I'm looking for and it has been handed to me. I think I should buy it."

In the morning, back to Naco we drove. At the suggestion of my sons, I had a compression check run by a local mechanic. Sam and I decided we should pop up the top since John had never done that. He sat on the floor in the doorway of the camper and watched with interest as we fumbled, unbuckling the holding straps then pushing on the two handles mounted in the roof with all our might. We got it up and found the canvas in excellent shape.

All of us marveled at how spacious that little camper seemed with the additional headroom. There were even two screened flaps that provided more light and ventilation when the top was extended.

John and I went to the bank, I called my auto insurer for coverage, and by 3 p.m. I was the proud owner of a Toyota

Chinook. It had been a wearing day and I suggested that we spend another night at the Copper Queen. Sam and I both slept soundly the second night and in the morning caravaned back to Las Cruces, Sam driving my car and I driving the Chinook whom we named "Tessie Toyota."

The trip home was uneventful except for the Mexican oranges and grapefruit John had given us rolling around in the back of the camper. The camper felt steady, tho' big, on the Interstate and purred along. We were in Las Cruces before dark. I parked Tessie on the north side of the house next to the garage and there she was — my means for making this journey in spite of the fact that I had no idea of what made her tick. Nor did I have time to fret about it. In that Spring semester of 1988, I was carrying 18 units of upper level work at NMSU.

And so it went. The semester ended the first week of May. In the meantime, I had read of an interim art and architecture session going to Italy for 10 days. Knowing full well that I really had enough to do, I checked into the session. It sounded perfect; only seven students and tours of Rome, Pompeii, Orvieto, and Florence. One should not pass up small pleasures when they present themselves. The opportunities may not come round again. I was off to Italy on my younger son's birthday, May 9.

I arrived home from Italy on May 25 after 48 hours in transit. That's another story, however. Enough to say here that my camera was stolen from my luggage somewhere between Rome and Dallas. Luckily, I had all my exposed film with me; however it hurt to find that my beloved Olympus OM-2 system was gone.

Mark had a business trip to Phoenix and he and his best pal, Jeff, arrived on the 27th about 3 p.m. We all had dinner, then the fellows loaded up the Chinook for a shake-down trip to the Gila. I knew Mark was anxious to see my toy named Tessie, and I was happy to have his assessment. After the boys left, I got some rest. Jet lag plus a heavy cold I had picked up in Italy were taking their toll. Ink was slowly forgiving me for having left her to celebrate her birthday alone. She and Mark have the same birthdate, May 9. We snuggled up on the bed and I assured her she would be with me on the next journey.

Mark and Jeff returned from the Gila on Sunday with the assurance that Tessie was one fine machine and would take me wherever I wanted to go.

It was when we were sitting out on the patio having our coffee on Memorial Day that Mark said, "God, Mom, you are an uncommon woman."

"Why do you say that, my son?"

"I don't have any friends with a mom that wants to take off in a camper like you do."

I recognize that our culture is very gender specific. Women aren't supposed to head out on their own. I could only point out to him that were it his father planning a trip in a camper, no one would think a thing about it.

Oh yes, I was being inundated with warnings: "You must carry a gun." "You can't do that all alone." "What if you break down?" All those constraints of fear. One of the hardest jobs in life is to be who you are. It's a right you must constantly fight for, and especially if you're a woman wanting to do something our culture has defined as male. You're going against the whole acculturation system. We women are the ones who defer, who play roles that are not really us, who always wonder if we have the right to seek our bliss. Most of the time, if we listen to anything other than our own inner voice, we're told that no indeed, we can't do that! Those voices of constraint tend to hold us in the status quo and the status quo can be very comfortable when compared to the unknown. Is it fear of the unknown that constrains so many people? I don't know. I only know I wanted to make this trip, that it felt right to me. I just kept plugging away. As Wayne Dyer so succinctly states in *Pulling Your Own Strings,* "It takes a great deal of self-confidence for people to consult their internal resources to determine what they want to do." How true. And I would add that by hanging in there, by following your own inner voice and doing what you know you want to do, you'll gain an insight into your own unique self you can gain in no other way.

Perhaps, this determination to do my own thing came more easily because three years before I had made the most agonizing decision of my life. I walked away from a 28 year marriage. My husband had only one goal in life, so far as I can determine. It was to retire at fifty, which he did. He left an excellent engineering job, I left my sons and we moved from Orange County, California, to Las Cruces, New Mexico. Unfortunately, we had never sat down and discussed what retirement meant to each of us. I was ready to run and jump, laugh and sing. He was ready to sit and drink in front of the television set. Not much commonality there. Inside, I was shrieking, "Is this all there is?" I was disintegrating and I knew it. After four years of "retirement," I walked.

It was only after I had moved from the family home to a tiny furnished guest house that I became aware of the plight of so many women in our culture. I had a constant stream of friends arriving at my door asking, "How did you have the guts to do it?" I had had no idea there were so many women, especially those with retired husbands, living in such quiet desperation. Really a sad commentary on the "golden years."

What could I say? I could only listen sympathetically and wonder what is wrong with this whole "retirement" set-up. One thing I had going in my favor was that I was still in my fifties — a power point for me, a great and awesome age. I have this cock-eyed theory that retirement age for men in the U.S. is predicated on the fact that their wives will be in their sixties when they reach 65, thus assuring the men of a built-in house servant. I had too many friends in their sixties tell me that they had resigned themselves to the creature comforts, the not uncomfortable status quo, and were just too tired to fight the system. I can relate to that; however, being in my fifties, I still had the strength and determination to fight for the right to some of my goals and dreams.

I had done my duty for my family. My older son, Scot, was married; Mark had a full research assistantship for his Master's degree at N.M. Tech. I felt surely it was my turn. A decision not lightly made nor easily taken, but vitally necessary to my growth and sanity. After grappling with that formidable hurdle, the rest has been relatively easy.

## II. Preparations for the Trip
## The Agony and the Ecstasy

On June 1, I began preparing for this pilgrimage. The logistics were not easy; in fact, they were damned hard. At that time, I was thinking in terms of a trip of approximately four months, returning to Las Cruces in December, and finishing my degree work in the spring semester of 1989. I had told Mark that I hated to think of looking for housing when I returned and he suggested that I just keep my rental house. I knew I couldn't afford to do that even though it would have been comforting to know I had a place to return to. I had a sub-let clause in my lease; however, I recognized that to rent out the house with all my furnishings might prove to be more of a hassle than a blessing. So I let it go. I decided to store all my stuff at Bekins' local warehouse. You can't have it all. You must set priorities.

First order of business for me was setting up finances. I called my investment company and got information on what must be done to have my monthly check deposited directly into a daily passport trust account I had. This account is a joy. It's tied to a Visa card. You can write checks on it, and it earns money market rates. Best of all, it can be used all over the world. All one needs to do is stop at any full service bank and get a cash advance and it's deducted from the account. I had used it in Italy and it seemed an easier way to take care of money needs than carrying traveler's checks or trying to get a check cashed. Indeed, I could have my check deposited monthly just as long as I sent off a letter to that effect. On the sixth, I sent a letter of instruction to the investment firm. I knew the sooner we got this direct deposit set up, the better I'd feel. I certainly didn't want to be on the road and not have money. It is, after all, a necessary evil in the plan.

Checked with Bekins and it would cost approximately $50.00 per month to have 3,000 pounds of furniture stored and insured. Way to go!

In spite of a hectic schedule — lots of friends stopping by to ask if I really was going to do this wild, crazy trip, lots of yard work, obedience classes for Ink, and lots of details to handle, I, at last, found time to get into Tessie and look her over carefully. She was small, but had everything I needed: a two burner propane stove, a sink, a refrigerator, and a potty. Oh, yes, the potty. It was a yellow plastic affair that I had started calling "Big Bertha" and it was really intimidating. As best I could determine, this yellow monstrosity was to be filled with water and chemicals, then from time to time lifted out of the head and dumped. At this point, I had never even seen a dump station. There was a lever at the bottom for dumping Big Bertha's eight-gallon water capacity. I kept looking at her and kept wondering just how I emptied that affair without soaking my feet but decided there must be a way.

The refrigerator did not seem to be working and I could get no lights in the camper when the engine was not running. It was time for help. I called the local RV garage and set up an appointment for June 16 to have the refrigerator, the potty, and the converter unit checked.

As is usual, the camper was in the shop until the 22nd. When I'd call, they'd tell me they had the refrigerator "on line and are burping it." Whatever that meant. When I finally went for Tess, the mechanic who worked on her was very helpful. He showed me how the converter unit worked and told me I needed a deep-cycling battery so that I would have lights when I wasn't plugged into electricity. The refrigerator was working and could be operated on 120 volts, propane, or battery. I inquired about a holding tank and found the cost too high. The mechanic said that the seals on "Big Bertha" no longer held. When I suggested that they would probably swell if she had some water in her, he looked at me rather quizzically and asked, "Are you sure you want to deal with that tank?" Good question. I left the RV place and went to Sears to check on deep-cycling batteries. They had them so I bought one. We set up an appointment to have it installed that evening and I also scheduled an oil change for Tessie. When I got home, I yanked "Big Bertha" out of the camper and filled it with water right there in the middle of the yard. I do believe that the seals would have swelled and worked, but I found that with the potty full of water, there was no way I could move it. My neighbor and I together couldn't budge it! Time for an executive decision. "Big Bertha" was relegated to the garage sale. That evening when I was at Sears, I bought a small hassock-type potty that a small woman could handle easily.

I spent the next morning trying to level the camper. The mechanic had told me that she should be level for the refrigerator to work properly. I put a small bubble level in the refrigerator, then I'd pull forward a bit, hop out and into the camper to check. Then I'd back a bit and into the camper again to check the level. I kept up this routine for two hours. Found the only place Tessie was level was out on the sidewalk. To compound the problem of leveling, when John had put new tires on the camper, he had had larger, wider radials installed on the back which meant that even if the site were level, the camper would not be. It never dawned on me, at that stage of my experience, to place a couple of boards under the front tires. No, I just kept backing and forwarding, laughing wildly as I hopped in and out of the camper to check the bubble. Thank God, I'm not easily discouraged, but it did cross my mind that I really didn't know much about this camping routine.

Some preparations were easier. I was sitting in Tessie after trying the bed for the first time and decided a sleeping bag was the way to go — no bed linens to deal with. I knew it would store easily on the deck along with a large plastic box for clothes. Tessie had come equipped with neat little blue denim storage bags hung in strategic places. There were two compartments for dishes by the stove. She had a shelf for canned goods and one for cooking equipment. The shelves in the clothes closet would accommodate two plastic storage boxes plus my toaster oven and still hold a few jackets and trousers. Ink's dry meal would fit below the hung clothes. I sat there and realized there was adequate space for one who wished to simplify her life. Just no room for excess baggage.

I had bought some of the rubberized matting that holds things secure and how sweet it was to pull out of the drive and not have everything rolling around in the back of the camper. It really does work. I even wrapped the clothes rod with it and never had the hangers slip off.

On the 27th, I popped the top. The spring was formidable. After a good spraying with WD40 it worked more easily, but I knew my arm muscles were going to get a good workout each day. I applied a coat of silastic to all the seams, around the zippers for the flaps, and to a few tiny holes I could see. Then I washed it and Armoralled it. While I was working away, I thought, I still don't understand how this damned convertor unit works. When I went into the house, I called the mechanic and wrote it all down.

On the 28th, I made arrangements for a post office box and joined Good Sam. My next door neighbors had lent me a copy of their Good Sam campground guide. It was such fun to read it and dream. I'm not sure I would ever have gotten myself together for this journey without the support of the Iveses. Ken and Maren were campers. They thought the Chinook was great. They kept assuring me that I'd have a ball, but, from time to time I did have my doubts.

The evening of the full moon, after alerting the Iveses to come looking for me if I was not back by noon, I loaded Ink and a few things into the camper. We headed 15 miles north of Las Cruces to Leasburg State Park to try this camping routine. Well, I'd forgotten a cooking pot and I couldn't get the refrigerator to work. I sat at the picnic table eating cold chili and watched the moon rise over the Organ Mountains. There was something so serene and peaceful about the setting, about this connection with nature, that I was totally unconcerned about the non-working of the refrigerator. I could operate the converter unit and did have lights; however, with that brilliant moon, we didn't need them. Ink hopped up to the passenger seat where I had put her feather pillow and I snuggled into the sleeping bag. We both spent a lot of time that night just looking and listening, savoring the beauty of the setting: the Rio Grande, the Robledo Mountains, the moon's peaceful white light. It was a lovely night. I thought, this is gonna be okay — just as soon as I learn how to operate all these damned gadgets in Tessie. Thank God for my optimism.

The first of July was a day of decision. I knew I wanted to make this journey, so I gave notice to my landlord that I would be vacating the house on August 1. The die was cast. If June was hectic, July was a total scruncher. Too many decisions to make and too many things to do. I vacillated between moments of total panic and moments of total elation; however, I kept plugging away, fighting anxiety attacks and handling all the knotty details.

Ken Ives had suggested taking the good Clarion speakers from my car and using them in the camper. He made boxes for them which fit behind the front seats. He also installed a CB unit for me. Mark had insisted that I have one. Of course, I kept thinking if I had to put out a call for help, I had no idea who might hear that I was a helpless sitting duck, but I did have a CB. When Ken installed those speakers, I knew I'd have great sound and jazz all the way.

I had a friend and previous neighbor, Berchie, who graciously offered to store my car in her lower garage. Since the insurance was scheduled to be renewed on the 15th of July, I took the car out to Berch's on the 14th and put her up, then dropped the insurance.

I was planning to finish my final semester of degree work at NMSU in the spring of '89, so I had packed the car with things I would need for that semester, if I decided not to get my furniture out of storage. I had promised myself this was the last time I was going to pack my life in boxes. This was the twenty-first time in thirty years that I had packed everything up and I made a covenant with myself that it would be the last time. Those boxes would not be unpacked until I was ready to settle in and never move again. I had to keep reminding myself that this time the packing was my choice, nobody else's. But I was really strung out doing all this, packing the car, packing the camper, packing for Bekins, sorting stuff for a garage sale. I remember waking one morning feeling so dragged out and thinking, what am I doing? This is a comfortable life. I have a pleasant little house, good neighbors. There's always that, what am I doing? It's always scary to let go of the cozy status quo. That fear of the unknown is always sticky. Perhaps, it's why so many women stay in situations they'd be better off without. Yes, the comfortable status quo is alluring. However, by this time I was sure I was doing what was right for me. That inner voice kept saying, "It's going to be a grand adventure, hang in there, Barb." I would say to myself, we're not what we eat, we're what we think. And I thought this was the way for me. It had become an inner calling. When Joseph Campbell stated on *The Power of Myth,* "We must all seek our own bliss," I knew he was talking to me.

I kept handling more details. Saw my lawyer and let her know about all my financial matters. Charlotte is my P. R. and needed this information. Besides, I had to recognize that I could have an accident. I wanted to be certain all would be handled properly for my sons. Life hangs by a tenuous thread. None of us has any assurances from one day to the next. Better to acknowledge that death is part of the whole process and have things in order.

I had a bunch of stuff that was too expensive to pay storage on: a ton of rocks my geologist son, Mark, had given me over the years, a potter's wheel, a loom, and porch furniture. Here again, good, kind friends offered to store it for me. On the 21st, Pam came by in her pickup truck and we took two plants I couldn't part with to the Boyces, my wheel and loom to Zindorfs and Pam took all the rocks to her garage. Iveses had offered to store and use porch furniture and a group of outdoor planters. I am very blessed with wonderful friends.

I had placed an ad in the Bulletin for a garage sale for Saturday only, in spite of knowing I really didn't want to grapple with it. Still, I had a bunch of stuff that I had weeded out and what better way to dispose of it? It was the Iveses who came to my rescue. Cheryl, their fifteen-year-old daughter, had said that she'd help me set it up. When Pam and I returned from delivering all my things to friends for storing, I was wise enough to go next door and avail myself of the help so kindly offered. Cheryl was a gem. No emotional ties about old cookie jars for her. She just priced all that junk, carried it to the garage, and displayed it. Her young brother, Ben, polished copper. In about two hours, the sale was ready.

Samantha and her daughter, Thelonika, came to help with the sale on Saturday morning. People were waiting outside when they arrived. By 1 p.m. most of what I considered a bunch of junk was gone. People will buy anything if the price is right.

The highlight of the sale for me was when a sturdy man picked up "Big Bertha," paid the price marked on her, and carted her off as if he'd been looking for a big, yellow pot all his life. Sam, Theo, and I celebrated by going out for a Chinese dinner.

I had scheduled Bekins to take furniture to storage on Friday, July 29. The final days of July were devoted to packing, yardwork, and talking with friends who dropped by. As the house looked more and more like some kind of storage depot, Tessie looked more and more homey. I had hung my cross-eyed retablo on the toilet door, my wooden butterfly over the bed, and even had a green plant with me. After all, this camper was going to be home for a while and she just seemed to expand to hold all the items I wanted with me. I was so tired, I was running on sheer determination, but when I climbed into Tessie, I just knew everything was going to be fine. Even the refrigerator started humming when I plugged it into 120 volt. Perhaps it had one last "burp" in it, but it was working beautifully now.

Ink certainly sensed that we were going to do something. I

worried a bit about how this young exuberant dog was going to fare on our travels, but I did know that this sweet girl would rather be with me than anywhere else. I had found a great 15-foot nylon lead that hooked around the bumper and gave her room to move and leeway to hop into the camper when she desired. Didn't want to lose this lovely travel companion. Samantha had brought Ink to me shortly after I had put down a lovely mutt I had had for 16 years. I had said with Ginger's demise, "No more dogs for awhile." Then, Sam arrived with this black bundle of joy and I was hooked. Ink had been whelped on May 9. Her mother was a purebred English Springer Spaniel and her father a pure-bred Gordon Setter. She was a mellow, sturdy dog. Ink had become an important part of my life and would be with me on the journey. I had a lot of people say she'd be protection; however, I knew Ink and realized that the only protection she might afford was kissing someone to death. This sweet gal was no guard dog. But she was such good company I wouldn't have left her behind for the world.

When Bekins arrived at 9 a.m. on the 29th, everything was ready. I had done all the packing with the exception of some large pictures, glass tops for tables, and one big mirror. It was just a matter of tagging everything and loading it. I was sitting out in the yard watching all this when my neighbor Laars came over. He asked, "Barb, how long will you be gone?" To which I replied, "I don't know. If I head out and find I don't like it, I may be back next week, Laars." By noon, the house was bare. I was so tired I lay down on the floor on my sleeping bag and went sound asleep.

I slept that night in Tessie parked up at the side of the house. Ink was in the back yard, but kept the camper in sight. Then, Saturday I tackled the final cleaning chores. It was infinitely easier with everything out of the way.

By this time, I was moving and looking like some kind of zombie. I was standing in the living room in a state of shock, leaning against the vacuum cleaner when another friend, Lori, arrived. She took one look at me, grabbed the vacuum and did the whole house while I finished more arranging in Tess. I really needed help and here it was. It was a good and generous gesture. We went out for lunch and a final visit. Lori said she thought I was so brave and courageous to set out all by myself. Strange, I didn't view my trip as an act of courage, but many people did. For me, it was just something I wanted and needed to do. I did realize that not many women in our society would make a choice like this. No matter. One must seek her own way, her own bliss. After all, life is a long, solitary road which we must travel alone and in our own way. We're all pilgrims.

The last day! Steve and Mary, my landlords, came by for a final check of their property and found it to their liking. Norma picked me up at noon for a good-bye party with friends. I had asked if she would drive because I feared if I drove away in Tessie, Ink would self-destruct. She knew we were going somewhere in that camper and she wanted to be with me.

With all these dear people, there was this necessity to inquire on my itinerary and schedule. We're all so conditioned to have a plan, to say this is Thursday so I must be in Anytown, USA. My refusal to commit myself to anything but the fact that I was heading North and then East seemed hard for people to accept. For that matter, I wondered if I could ease off and just meander as I hoped to do. I had promised myself that this journey was to take me anywhere I decided to go with stops anywhere that looked inviting. I did not want to set up certain distances each day, just wanted to meander and enjoy. I was so blessed to have the time to do it — no two week vacation from work to see as much as possible. I had time and planned to savor it.

The party was fun. I knew all these friends were concerned about my zany undertaking and I was touched. I assured them I'd not place myself in any compromising positions. Norma gave me a foot-operated tire pump in case of a flat a million miles from help. The Boyces gave me a compass so I'd know whether or not I was headed north. Zindorfs presented me with a bucket and shovel for any archeological studies I might undertake. And Seimers gave me two key rings; one with a big thumb for hitch-hiking, the other with a whistle for protection. Fun things from fun people whom I'd miss.

Returned to the empty house and placed final phone calls to both my sons. Mark had sent me one of his AT&T credit cards and told me he expected a call once a week. I told him I'd not promise that, but would check in. Scot was admonishing me to drive carefully. There was a total role-reversal here. I assured my sons that I would be fine, would drive carefully, and would stay in touch. I had given them my license number and knew if they needed me the State Police would find me somewhere on the nation's highways. I reminded them that no news is good news and that I loved them very much. Took the phone off the wall and packed it in Tessie. After hugs and tearful good-byes to the Iveses, I drove out to park up in Pam's driveway for the night and ease my jangled nerves in her jacuzzi.

Pam Smith is an archeologist with the Bureau of Land Management in Las Cruces. A delightful young woman whose friendship is very precious to me. It was Pam who was going to forward mail to me while I was traveling. Pamie understood my need to do this journey and was so supportive. It was nice to have a quiet evening with this good friend. We stretched out in the jacuzzi, listened to Beethoven, and discussed mail drops. I had to admit to being too frayed to make any more decisions — the synapses would not function. We both knew that mail sent to General Delivery was held for 10 days then returned to the sender. I had decided that small towns with only one zip code and one post office were my preference. Pam said she'd check my local box once a week, sort out magazines and junk mail, and forward to me once a month. Not too definitive, but okay for starters. Pam and I hugged fondly, agreed we'd talk more about mail in the morning, and said our good-nights. I eased on out to Tessie where Ink and I conked.

Pam woke me a little past 6 a.m. with a steaming cup of good, strong coffee. I felt like a truck had run over me, but tension will do that. We decided that Greeley, Colorado, should be the first mail pick-up. I could not make any further decision so told

Pam I'd just have to let her know of future drops once I was underway. With that, we hugged, said "See you later," and Pam left for work. I laboriously got the caravan together for the last details to be handled in Las Cruces. I left Pam's by 9:30 a.m. Stopped at the bank, filled Tessie with gasoline, checked the tire pressure, and noted the odometer read 38,361 miles. Then, to Bekins to pay the moving bill plus three months of storage. Last stop was the veterinarian's for heart-worm pills and a duplicate vaccination certificate for Ink. We were on our way north by noon. I had made it! So far as I could determine, everything was handled. I was now responsible only to myself, my dog, and this neat little Toyota Chinook. Oh, Joy!

# III. On the Road But Close to Home

I was deadly tired, not really with it, and probably should not have been driving; however, this was familiar territory and I was in no hurry. We were driving only as far as Manzano State Park our first day on the road. There were heavy rains north of Truth or Consequences and the arroyos were running full. We stopped on campus at Tech where Ink had a run, then a swim in Turtle Bay. I picked up a few supplies at Safeway, then drove north to Route 60. Felt more with it as we climbed out of the valley and into the cool Manzano country. We arrived at the park about six, took space #16 with electricity, and after backing and forwarding for ten minutes, got Tessie level and plugged in. I had known intuitively where I should go. I had never been to this park, but at 7000 feet, the sites were green with ponderosa and juniper and the air was refreshing and smelled heavenly. It was a perfect place for soothing jangled nerves, getting some rest, and settling into camping life.

Baked a pork chop in the toaster oven, fixed a big salad, and ate at the picnic table. There weren't many campers, but those who strolled past all said hello and fussed over Ink. She roamed and explored a bit, but kept me in sight. At dusk, she hopped into the camper on her own, curled up on her feather pillow, and said good night. I curled up in my sleeping bag feeling fatigued, but happy. We were on our way and thankful to be in this still, serene, cool area.

I woke with the sun. The birds were chirping in the pines. I had had the best night's sleep in ages. Ink wanted to get outside to see what was happening and I put her on her lead. Walked up to the restrooms and had a good, hot shower. Fixed breakfast and ate outside at the picnic table. The hummingbirds were zooming around, the air was heady with the scent of pine, and I felt at peace with the world. It was a day made for rest and relaxation.

I had never washed dishes in the camper, but found a method that worked. Filling the small sink with hot water, I washed everything, put the scrubbed dishes into a bucket on the floor between my feet, drained the sink, put the dishes back into it, then scalded them, dried them, and put them away. All this was done while sitting and enjoying the view. I also walked over and inspected my first dump station. It wasn't very exciting, but when I saw the small drain space, I was really happy I had gotten rid of "Big Bertha." No way I could have drained that monster into that hole without soaking myself. My honey bucket was simple, light, and easy.

Shortly after lunch, the clouds started building and the thunder started rolling. When the rains came, Ink and I curled up and took a nap. Tessie felt snug and cozy and there was no sign of a leak. The rains were with us all evening, so I ate inside. I read awhile. Went to sleep early, feeling my guides were telling me that I really did need the rest. The sound of rain on Tessie's roof was so soothing. Ink was as tired as I. She curled up and seemed content to listen to the rain and snooze, too.

Another beautiful morning. I was gathering strength and feeling more rested, but knew I must move from this idyllic spot. Friends were expecting me in Placitas that afternoon: however, I didn't feel rushed, didn't feel pressured. I had a visit with a couple from El Paso who owned a Dolphin. They told me that the 12-volt connection on their refrigerator did not cool well either. They suggested running the refrigerator on the propane tank, said they'd found that the easiest way. Ink and I walked and gawked, listened to the hummers zooming and enjoyed. About noon, a large group moved into the campground, so we packed it up and headed on.

We drove north through the Manzano Mountains and caught the Interstate at Tijeras Canyon. Zipped through Albuquerque and on north to Placitas. When we got to Bert's house about

3:30 p.m., there was a note on the door saying he'd be back about four. I used the time to find a level spot for Tessie. It still was a difficult task: backing and forwarding and hopping into the camper to check the level. I had thought I might gain weight on the trip just sitting and driving every day. This leveling Tess would provide me with more than enough exercise.

Bert had been a former neighbor in Ranchos de Placitas where we had lived when the boys were young. They have always called him "Uncle Bert." He has remained a constant friend over many years and many moves on our part. He'd told me that he'd not let me leave until I was sure of the workings of that camper. When he rolled in about four, he examined her well. He told me she looked fine, but he didn't think he'd want to make the journey. Since Bert turned 80 this year, I could relate to that. I was blessed to have the opportunity to do this trip while I still had the energy and stamina it would require. Bert did like my little Tess. I was pleased with his assessment.

I hooked into electricity and told him I'd just sleep in my own room. After all, I had to get used to this lifestyle. Ink was bounding around and making herself very much at home. We put her in the house. Then Bert and I went out for Mexican food. We returned early and I did take a long soak in the tub. Said our good-nights and thank-you's and Ink and I settled in for another peaceful night.

It was the next morning when Bert and I were sitting discussing the world's woes that he asked me if there was anything I needed to do before I left the area. I told him that, although I knew it was like looking for a needle in a haystack, I did want to phone camera shops in Albuquerque and see if one of them might have a used Olympus OM-2. I still had no camera to record this journey, mainly because they no longer made the camera I had had stolen. I wanted another like it, but had been told they were impossible to find, so I had put it on the back burner.

A young lad answered at the first shop I called. When I inquired if they might have a used Olympus OM-2, his reply was, "Don't I wish!"

I continued calling, and would you believe, one young lady said, "Hold on." She came back on the line in a few minutes saying, "Yes, we do." Bert and I went into town that afternoon and checked it out. It was fine, a bit more sophisticated than my first one and it had a dating mechanism on it. I bought the camera and a Vivitar lens. I had my means of documenting this trip. What a good omen. Bert and I had a delightful dinner and were home in time to walk Ink and watch a magnificent sunset over the Jemez Mountains. Friday, Bert joined me for lunch in the camper. Tessie will accommodate two people, at least when the table is set up. We drove down to Bernalillo and I topped off Tess's tank. I asked Bert to compute the gas mileage and he found that I was getting approximately 23 m.p.g. That didn't seem bad. When I was ready to leave Bert's and go to visit the Klemzes, he asked, "Well, do you know all about this little machine?" To which I had to answer truthfully, "Hell, no, but I'll learn as I go." Fools rush in where angels fear to tread!

I spent Friday evening with Chuck and Victoria Klemz. Vicky and I talked late. They had just put their lovely old adobe up for sale, so, of course, most of the conversation was about their plans. Chuck gave me some boards for under the front tires so that I could level Tessie on a level site. I put those boards on top of the tape rack on the floor up front. Thank God, I have knowledgeable friends.

I was asked what my itinerary was. It was still North then East. By this time, I was thinking about going to Pennsylvania by way of the north shore of the Great Lakes on the Trans-Canada highway. Nothing certain, but I kept reading my camp guide and having flights of fancy. It was a section of the country I had never seen. I told both Bert and the Klemzes I was not going to get too far from friends until I felt more certain of myself and the camper. Planned to stay on familiar turf until I was more secure.

Saturday morning we said good-byes, and wished the Klemzes

good luck on the sale of their property, if it was what they wanted. And the "gypsy caravan" headed out. I knew I wanted to go through the Jemez country with its magnificent red rock scenery. It's always been an especially pleasant area of New Mexico for me. But, then, most areas in New Mexico are. This state has always been a power point for me.

Told Klemzes, "I think I'll only drive as far as Fenton Lake today." Remembering Fenton as it had been twenty years before: a dirt road into it, a quiet, little lake, and never many people. So I headed west on Route 44 to the Jemez country, through a whiz of a rain storm. Tessie didn't mind the rain a bit, but Ink sat and tried to bite the windshield wipers as they waved back and forth.

When we got to the turn-off, the road was paved. Headed on back only to discover that Fenton Lake is a State Park now. There were wall-to-wall people. It was a Saturday afternoon. I drove through and looked. There weren't many spaces, but I did find one and pulled into it. However, I thought, No, I can't stand this zoo. And it was a zoo — people drinking beer and pitching horseshoes, kids screaming and running everywhere. This wasn't the Fenton Lake I had known. It was early and I decided to drive farther, which was probably a mistake. But I made a lot of errors in judgment on the trip. On we drove.

Got to Bandelier and everything was jammed up there, too. It was a fact I hadn't taken into consideration. August is vacation month and there are a lot of people in our forests.

I decided we must get to The Ranch. That quiet, wonderful place, The Ghost Ranch. I had never camped there, but knew there was a campground. Rolled through Los Alamos, Española, and on north to Abiquiu and The Ranch.

It was about 6 p.m. when I pulled in and stopped at the office. I was tired and a bit frayed. I wasn't used to all the driving and was very new at this whole routine. Charles greeted me warmly, but said there were no campsites available. I said, "I just can't drive any farther tonight, Charles. Please would you call the Grahams and see if there's not someplace I can just park up?" I think he sensed the small panic in me because he suggested driving on up to the campground to check on any spaces. Sure enough, I did find a great spot among the junipers and proceeded to settle in, thanking my God for little favors. I was still setting up when here came Chuck and Ginny in a golf cart. These two wonderful, supportive people had left a house full of dinner guests to zip up and greet me with, "How great for you to surface, we haven't heard from you for a while. What's going on?"

When I told them I was heading out in the camper, they understood perfectly and affirmed my decision to make this journey. Then, they told me they were leaving the Ranch, had bought a house in Durango, Colorado. After seven years of service to the Ranch, they felt that they must take another route. It was a short, but meaningful, visit with two very special people.

I stayed through the week-end in this magical place. The Ranch is one of those uncanny spots where I feel totally centered. All the trivia of everyday living seems so unimportant here. I wasn't in any hurry. I had no place I had to be. So I stayed Saturday and Sunday nights and replenished myself. Ink and I took long walks over the mesas and enjoyed the glorious scenery. I unwound even more.

I am a *Comadre* of the Ghost Ranch. It was pleasant to see the picnic tables in the campground that I had helped paint one summer when I had spent two weeks in Service Corps. The Ghost Ranch is owned by the Presbyterian Church and bills itself as an adult learning center; however, it is much more. I'm not a Presbyterian nor affiliated with any formal religious order, but this is a special place for me. There is no proselytizing and there are always wonderful, interesting people.

Monday, August 8, the gypsy caravan headed on North. We were getting farther and farther from home base, but I had a week of driving under my belt and was feeling better all the time. I certainly felt more rested than the previous Monday when I had left Las Cruces. I felt no hurry on setting out. I liked to have my coffee and look at the scenery, just slow and easy.

Usually, other campers would stop to visit, so I never left at the crack of dawn, just whenever I was ready. And, there were necessary details to attend to before leaving; wash dishes, secure all the stuff, pull the top down and belt it, unplug the electrical cord — lots of details for safe traveling. I felt it was better to take my time and know that all was done.

# IV. Rocky Mountain High

We didn't get away from the Ranch until eleven. Drove on north on Route 84 through the little town of Chama. It hasn't changed much over so many years; a good fishing town with a beautiful old train station which is the terminus for the Cumbres Toltec narrow gauge railroad. I have taken the trip and so decided that we'd follow the route over La Manga Pass which parallels the train tracks. Tessie climbed La Manga with no trouble. The meadows were a riot of yellow and blue wildflowers. Cattle were grazing on green grass.

On the downhill side of the pass, I pulled off the road to fix some lunch. I would just pull off somewhere comfortable, sit down in the back and fix myself a sandwich while Ink roamed and got some exercise. I went outside to eat and enjoy the heady aroma of those lush alpine meadows and, Lord, I heard the train whistle. Thought, oh boy, it's gonna come right by us. For I had parked above a glorious meadow with the tracks running right through it. Finished lunch, then sat there knowing the train would be coming and thinking what a great picture this would make. After about 10 minutes, the little train came chugging over the hill billowing great clouds of steam looking so picturesque. I was all ready to snap a great photo, only to discover I was out of film. I had bought a roll of only 12 exposures at the camera shop for the initial tryout of this new system and hadn't thought to check my counter. So there I sat, ready to take the picture and no film. I used a few choice expletives: Well, damn. Well, hell. I don't believe this! But such is life. Didn't get a picture, but watched the train slip by and on down the hill out of sight. Then we were on our way. I kicked myself mentally a few more times for not checking my exposure gauge. Promised myself to see to it that I had a supply of film at all times while on this journey.

We coasted down La Manga Pass and into Alamosa, Colorado, where I decided I had better get food, money, and gasoline. While I was gassing, I inquired about a full service bank. They directed me back through town. Went in and used my Visa for a cash advance with no problem. Surely did find this a much simpler way to handle the finances than carrying traveler's checks or large sums of cash. Any bank in any town would advance money against my Visa card; however, it was just deducted from my passport account and I didn't have to worry about paying the charges. So simple.

I had decided to spend the night somewhere around Creede by the headwaters of the Rio Grande. I knew I wanted to make the trip over to Lake City. It's a paved road now, but I can remember when it was dirt and a bear of a drive. The scenery is magnificent. Seemed that Creede was the logical place to spend the night and then head over the mountains to Lake City in the morning.

We turned off the highway at South Fork and headed northwest on Route 149 towards Creede, driving along the banks of the Rio Grande. It's such a different river in this area. A clear, pure tumbling mountain stream filled with trout. Not that sluggish mud-silted river in southern New Mexico. A glorious river and glorious country.

Here again I kept running into the problem of all the campgrounds being filled. I had never thought about this, had not realized how many campers there were out there, especially during the summer season. It was getting late and I was getting tired. I still wasn't used to driving the Chinook all day long or even partial days. Kept pulling into campgrounds all along the river. Everything was filled.

When we got to Creede, where according to my camper guide there was a campground, I couldn't find it. It was about 5:30 p.m. and I thought, My God, I can't possibly handle that tortuous mountain road to Lake City tonight. What am I going to do? I did take comfort in knowing that I had shelter, food and all I needed right there on wheels with me.

However, as I had assured so many people who had questioned the safety of traveling alone, I would not place myself in any compromising positions. At this point, there was no way I was inclined to just pull off the road and be a sitting duck for anyone; if indeed there was anyone out there. It did not seem a wise thing to do.

We were on the highway out of Creede driving towards Lake City when the solution came to me — I'll just pull into the Wetherill ranch, a place where we'd had delightful times when the boys were young. A special place to me, as were the owners, Charlie and Hilda Kipp. I thought, surely I can park up somewhere at the ranch for the night, Charlie and Hilda won't mind. So into Wetherill Ranch we rolled.

I stopped at the ranch house and went into the office. A nice looking man came up and asked, "May I help you?"

"Might the Kipps be here?"

"Well, they have the cabin across the river now, I don't know whether they're there or not."

I had known that their daughter Barbara and her husband were running the ranch and Hilda and Charlie kept the cabin across the Rio Grande. They were no longer handling the daily operations. Hilda had mentioned matters were a little iffy since Barbara and her husband were contemplating a divorce. This gentleman said, "I don't see a car over there and don't think Charlie and Hilda are there today. May I give you a hand? I'm the new owner of the ranch."

"Oh, I thought Barb and her husband were running the ranch."

"I'm her ex-husband."

I thought to myself, well, you've stuck your foot in your mouth again, Barb.

He introduced himself as George Hughes. I explained my problem, "George, I've been a guest here at the ranch many times and know Charlie and Hilda well. We brought our older son, Scot, here first when he was a year old. He slept in the crib

Charlie had made for his kids. I've found all the campgrounds along the river are full, and I know I can't make it to Lake City tonight. Is there someplace here at the ranch I could park up?"

George and I walked out to Tessie and he asked, "Is that little thing all self-contained?"

"Oh, yeah. I have electricity, a potty, stove, and refrigerator. Yeah, no problem there. I don't have to plug in anywhere or need anything but a little space."

George was quite intrigued with my camper. "Gee, that's just exactly what I'd like to have."

"Well, she certainly seems fine to me. I don't know much about her yet, but so far, so good." I told him about my plans.

George, bless his heart, offered, "Just pull up any place you like. Over by the far cabins there, just wherever you want to be. It's fine with me." I, of course, offered to pay him for the space, but he wouldn't take a cent. Sweet man.

Since the restaurant was open, I thought the least I could do was have dinner — this seemed a way of repaying George for his kindness. Ink and I drove over and found a good spot for Tess beyond the far guest cabin. Parked up, popped the top and got her settled. Ink was exploring the meadow and having a ball. George had said she didn't need to be tied. We walked over to the restaurant where Ink immediately met a dog and was happy to visit and romp with him. Although she wasn't sure about my going into the restaurant and leaving her outside, she stayed close to the door and waited for me. No chance of losing this young gal. I had a delicious steak dinner.

After dinner, Ink and I wandered back to Tessie. It was getting dark and cool. The ranch is at 8600 feet and the nights get chilly even in August. The stars were brilliant and seemed within reach. We were parked off the highway in a very special place. I was only sorry that the Kipps had not been there. Tessie felt snug and cozy. I slept soundly, feeling safe and secure and knowing my guides had led me well.

I woke with the sun, only to discover ice on the windshield. It must have been a cold night. When I put the kettle on, the camper warmed quickly. Had breakfast inside, gazing at the great granite cliff southwest of the ranch — solid and sparkling in the sun. Ink loved the cold. She was outside exploring, chasing lizards, and enjoying her total freedom. We finally got on our way about 10 a.m. Took Route 149 toward Lake City. The road is paved now and that is quite an improvement. The scenery is as spectacular as I had remembered. The speed limit was 35 mph, but I don't think we even went that fast. Tessie chugged up and down mountains with style and grace. We stopped in a lovely alpine meadow where Ink had a run. San Luis peak was directly in front of us, its great dome looking orange against the azure sky. I took some pictures and walked a bit. No people, just nature at her best. Heard the call of a flicker somewhere in the distance. I could have been the only person on earth. The solitude was delightful.

Farther along, a road crew was working and traffic was stopped — not much traffic on this narrow, winding back road — certainly none of those great big rigs. We had to wait. I could look down over the ridge to the little lake for which Lake City is named nestled in the valley shimmering blue and lovely.

Wound down the mountain slowly, through Lake City and continued on Route 149. It was getting close to lunch time. As we came over a knoll, in front of us was this huge body of water. The sign read Curecanti National Recreational Area. To the left was a large parking lot, grass and picnic tables, restroom facilities, and boat ramps. Looked the ideal place to lunch, so in we pulled. Very few people here. This area of Colorado was really quiet and unencumbered with lots of tourists, for which I was grateful.

I had lunch, then stretched out in Tessie and reflected a bit about my first full week on the road. I had averaged only about 100 miles a day. I thought to myself that at that rate I'd be years getting to the East Coast. Then, I had to remind myself that the spirit of the journey was to meander and enjoy. There was no need to hurry, no need to worry — just slow and easy. What a great feeling. In our culture it's hard to slow down and smell the roses. I had to work at this from time to time.

The caravan headed on after about an hour. When we came to an intersection just beyond the lunch stop, it was decision time again — shall I go left or right? Checked the map and found that if we turned right we'd be in Gunnison, which is a very cold area. So I opted for turning left and on west. Followed the road beside Curecanti until I spotted a sign which read Black Canyon of the Gunnison National Monument. So, of course, we went up the hill and into the monument where we drove the south rim of this awesome gorge.

The canyon was formed by the slow but continuous and unyielding process of erosion; by one drop of water at a time or by floods when the river ran. My God, what the forces of Mother Nature and a little water can do. It took about two million years to carve the gorge as it is now. And it's still carving but not as fast because of dams upstream. I learned that the Curecanti Reservoir is a result of the damming of the Gunnison River. The Gunnison within the Park drops an average of 95 feet per mile. This is one of the greatest rates of fall of any river in all of North America. That's a lot of force, a whole lot of force.

It was a warm, sunny afternoon and we meandered along the south rim. You had to park up and walk to overlooks to see the full grandeur of the canyon. I did do some, but didn't want to leave Ink too long in the hot camper. Her comfort was important to me and I just couldn't have her too hot. I did walk down to see the formation called the painted wall. This was at Dragon Point. I learned from a sign here that the canyon is always in shadow because of its depth, hence the name Black Canyon. Dragon Point is 2200 feet above the river and the views were breath-taking. This painted wall, which rises so majestically from the bottom of the canyon, is the result of molten material forced under great pressure into the cracks and joints of the base rock. The molten material is pink and shows vividly against the dark, somber grey base rock which I suppose is granite.

It was at this observation point that people were pointing to the sky and asking, "What is that bird?" I looked up and recognized a big, free golden eagle soaring on the thermals. The eagle started to fly off. Not thinking about the people or anything, I yelled out loud, "No, don't leave yet. I want to take your picture." It was uncanny, because this eagle circled back around and I have a picture of him in flight against that incredible blue sky. The people at the point were all muttering, "My God, he acted like he heard you." I don't know about that, but I did get his picture.

We drove to the end of the south rim and then returned. There is a north rim road; however, it's inaccessible and remote. I was still too uncertain at this period in my travels to tackle it. The area shows little imposition by man. Lots of birds: swifts and swallows, vultures, red-tailed hawks, and golden eagles. Gunnison has been a National Monument since 1933 when Herbert Hoover proclaimed it as such. It's quite a large hole, quite an awesome gorge, and quite lovely. Mother Nature does such outstanding design. It was a meaningful, enjoyable side trip.

Back to Route 50 and on west through the town of Montrose, then north to Delta were we spent the night right on the banks of the Gunnison River. A laid back day of traveling west instead of east, but seeing some beautiful country that I had decided I wanted to see.

This was a commercial campground right on the banks of the Gunnison with nice grassy areas. I plugged into electricity, after backing and forwarding in my usual style to get Tessie leveled. Then Ink and I took a walk. She, of course, went down the bank and into the river. Ink was always in the water; loved to swim and cool off and bite at the water after a long day's ride. Although it surely did make a mess in the camper, I could not deny this pup her pleasure.

There were a lot of campers here who were summer residents. They came for the great trout fishing. These fishing people sometimes acted like you were imposing on their space and so they were not always overly friendly. However, it was a nice park. Popped dinner into the toaster oven then leashed Ink and went over to the restrooms for a good, hot shower and shampoo.

Ate dinner at dusk out at the picnic table overlooking the Gunnison River. Then prepared to settle in for the night. The campground was close to the highway and a bridge over the river which was noisy. Every time a car drove over it, it made this funny "brr brr" sound. Ink had crawled into Tess. Some nights she would curl up next to me and some nights she'd go up front to her feather pillow which I put in the passenger seat. She could sleep up there and look out to see what was going on. Some nights I guess she didn't care and would curl up near me. She did her own thing, and appeared to be holding up well. We had over a week of our journey in and we were both doing fine and accommodating each other in our small space. She really did enjoy the cool, clear streams of Colorado. It was much warmer in Delta than it had been at the Ranch. In spite of the "brrr brrr" of the bridge, we both curled up together and were asleep in minutes. My last conscious thought was of that magnificent eagle circling back so that I could get his picture — how lovely!

We didn't get an early start. Headed out of Delta about 11 a.m. on State Route 133 going northeast. It was a two lane, little traveled road winding by clear mountain streams, flower strewn meadows with views of the majestic mountains in all directions. We stopped at a fruit stand and bought fresh peaches, talked with the people there, then meandered through this glorious scenic part of Colorado.

I had looked at the map and noticed a road leading to the right which went to Crested Butte and thought that might be fun. I had never been to Crested Butte and just loved the name. Sure enough, the road was marked. We headed down a hill and past an interesting guest ranch. About three blocks later, the pavement ended. Nothing but gravel. I wasn't sure Tessie was ready for 20 miles of mountainous gravel road, nor did I feel I was ready to tackle it either.

We turned around and went back to Route 133 which led us on north through beautiful country. The weather was great — air like champagne, cool and invigorating, the sun beaming down from an azure, cloudless sky. I had such a sense of well-being and total freedom rolling along in my little home on wheels.

This sense was shattered when we drove by a huge molybdenum plant here in the midst of nature's beauty. It was a total wasteland — acres and acres of desolation from, I suspect, the processing and dumping of waste products. Nothing alive, just nothing. No vegetation, no trees, just evil-looking pools of water. Really gross! I had to wonder what in the world we are doing to this magnificent planet of ours? And, also, is this stuff leaching into the water supply? It was ugly, really ugly. We as a species are being horribly hard on Mother Earth, on Gaia, and we are all losing because of it.

Next thing I knew, we were in Carbondale. It was just a few miles up to Interstate 70 and a straight, easy drive east to Denver. But I didn't like driving the Interstates, they're noisy and crowded and not my bag. So we headed south toward Aspen on Route 82. This was lovely country, except for molybdenum plants, and I had not had my fill of all this beauty.

It was south through Basalt and into the Aspen area. I started complaining about all the traffic and people. It is a charming tourist village, however. As we were passing through town, I spotted a sign for the local college. We turned up to the campus where Ink and I had a leisurely walk and I shot some pictures. Campuses are great rest stops; easy parking, no one around in the summer, and nice walking areas. This small campus of the College of the Rockies was an oasis in the midst of all the tourists. Ink and I enjoyed it.

Next, we tackled Independence Pass. Wow! It's a high one — elevation 12,500 feet and the name seemed appropriate. The highway was excellent — three lanes going up and up and up. It was here that I began to believe old Tessie was going to take us any place we wanted to go. She chugged along, slow, very slow, but steady. No overheating, no problem except that that little 4-cylinder engine does not lend itself to speeding up mountain passes. Tess kept chugging away like the little engine that could, and indeed we did. Arrived at the summit with style and grace and my respect for this engine under me increased. Stopped in the observation area and took some pictures of the snow still lingering in this high country in August.

I was glad I did that pass. I began to have great faith in my Tessie and put aside fears of her breaking down on me. One can waste energy and agonize over this sort of thing. I had to take the tack that it's foolish — another "what if" construct. So I put it up on the Pass and reconciled myself to "if she does break down, I'll handle it." But my faith in that Toyota engine was building. Independence Pass, besides defining how I was feeling, was a great confidence builder for me.

The afternoon drive on Route 82 east was lovely. Meadows lush with wildflowers and tumbling mountain streams. St. Elbert, the highest peak in Colorado, dominated the skyline. A quiet, traffic-less drive; good for the soul. In late afternoon, almost to the Buena Vista-Leadville highway, we passed the Twin Lakes. They were beautiful — not a ripple on these lakes and they mirrored the clear, blue sky so handsomely. We pulled off the highway and enjoyed the serenity of the lakes and mountains while we walked a bit.

When we intersected with Route 24, it was time for another executive decision: left or right? Decided on right and south to Buena Vista for the night. Knew I wanted to go on north through Leadville, but knew I didn't want the cold night that Leadville's elevation promised. I hate to be cold. We followed the Arkansas River down the highway to a commercial campground on the outskirts of Buena Vista.

When I had met with my lawyer, Charlotte, she had mentioned that she and her husband had been renovating an old hotel in Leadville. She inquired, "You're going north, Barb?" I told her that yes, I'd head north first into the high country and Colorado to escape the deadly heat of the valley. She suggested, "If you go through Leadville, stop and go into the Delaware Hotel. Tell them you're a client of mine and they'll let you look around. We've done so much work and I'd love for you to see it."

We were in Leadville about noon on Thursday, August 11. It's a great old mining town at an elevation of 10,150 feet. It's now quite a tourist mecca. A charming town, cool and picturesque. Parked Tessie and knew I didn't have to worry about Ink being hot, so left her to guard the house. I wandered down the main street. The sun was warm and the air crystal clear. The solid brick buildings were a joy. You had to climb two steps up from the street to the sidewalks. I felt like I was back at the turn of the century. There were lots of interesting shops and flowers everywhere. I had spotted the Delaware Hotel on a corner of the main street as I was driving. Slowly made my way back to it, stopping to gaze at fascinating rock specimens in some of the shops.

Knew I had regressed to the turn of the century when I entered the lobby of the Delaware Hotel. I went to the desk and told them I was Charlotte's client. They gave me free rein to look around. The clerk told me they were cleaning the rooms, but to go upstairs and browse. I climbed a solid flight of wooden stairs with lovely newel posts and a wooden bannister that made me wish I could slide down it. Walked up and down the hallways peeking into rooms that had been decorated with care and love. Each room had a handmade quilt hanging on the wall; usually above the bed.

I recognized many of the old designs: wedding ring, around the world, old designs that are a part of our heritage. Charming rooms, some with iron beds and coverlets, but all done in authentic Americana. It was great fun nosing around the Delaware. I was glad Charlotte had suggested I stop. She and her husband have created a unique hotel.

When I got back to the lobby, I went into the deli and bought a corned beef sandwich to take with me for lunch, whenever I decided to have lunch. I had no set schedule for eating either. I ate when I was hungry and stopped when I was tired. Some evenings dinner would be at seven, some at nine — just whenever I got to it. I didn't have anyone to please but myself. Ink didn't seem to mind at all — if she had dinner at six, she ate; if she had it at eight, she ate. But then, Ink was a great travel companion. She never asked "What are we going to have for dinner? When are we going to eat?" It does seem to be one of man's favorite questions. Thank God, my dog didn't burden me with it. We had a free and easy lifestyle.

In front of the hotel was a statue of a miner standing by an iron mining cart filled with flowers. I took a picture of him, then meandered up the street toward the camper. Ink assured me she had been quite comfortable. After a stop for supplies, we headed up Route 91 to connect with Interstate 70 and Denver. I had promised a friend that I'd stop for a short visit, if I got to Denver. We stopped by a bubbly stream where Ink took a swim while I ate my corned beef sandwich. I took a short rest, did a little mind adjustment, and girded my loins for the noise and traffic of the Interstate. Away we went after a rather zig-zag route through some gorgeous Colorado countryside.

I probably would have avoided Denver totally, except that I had promised Chris if I was in the area I would touch base.

Chris Carpenter, a young, intense lad who had been in a creative writing class with me at NMSU. Chris had graduated with a degree in Electrical Engineering and had taken a job with Hughes in Denver. He had written me saying that he expected me to call and have a visit before I headed for the unknown. So, into Denver we rolled on Interstate 70 and then onto Interstate 25, once again heading north.

We pulled into KOA Denver North in late afternoon of August 11. I called Chris, who accepted my invitation to dinner in Tessie. Therefore, it was clean up the camper, set up the table, give Ink a good run, shower, and get ready for my guest.

The campground was typical of so many commercial campgrounds in the United States. Good laundry and shower facilities, a pool and playground for the kids, all those creature comforts for a nation on wheels; however, the traffic noise from the Interstate was horrendous and it suffered from what I term the "sardine effect" — spaces so small that if you stuck your arm out the window, you were touching the camper next to you.

When Chris arrived at 7:30, the table was set with place mats and a candle, Tessie looked cozy, comfortable, and clean. We had baked beef patties, baked potatoes, and artichoke salad with poppy seed dressing, cookies and tea for dessert. Chris chided me a bit, saying, "Boy, you're really roughing it, aren't you, Barb?" To me a good meal at the end of the day was a means of nurturing myself, of saying, "Hey, this has been a good day. I'll have a good meal and give thanks to my God for the blessing of a safe journey."

I did make it a point to eat well on my journey and found it a replenishing ritual. It was a fun evening listening to this intense, intelligent young man's dreams, hopes, and ideas for the future. Still, I don't envy youth the agonizing questioning time it is in everyone's life. So glad that era is over for me, but was happy to let Chris verbalize. It was a good visit, worth fighting the traffic in Denver for. We said our good-byes with an agreement that if my mail wasn't at Greeley, I'd call him and we'd spend the weekend camping in the Rockies.

Next morning, by eleven, we were back on Interstate 25 heading north. Within ten miles, I found a lateral over to Route 85 and took it into Greeley. As we were driving down the street, I spied Old Glory waving grandly and thought there's the Post Office. So we turned right and ambled over. Went in and inquired if they had any General Delivery mail for me. There was a whole packet of mail from Pamie. Shazam! I had to show the postal clerk my driver's license before he would give me the mail, but it looked like this method of staying in touch was going to work.

# V. Black Hills, Badlands and Drought

It was still early after mail pick-up, so we rolled on north through Cheyenne, Wyoming. Route 85 had re-connected with the Interstate — just couldn't avoid it — but here in Wyoming there wasn't much traffic. The mountains were leaving us. They were far over to the West now. We were heading into the grasslands of the United States, the wheat belt, the bread basket of the nation, cow-land, USA. The plains were stretching out before us. The driving was easy, but boring, just a ribbon of highway through this vast expanse. I sat there driving and thinking, gosh, how blessed I am to be able to do this. How good it feels. What total freedom. No hurry, no schedule, just rolling along listening to good jazz as the miles ticked by.

Rolling along in this contemplative mood, I saw a sign for Chugwater. Loved the sound — Chugwater. So we detoured from the Interstate and 85 and drove through Chugwater. There wasn't even a gas station and definitely no bank. It had dawned on me that this was Friday and I should get some money. It was not going to happen in Chugwater, however. There were only two buildings on the main street, a two story saloon and another bar. Great name, though.

It was onward to Wheatland, Wyoming, where I did find a bank and got a cash advance. Wheatland was picturesque; big trees, wide streets, and solid brick houses. We drove north through the town to a small campground written up in my camper guide. There were no campers there, not much going on, very quiet. Went into the office and the lovely lady behind the counter assured me she had space, lots of space. I didn't seem to be on the tourist path. Made arrangements to spend the night, then explained to her that I was going back down the road to a

46

market before I set up. She said I could park up any place I wished and assured me there would be space when I got back. At the market I was struck with the nice, kind, and friendly people in Wheatland. Everyone smiled and said hello. No one seemed in a hurry. How refreshing. When I was checking out, the clerk asked where I was from. I told her and mentioned that I was just meandering and camping and having such a good time. She said, "Oh God, how I'd love to do something like that!" I told her I thought everyone should.

We were back at the campground by 5:30 p.m. There were still no other campers, so we chose a grassy site with a small tree and set up. Ink and I had a long walk, then dinner outside at the picnic table. Watched the sun sink into the vastness of the plains and listened to the birds muttering their goodnight songs. It was quiet and peaceful with no one around. I was beginning to realize that I didn't much care for the sardine effect; people jammed up side by side; however, I still felt the need to pull into facilities that were in my camper guide. I needed the assurance of having someone near by.

After dinner, I put Ink on her lead and walked over for a hot shower and a good scrub. The restroom was blessedly quiet. We turned in early and slept well in this quiet little campground in the friendly town of Wheatland, Wyoming.

Woke in time to watch the sun rise over the plains. Had my coffee and breakfast outside, then washed dishes and policed up the camper for the day's journey. Decided to check in with Mark and Lois as there was a phone booth outside the office. Mark was so right in insisting that I take his AT&T credit card. It was a joy not to have to worry about change for the phones. The kid's first question was, "Mom, where are you?" Told them about my travels so far and that Wheatland was charming. Assured them all was going well and not to worry. Then called Pam and let her know I had received the mail. Suggested Hibbing, Minnesota, as the next pick-up point. I had thought to pack information on zip codes throughout the nation, so I could give Pam a full mailing address. It was wonderful to touch base with loved ones who were always very supportive and encouraging.

We didn't leave until about 11 a.m. I didn't even have the excuse of talking with other campers, just this leisurely, unhurried routine I was settling into so well. Besides, when I didn't hurry, I had everything checked on Tessie and pulled out of the campgrounds knowing all was secure. I had this fear of driving off some morning with the top up.

It was north from Wheatland on Interstate 25 which wasn't trafficked in this area. We drove through fields and fields of cattle, lots of cows. In the fields were huge wooden fences which I assumed afforded the cattle some protection in the winter from storms, snows, and winds. We saw a lot more cattle that morning than we saw people or traffic.

We turned off the Interstate onto Route 18/20, rolling along through plainsland and wide open country. There weren't many towns and the few there were, like Hat Creek and Mule Creek, had populations of less than 100. There was an energy, a flow, in this eastern part of Wyoming for me. It was big sky and vast. We rolled along with ease.

This Saturday there were a lot of motorcycles on 18/20 going both east and west. They would wave and it was nice company. When you're driving along alone, it's really nice to be in an area where the people wave and are friendly. We had just crossed into South Dakota when I spotted a nice picnic area with a shade pavilion and lots of parking space, so we pulled in for a lunch break. There were some bikers there and they informed me that they were having a rally. They all fussed over Ink which made her happy. We visited as we ate, wished the bikers safe journeying and were on our way again, heading for the Black Hills and Custer State Park.

The Black Hills of South Dakota are a fascinating geological formation. This dome that was created years and years ago rises above the plain and I could see it in the distance. The hills are covered with ponderosa pines, about 90% of the pines are ponderosas and from a distance they do look very black. Here's the escarpment, this mountainous area just plunked down by Mother Nature rising above the grasslands like an island. It was formed at least 60 million years ago when the pressures from below pushed these layers up and created this dome about 120 miles long and 60 miles wide here in the prairie. Erosive forces have worn it down and the core of the hills is now revealed as granite.

It was warm, but not oppressively so. Edgemont was the first town we came to in South Dakota on Route 18. It was at an elevation of 3500 feet, but we climbed steadily as we went on north. Drove through Minnekahta Junction and Pringle. The road was winding and mountainous with lots to look at, so we didn't make good time; however, we arrived in Custer fairly early. Here again, I opted for a commercial campground. Obviously, I wasn't ready for camping on my own yet. We found a delightful campground in the heart of the Black Hills close to an entrance to Custer State Park. The grounds were meadowlands at 5000 feet covered with ponderosa pines. This was a family style park, something for everyone — miniature golf, horse shoes, a swimming pool, programs in the evening, and cabins for those who didn't have their house on wheels with them. There was an area with electricity only down by the tent sites amongst the ponderosas which seemed just right. We registered at the office, then parked down in the meadow, cool and smelling of pine.

It was on this evening when I plugged into the electrical outlet that it kept tripping off. I thought possibly there was something wrong with the connection. I'm not much on electrical problems. The extent of my knowledge is that when you turn the switch on, you have light. I walked up to the office and explained my dilemma to accommodating people. The owner came down and tested to see if the connection was working. It was, but my system wasn't. The owner suggested I have the wiring in the camper checked. He also offered, "Well, since you're not using electricity, that's a dollar less and you can stay here in the same place." I said, "Sounds good to me." So there we stayed. Having no connection meant that I could not use the toaster oven nor the radio, but it didn't seem very important. Somehow, life's little frustrations just seemed to fade away for me on this trip. I fixed a big salad and had dinner under the ponderosas while Ink frolicked in the meadow.

There was a couple from Alaska tenting down below us. They had a small hand built trailer in which they carried supplies. It was quite handsome, and over the top, as a hold-down for their canoe, they had used large moose horns. They also had a cute five year old boy who thought Ink was great, and Ink in turn loved his attention. We had a pleasant chat as is par for the course. Campers seem a pleasant lot as a general rule.

When I woke Sunday morning, the sun was beaming and the air was fragrant with the smell of pines. There were distant noises of people tending to their chores. I felt so good, so in sync, and happy to be right where I was. I had heard a camper pull in the night before after dark. Ink had barked and there was an answering bark and the sound of an engine chugging around the meadow. I hadn't bothered to check, but this morning when I looked out, over to my left — not too far from us — was a rather unique camper: low-slung and green — an old Dodge that had been customized. I put Ink out on her lead, had more coffee, stirred about, and finally got out of Tessie. There was a young lady, a beautiful young lady, probably in her thirties, at this unique camper to my left.

She was traveling with her nine year old son and a big dog. But she was the first woman I had met traveling without a man, so we kindred spirits started talking. This young woman was divorced, had been living in Los Angeles, and told me quite frankly that raising a son alone on the L.A. scene was more than she could manage. She was going back to Long Island where she had family and support.

She had bought the camper in Los Angeles from the man who had customized it and she invited me in to see her house on wheels. It was something — big and roomy. She had a washer and dryer, even a roll-top desk in there. She had all the comforts of home. The previous owner had checked her out and she knew all about maintaining that van. She was much more with it on maintenance than was I with my pig in a poke. She did mention that she was getting only 9 mpg on the trip. She planned to head on north and take the Trans-Canadian highway across. I told her I was planning to catch it, too, but wasn't sure where or when. She was a dear and we had such a good talk, one of those wonderful visits women can have — full of support and sisterhood and best of wishes. She did some work under her van and obviously knew what she was doing. Finally pulled out about 3 p.m. after warm hugs and fond good-byes. I was sorry to see her go, she was such a lovely young lady. I didn't see her again. I've often thought of her. Hope she made it home to Long Island and found the support and happiness she sought.

I had decided on that glorious Sunday morning to spend the day in this lovely setting and did just that. Got out my mail and did my paper work at the picnic table. I had a briefcase which served as my office since one must, from time to time, check up on those obligations one cannot avoid. So I balanced my passport account, read and sorted the mail sitting in the pines and enjoying the sun. Ink had met a little dog who had come into the campground. They were romping and chasing. It was a perfect place to take a day off. I did a load of laundry, then strolled up and took a swim. It was a laid back, lazy, lovely day.

I read some brochures available at the office and learned that Custer State Park is a specified area within the larger area designated Black Hills National Forest which straddles the South Dakota-Wyoming border. Lots of touristy stuff to do: helicopter rides around Mt. Rushmore, fishing, buffalo jeep rides, gold mine tours, even Old MacDonald's farm. There are museums of geology, a dinosaur park, old Ft. Meade Cavalry Museum, Black Hills National Cemetery, stage barns, passion plays, and, of course, Mt. Rushmore, which is not within Custer State Park but just north of it.

You can visit the Borglum Museum and learn about the Danish man who was responsible for the sculptures of the four presidents on Mt. Rushmore. He conceived the dream, obtained a grant from the government, and did the sculpture work on this granite mountain. He had worked at Stone Mountain, Georgia, where he learned some techniques that helped him greatly in this outstanding job. He died in 1941 and his son, Lincoln, finished the work at Rushmore. Lincoln became the Memorial's first National Park Service Superintendent.

The federal government and South Dakota authorized the sculpture in 1925. In October of that year the dedication of Mt. Rushmore as a National Memorial occurred. In 1927, the first actual drilling started. On July 4, 1930, the dedication of the Washington figure took place. On August 30, 1936, the Jefferson figure was dedicated; September 17, 1937, dedication of the Lincoln figure; and July 2, 1939, the dedication of Roosevelt. On October 31, 1941, the last work at Rushmore was completed. Originally, the figure of Jefferson was blocked out to the left of Washington, but because of variations in the rock, the Jefferson face was removed in the summer of 1934 and put in the spot where we see it now. This was a great set-back in both time and money. Borglum also realized the damaging effects of water on the granite with cracking and water accumulation freezing and contracting. He devised a putty consisting of white lead, linseed oil, and granite dust to fill the cracks. Each year since the memorial's completion, National Park Service personnel perform a routine inspection of the carvings, still using Borglum's mixture to seal the cracks.

I didn't want to avail myself of the tourist traps. I preferred to stay with Mother Nature. And Mother Nature seemed to be in fine fettle here on this high escarpment in the middle of the plains. She supported such varied wildlife as elk, white-tailed deer, mule deer, prong-horned antelope, mountain goats, coyotes, prairie dogs and lots of small mammals such as raccoons, skunks, marmots, squirrels and chipmunks, plus a great bird population and multitudes of fish in the streams.

I was especially interested in the bison. Read that the herd within the park is controlled. The newborn come in April, May, and June. Generally, 400 to 500 new bison calves are born. They are reddish brown when young rather than chocolate brown. In July, the older bison rejoin the main herd and the grazing season begins. This is when the adult bulls rival one another for breeding rights. The rut lasts until late August or early September. Then the bulls leave the herd once again. The animals are rounded up in October. The surplus animals are sold at the park's live bison auction which is held the third Saturday of November and brings in buyers and spectators from all across the country. The bison have no problem with winter on the open prairie. When it snows they use their short, flat noses as a snow plow to brush the snow aside and expose the grasses.

After a pleasant Sunday of loafing and reading, we had a quiet dinner at the picnic table before dark. Ink's friend came for another good romp. We turned in about nine. I said a special prayer for that courageous young woman on her way back to family in her green, low-slung van.

Delightful as it was, we did pack up and leave this spot late Monday morning. I was ready to see more and drive more. We went past Gordon Stockade to the entrance of Custer State Park. I wanted to take the Wildlife Loop Road which we did. It was mid-day and not the best time to see wildlife, but I hoped to catch a glimpse of some buffalo. We managed that as there was a whole herd of the cumbersome beasties over in a meadow far from the road. I stopped and watched them for a while, regretting that they were not closer. But, at least, we did see buffalo. As we came over a knoll, the traffic was stopped in both directions for there was a group of burros standing smack in the middle of the road. There were ten adults and three cute, furry babies just milling around on the highway. The park personnel call them their "begging burros" and that's exactly what they were doing. They were walking along sticking their big heads into the windows of all the stopped cars as if asking, "Do you have anything for us to eat?" One came right up to our window. Ink wasn't sure what to do about this shaggy creature peering in at her. All of us who had to stop enjoyed the antics of the "begging burros."

We continued around the wildlife loop and then took Route 16A. At an intersection, we came upon a lovely park: pavilion, picnic tables, restrooms, and a neat little pond. There was no one there, so we stopped for lunch. I ate and Ink took a swim. I recognized the flicker's shrill call among all the various chirping and chipping sounds of many birds. We loafed around that lovely spot for an hour or so, then traveled on north and stopped at the Peter Norbeck Memorial Overlook. Peter Norbeck had been a governor and a U.S. Senator of South Dakota. He was a conservationist, a friend of Teddy Roosevelt's, and was responsible for designing the tunnels along Iron Mountain Road. Fascinating tunnels — there were three — which framed Mt. Rushmore in the distance as you drove through them. And there were beautiful wooden trestle bridges. It was a very scenic road in most areas, but there was also along this road graphic evidence of the burn-off from the fires they had had that summer. It was the summer of the great drought in the northern United States. It was the topic of conversation everywhere. I don't know how many acres were burned. It wasn't close to lush gameland, but it was a destructive fire in what had been a heavily forested area. I did walk up and view the scene from the overlook. The elevation here was 5500 feet and it was cool. So I took a short stroll and enjoyed the sweeping panoramas of the Black Hills and Mt. Rushmore that the observation deck encompassed.

We continued on up Iron Mountain Road and through the tunnels. I kept wanting to stop in one of them and take a picture of Rushmore framed directly in front of me; however, this was a two-way road. I decided for the safety of all concerned not to try such a thing. Instead, I pulled off under one of the lovely wooden trestles and shot pictures of the tunnel from beneath it.

We arrived in the parking area at Mt. Rushmore about 1 p.m. and it was hot, about 95 degrees. The area was wall-to-wall people; a seething mass of humanity. This is an attraction for visitors from all over the world and rightly so. Those four presidents' faces up there on that mountain are very impressive. I had hoped to walk up the avenue of flags and view the sculpture from the upper observation platform, but decided against it. I decided not to leave my dog, since it was hot and crowded. Therefore, I climbed a sturdy fence in the parking lot and shot a couple of pictures, went back to the camper and said to Ink, "Let's get out of here!" I found it significant that the three presidents — Washington, Jefferson, and Roosevelt — were together and Lincoln was positioned over to the right, set off a little by himself. It seemed to me an appropriate comment on the presidents. I was happy to have gotten to Rushmore in spite of the brevity of our stay. That granite mountain sculpture is worth seeing.

Just south of Rapid City, we took Route 44 east to see the Badlands. Wow! Were they ever bad that day! The wind was blowing furiously and we were dropping in elevation. Sand was swirling through a surrealistic landscape: tall cliffs carved from erosion in a stark, desert setting. I had considered spending the night at Interior which is in the center of the Badlands. We arrived in that small town about 5 p.m. after a hot, hot drive. Tessie was hot, I was hot, and Ink was hot. No wonder. When we stopped for gasoline in Interior, the temperature was 105 degrees and the wind was gusting at 60 mph. I looked at the campground with the wind swirling and the heat waves rising and gave up my desire to take sunset pictures of the Badlands. We drove on out of the inferno looking for a cooler, calmer place to spend the night.

We kept driving, fighting searing winds all the way, and pulled into Circle 10 campground just off Interstate 90 about 6 p.m. It was still hot and windy, but there were some trees and the park wasn't crowded. I set up Tessie under a tree. The electrical connection worked fine when I plugged in here. I just ignored it, still not knowing why it wouldn't work at Custer. Ink and I took a stroll.

There was a compatible group of people at the campground. We met twenty-three Germans who were touring the United

States in a beautiful, functional Mercedes bus: bright red with a black strip and powered by twin Mercedes diesels. In front, there were large observation windows and seats for the passengers on board. In the back, there were sleeping bunks for each of them. They carried supplies with them and laid out a sumptuous picnic dinner.

Ink and I visited with a few of them and learned that they had flown into Los Angeles where the bus met them. They planned to see all of our country from west to east. They had seen thus far the Grand Canyon, Phoenix, Albuquerque, Denver, Rocky Mountain National Park, and Mt. Rushmore. It was a diverse group — young girls, older women, a few men, and a charming German gal who was driving the bus. They were taking an in-depth view of our nation and surely did seem to be enjoying themselves.

In spite of the heat, Ink and I settled in and had a good night's rest. I felt like I had driven through a portion of hell that day. The Badlands were appropriately named.

After waving good-byes to the Germans in their fabulous bus, Ink and I pulled out of Circle 10 about 9 a.m. We followed Interstate 90 east for a bit, but pulled off and went into Kadoka, South Dakota, since we needed supplies. It was a typical plains town, the heartland of America; wide streets, big trees, brick buildings. It was a small town and moved at a leisurely pace. I found the bank, then stopped at a grocery store that made me feel as if I was marketing fifty years in the past. An old fashioned grocery store. I always found enough for our simple needs. We couldn't store a great lot and didn't need a great lot, just enough for Ink and me. Dog food, always dog food because I had room to store only five pound bags and Ink went through one of those quickly.

This was an old time store and it smelled good. I kept looking for a pickle barrel; there wasn't one, but it seemed there should have been. When I was checking out, the young clerk asked, "You're not from around here, are you?" I explained that I was just traveling through. She was a pretty young girl and wanted to know about my journey. We chatted for a while. Women were so supportive on this journey, except for the feeble-minded ones — and they were few, thank God — who were sure I had to be looking for a man and felt threatened. Having observed their mates, I just thanked my God for not being encumbered. They had nothing to fear from me. Most women were kind, encouraging, and supportive. We women have such a sisterhood. What a pity men have never learned how to connect on our level. It would be good for them.

Left Kadoka feeling I had been in a town that still lived by simpler, easier, more basic standards than most of the country. Back on the Interstate until I turned north on Route 83 towards Pierre. We were about midway across South Dakota. I wasn't quite sure where we were going, but north seemed appropriate. It was easy driving on open roads.

As we were going through Ft. Pierre just across the Missouri River from Pierre, the capital of South Dakota, I read a big sign advertising a city park on the banks of the Bad River and saying, "Campers Welcome — pull in." I had gone by before it registered, but turned around and went back. We followed the signs and came to a lovely city park which welcomed campers.We decided this was the perfect spot for a lunch break. Ink hopped out and had a run then took a swim in the Bad River. It connected with the Missouri River about 100 yards from where we were parked. We could see the bridge over the river leading into Pierre. I had lunch at a picnic table and enjoyed the view while Ink explored. There were restrooms and water faucets. The rivers were beautiful. We left Ft. Pierre's City Park feeling rested and impressed. The city's sign of welcome was so hospitable and friendly. We appreciated the gesture.

We drove through Pierre and continued north on Route 83. It was this area, just north of Pierre, that showed the devastation of the drought. Fields and fields of seared corn stalks — brown and not an ear on them — just standing there in mute testimony to what Mother Nature can do in spite of all our technology. It was sad. No corn in the corn belt this summer. However, there were also fields and fields of sunflowers and it was joyful to see them after the seared corn. They were looking well with their cheerful yellow heads turned directly to the sun. Beautiful, huge fields of sunflowers. A welcome cheerful note to counteract the drought's devastation.

It was easy driving through open country. There was little traffic and we just tooled along. I decided to turn on the radio. I listened to it from time to time, or tried to. I'd tune in, check stations, and find that the news was always bad. I think in the United States we have possibly four genre of radio stations: the contemporary station where the beat after ten minutes has you throbbing with it and the announcers come on beating in the same manner, exhorting you to rush right down and take advantage of some kind of sale. They break often for the bad news. Over and over again they hit you with the bad news.

Then, we have Country and Western. It's a very popular music style in our nation; however, one refrain of "I'm down on my luck and I've lost my truck" is as much as I can handle. There's "Easy Listening." Aye, the "jammy" stations. Most of these are huddled around one hundred on the radio dial. I read an article years ago in the *L.A. Times* on the Mormons which stated that they own this network. I don't know if it's true, but I do know that after ten minutes of "Easy Listening" I feel I'm in a dental office. It seems they have only one tape which they play throughout the nation.

Finally, thank God, we have PBS. Granted, they get into some esoteric, funded programs on the problems in Zimbabwe, but, overall, the stations are great for me — a wonderful mix of classical and jazz music, and the news is low-key. From time to time, I could find a PBS gem and listen for a while.

That afternoon as we were rolling over hills and dales, found a PBS station playing *Concierto de Aranjuez*. It was lovely and appropriate as we ticked off miles here in the middle of the nation. I did like having music while I drove, but generally stayed with my own tapes. Since I found the constant inundation of bad news and hype from most stations not to my liking, I didn't bother with it. I did not buy newspapers either. Needless to say, I never saw television. I found my personal balance and my outlook getting better and better. Perhaps the entire country would feel better, less paranoid, if everyone limited the dose of daily poison the media throws at us. But everyone seems to dwell on bad news. It's commercial, it sells.

Strictly my thoughts on the media. Surely the mentality of the nation is greater than the level of trash thrown out over radio and television. They certainly place listeners and viewers in a category of stupid bumpkins. I don't think this is true of the American public.

We continued north on Route 83 until we got to Highway 12 leading into Mobridge on the banks of the mighty Missouri River. There were many handsome bridges in Mobridge, lots of water and lots of bridges. The town seemed geared to fishing and water activities. We crossed over one of those big bridges going west on 12 and found Indian Memorial State Park situated on a peninsula jutting into the Missouri River.

It was early, but this looked like a great stopping place. We pulled up to the office and inquired about camping for the night. The nice lady asked me The Question: "You're all alone?" To which I always responded, "No, I have my dog." And then, of course, "Aren't you afraid?" To which I always asked, "Of what?" She assigned us a space near the restrooms.

It was a beautiful park, few people, big shade trees, grass, paved parking spaces with water and electricity. We set up in the shade of a tree with a lush meadow stretching out behind us. It was hot and muggy, so Ink and I hiked across the meadow and down to the river. She was swimming and splashing immediately. I kicked off my Burks, rolled up my trousers and waded. I picked up some river-washed pebbles and watched the birds. We both dawdled and savored the grandeur of the Missouri River.

Since the electricity was working that night (no, I still hadn't done a damned thing about having it checked) I threw a pork chop and potato into the toaster oven, then sat in the grass with Ink. I did eat well. After all, I had to take care of myself as Ink didn't know how to drive. She told me that she preferred I handle that job. We ate outside and watched the lingering, scarlet sunset, then had a leisurely stroll at dusk. The birds were twittering and settling in for the night. It was quiet and peaceful, good for the soul. Ink insists on her walks, for she will not foul her own space. She never in all of our journey would condescend to doing her business while she was on lead or her long line. She just won't do it. She waits until she is free to take care of business and never fouls the foot paths. She has an innate sense of propriety, bless her.

After our golden twilight walk, I headed to the ladies room for a shower and shampoo. Had a great, long, hot soak and a visit with a native woman who told me that the corn failure that year had been devastating for many farmers. It was doubly sad because some didn't feel they could afford to replant corn the following year. Bad news. Bad news for the farmers, for the state, for the nation. We had a nice chat, as was always the case in the restrooms. They were an ideal meeting place. She and I were showering and exchanging views. The water was hot. It was pleasurable standing under a good hot stream of water after a day of travel, visiting with a friendly woman.

When I got back to Tessie, the few people in the park had settled in. It was still quite warm and muggy. Ink decided she did not want to be inside. She was stretched out in the grass, happy on her long lead. I decided to let her stay outside and I just left the door to the camper open. I thought, my God, I'm perfectly safe. No one is going to come up to Tessie with Ink out there. Besides there was a nice breeze blowing across the meadow. I went sound asleep. When I awoke sometime in the night, Ink had come in and was curled up next to me. The door was still wide open. By that time there was a cool breeze from the river, so I closed it. The sense of security in the campgrounds is a wonderful thing. I felt absolutely safe: surrounded by good people, quiet and private, mostly families or retired couples. It's a family oriented activity and this does make a safe haven for a solitary woman.

We left Indian Memorial State Park on Tuesday morning, August 17, feeling refreshed and replenished. Made the trip across the river and along the bluff to the burial site of Sitting Bull. I had noticed it on the map. Since we were so close, thought we should go take a look. There was a huge granite marker with a bust of Sitting Bull on top placed on a hill with a view of the Missouri stretched out before it. Sitting Bull's real name was Talanka Iyotake. He was victorious against Custer at the Battle of the Little Big Horn in 1876 and sought asylum in Canada in 1877. He returned to the States in 1881. In 1885, he toured with Buffalo Bill's Wild West Show. He was shot while being arrested because of his involvement with the Ghost Dance craze in 1890. He had originally been buried at Ft. Gage, North Dakota, but he was moved to the present site in April, 1958, when the memorial was dedicated. The bust is there with a marker with these historical details. Custer should see him now.

Just down the lane from Sitting Bull's statue is another memorial — a slim obelisk — in honor of Sakajawea, the Shoshone Indian woman who was so instrumental in helping Lewis and Clark make their expedition. It's a touching and serene grassland hillside overlooking that magnificent river. A fitting burial site for two of our notable native Americans. May they both rest in peace.

We continued on northwest and stopped at McLaughlin, South Dakota, where I posted mail. Just north of McLaughlin, we entered North Dakota. We were on Route 4 driving through the Standing Rock Indian Reservation. It was rather typical of the country our government has handed the Indians: barren, hard to eke out a living, but nevertheless theirs. It was bounded on the east by the Missouri River, so they did have water. Not much going on, no sign of people, just desolate, barren country. No evidence of irrigation farming along this route, even though there were lots of dams and reservoirs on the Missouri River.

We had lunch at another city park in Mandan, North Dakota.

They, too, had a welcome sign out for campers passing through. This one was next to a golf course, so we watched the golfers while we ate. Ink found a golf ball and bounced it around. We used the restrooms and availed ourselves of this friendly hospitality the Dakotas extend to campers.

We continued north to Interstate 94, drove into Bismark, the capital of North Dakota, where we caught Route 83 heading still farther north.

It was an uneventful day of driving through rolling hills and wide open country. My sensibilities were jarred once again by man's rape of our beautiful planet when we passed the Coal Creek Power Generating Station just before we got to Minot. The mining corporation, in conjunction with the generating station, had some of the meanest looking earth moving equipment I have ever seen. The earth had been gouged horribly to supply fuel to the generating station. But, who among us is willing to give up all our creature comforts?

We spent the night in Minot at a commercial park out a bumpy road in a nice country setting. There was a fishing pond and lots of space, no traffic and no traffic noise either. The hosts were a delightful couple, friendly and pleasant. The usual question was asked, "You're traveling all alone?" I gave my same replies, then checked in and parked up.

In spite of the setting and the pleasant hosts, there was an uptight group of people in the campground that night. Indeed, campgrounds varied greatly. This was hostile city all around. While I was setting up, running back and forth checking my level, Ink was out bouncing around saying, "Hi, I'm Ink. Wanna be friends?" Some man in one of the largest rigs in the grounds was aghast that this dog was running loose and complained to the hosts. I'm sure he felt he had high status because of the size of his rig. There is a kind of pecking order among some of these people; at least in their minds. I didn't bother to try and comprehend this order and rank aspect. Really didn't see it much except in commercial campgrounds next to Interstates.

I didn't mean to cause any trouble and got Ink on her long lead as quickly as I could. I went over to the restroom. There were two older women in there looking like a Grant Wood painting. I mean rigid. I said, "Hi." They glared at me as if they wanted to ask, "What in hell is wrong with you?" If they had smiled, their faces would have cracked. The whole group seemed very unhappy with the exception of a delightful, red-headed young lady, her husband, and their two children. The kids loved Ink and she was happy with their attention. They came to pat her and their cute, young mother told me they'd been to Disneyland.

They were camping and were on their way home to Wisconsin. She was intrigued with my traveling alone and just meandering. I admired her courage to camp with little ones all across the United States. She was the bright spot amid the gloom in the campground. Think the people at this place were the most uptight, miserable group I encountered. And it was the people that made the campgrounds foul or fun. Most were friendly and kind. Occasionally, I'd get quizzical looks and could see the question forming, "Why would any woman be traveling alone?"

I gave up on socializing here. Just had dinner, a hot shower, and settled in early. Had turned off my lights when I heard a man talking outside. He sounded friendly: visiting a bit with someone. I'm sure it was the Grant Wood women who yelled from somewhere, "Don't you know we're trying to sleep!" Wow! They must have been having a lousy vacation with such negative attitudes. This was a transient park — everyone in for a night, then on the road again. They all rolled out bright and early the next morning. Ink and I then had some time to take a long walk, enjoy the scenery and the setting, and question why in the world all those people were so miserable. Bless the hosts, they bid us a fond farewell and safe traveling and said they'd love to have us back anytime. I surely didn't envy them having to deal with a different group of people each and every night. Do hope they didn't have many more such negative conjunctions as the ones on the night we spent there.

There were lots of wheat fields in this section of North Dakota. They showed no ill effects from the drought. I noted different ways the wheat was stacked after it had been harvested. There were the usual rectangular bales, but then there were fields with the wheat stacked like big loaves of bread — huge stacks looking like big loaves and, eventually, that wheat was going to be bread. Then, there were neat little mounds of wheat, and, most intriguing of all, there were some baled in triangular shapes. Nice wheat fields and nice country, in spite of it being overcast and cloudy. Could not complain, this was the first cloudy day we had had.

Route 2 took us through the town of Rugby which has a marker denoting the geographic center of North America. It was a stone obelisk in front of a gas station, so we stopped, gassed up, and took a photo. Standing there at the exact center of the North American continent, I too felt very centered.

We rolled on down the highway through miles and miles of open plains, wheat and cattle and not much else. The Dakotas are vast and we had covered them fairly well. Since it was easy driving, we kept going a little later than usual and crossed into Minnesota.

Was happy to be tackling another state since it seemed we had spent a long time in the Dakotas; however, it was quality time in an area of the nation I had never visited before. Ink and I fondly remember the hospitable signs welcoming campers to the city parks in the heartland of our nation.

# VI. Land of 10,000 Lakes and 10,000 Friendly People

Once into Minnesota, I stopped and checked my guide. Noted an ad for a campground in Erskine on the banks of Lake Cameron. Since it was almost 6:30 p.m., decided Erskine would be our destination for the night. Initially missed the site, so rechecked directions, back-tracked about a half mile and found a small sign. We turned down a dirt road and came to the campground: a splendid setting, lots of grass, big oak trees, a two-story, white wooden farm house, and the lake in the distance. But the place looked deserted. There were no campers parked and no sign of people. We pulled in. Off to the left was a trailer with a small handpainted sign reading "Office," so I pulled up and stopped. But still no people anywhere. About that time, the trailer door opened and out came a sturdy man in a pair of bib overalls. A pleasant looking, sturdy man, not young. Beside him was a sturdy dog which looked like a bear — big head and big, furry body. Ink was looking her over and she was quietly eyeing us. I rolled down the window and asked, "Are you open?"

"Oh, yes ma'am, sure are. Doesn't seem to be anybody here tonight though."

It seemed an obvious observation on his part. I smiled and said, "Well, we'd like to spend the night."

"Yes, ma'am. That's just fine. Come on in."

He looked at Ink and asked, "Your dog fight?" I assured him Ink was no fighter, just a good, friendly dog. He said, "Well, my dog doesn't fight either. Why don't you let her out?" Which I did. Ink and the wooly, bear dog nosed each other a few minutes, then decided they should play. The dogs ran and romped while I went in and registered and got all the info on the facilities. This kind man did not ask The Question, just said, "Park up and plug in wherever you like. No one here. Old dog's name is Sasha. She's a good one."

I chose a grassy spot looking out over the lake. Got Tessie parked up, popped up, and plugged in. Then I walked over to see if I could buy some ice. Ice was a problem: couldn't store it in my small freezer compartment, but I did like my quinine in the evening after a day of driving and I did like it with ice. When I inquired about buying ice, he said, "Oh, ma'am, I don't have any ice for sale, but here's a tray full of ice cubes, just use 'em." This was the first time I had been given ice on the journey. Most of the campgrounds charge $1.50 for a bag of ice. I'd use about 25 cents worth and have to toss the rest.

When I returned the ice tray, my sturdy friend said, "Well, you know, ma'am, I don't think anybody else is coming in tonight and the dogs sure seem to like each other. Why don't we just let 'em play out there? Now if someone does come in, I guess you ought to put her up, but otherwise, Sasha and Ink oughta have some playtime." These two female dogs did just that. Rolling and tumbling in the lush grass, chasing each other all around the park and having a ball. Ink was delighted. It certainly was a pleasant change after our experience in the Minot campground the night before.

I had a quiet dinner sitting and gazing at Lake Cameron. It was a lingering, golden sunset, there were two blue herons skimming the water, an almost-half moon in a clear sky. I drank deeply of all of nature's beauty that evening, feeling so at peace, so full of joy, and so grateful for the blessing of this lovely journey. Somehow, that setting made all my struggles and efforts getting ready to head out worthwhile.

I'm not sure why there were no other campers at this sweet campground. It was off the beaten path and many people seem to prefer to be right next to the highway; however, I love the tranquility of the small, hidden away sites and found this night one of the most memorable of my journey.

While I ate a leisurely breakfast and listened to the birds muttering contentedly, Ink and her pal, Sasha, had a final romp. Felt no compunction to hurry, but we seemed to get squared away early — perhaps because there was no line-up in the restroom. About 10 a.m. we were ready to roll on.

We were still on Route 2 heading east, directly east, and the country was changing. We were out of the plains and the wheat fields and coming into the area that is the headwaters of the Mississippi River. Drove through Bemidji and enjoyed seeing the statues of Paul Bunyan and Babe, the Blue Ox. Then, it was through Chippewa National Forest which was dotted with lakes. I counted for awhile, but tired after noting 73 lakes in less than an hour. We really were in the land of 10,000 lakes.

Still rolling along on Route 2, we crossed a tiny, meandering stream that belied its big name — Mississippi River. I think with a little effort on my part I could have jumped clear across it. And I did think about letting Ink take a swim in the Mississippi, but it wasn't time to stop. So we continued over the bridge that spanned the mighty Mississippi which was nothing more than a little tad in this area.

Turned off Route 2 at Grand Rapids and followed another Iron Mountain Road up Iron Mountain past Iron Mountain Man, a huge statue of a mining man complete with pick and shovel. Arrived in Chisholm about 2:30 p.m., found the post office, and Pam and I connected once again on mail. How welcome those packets of mail were.

The lady at the post office was gracious and helpful. Told me there was a market about four blocks directly up the street. We picked up some supplies at another interesting, old-fashioned grocery store. Not much of a selection of fruits and vegetables here; certainly no avocados and the lettuce was worn. But there was a wonderful variety of cheeses. Shopping was always an adventure.

We decided to spend the night in Hibbing, the home of the world's largest iron ore pit; an open pit 535 feet deep. The Minnesota Museum of Mining is also located in Hibbing. The mountains looked like solid iron, sort of a dull red color. In fact, the whole area looked like one big solid chunk of iron. And it was. We were in the heart of the Mesabi Range which held a mother lode of iron ore and gave birth to cities such as Hibbing and Virginia in the early 1900's. It was a solid sturdy town which looked as if it could withstand the frigid winters of this region.

We found a theme type campground located next to the area of the Minnesota Museum of Mining where all the heavy mining equipment was displayed. There were some awesome earth-moving giants in the field next to us. I made arrangements for a space, then headed up the street to a gas station to get the oil and filter changed on Tessie. I was very disciplined about regular oil changes on the trip. Felt if I wanted good service from my little camper, I should see to it that she got good service, too.

Just two blocks from the campground, we located a station. There was only one lad working. He was pumping gas and trying to get the oil changed, but we weren't in any hurry. Stood and observed the local color. My God, the cars were horribly rusted, nothing left underneath them. I surmised it was from salt on the highways during their frigid winter. Being from a dry, desert climate, those rusted cars looked very strange.

Ink and I walked out behind the station and, of course, Ink met a couple of dogs. She frisked and flirted with them. This animal of mine never walked up to anyone or any dog aggressively. She'd stand and look and wiggle a bit as if to ask, "Hey, you want to be friends?" Ink could teach humans a lot. She had a number of rebuffs — people didn't want this big, black dog bouncing around them; however, it didn't seem to matter. She'd try again and again and more often than not would get a friendly pat and the attention she loved. With other dogs, she never came on as alpha dog, just moved in, wiggling and wagging her tail. She really is a vamp. Had great fun that afternoon with two handsome mongrels while Tessie got her oil changed.

We were back in the campground early and set up with no

trouble. Our space was way up back and had a slight upward incline which made leveling Tess easy. I was finally learning and not hopping into the back so often to check my level. Just on the other side of a chain link fence was all that huge earth moving equipment looking like a herd of dinosaurs.

I was getting some wash together — the campground had an excellent laundromat — when I was honored by a visit from two darling little girls. Jennifer, who was six, and her older sister, Charlotte, who was about nine. They came up and started to fuss over Ink. Before long, they were peering into the camper and I invited them in. All the little girls loved Tessie because she was like a little doll house. These two were from Wisconsin and they thought Tessie was the neatest camper they had ever seen. They told me they had only a pop-up tent camper. They thought they really needed one like this. Their mama came by and I assured her they weren't bothering me; they were just fine. Jen climbed up and sat in the driver's seat saying, "I'll drive us somewhere." Charlotte visited with me while I was getting dinner ready for my oven. Yes, the electricity was operating that evening, so I had decided on a baked chicken thigh and potato.

Jennifer and Charlotte were earthy little girls who lived on a farm. They told me about their grandma, their dog, and their vacation trip. They said they were on their way home, but had come to see the Iron Man and the mining museum. Jennifer was up front "driving": sitting there turning the wheel and taking us to marvelous places. Charlotte looked up saying, "Jen, you just stop that!" She asked me, "Did you hear her?"

"No."

"Well, she just farted! She's gonna blow a hole right through that seat. Now listen, Jennifer, you just stop that farting right now, you hear!"

I somehow managed to keep a straight face throughout this exchange. You know, this wasn't anything I was allowed to say when I was a kid. Nevertheless, the young ladies were charming. They went down to the laundry with me and were my constant companions for the evening. Their mother couldn't get them to come home. She finally came down to the laundry and collected them.

I thought I'd have some time to myself, but five minutes later Jennifer was back. She had decided it would be more fun to go with me and Ink in that neat little camper. Ink was in the laundromat, too, and it was getting hectic. After a number of warm hugs, I convinced Jen that she really should go back to her tent and go to bed. She reluctantly consented. Ink and I finished the folding of clothes and headed up the hill.

We closed the door just in case Jennifer decided to stow away. Had dinner and read my packet of mail. Ink curled up on her feather bed. I turned in early, too. Felt satisfied that Tessie was ready for another 3000 miles and felt I was, too.

Saturday morning was cloudy and rainy in Hibbing. Got out my poncho and boots and took Ink for her walk. She did collect a lot of mud. The camper swept out easily and Ink's companionship was much more important than mud. My Wisconsin friends had gone before we were stirring, but the memory of those sweet girls will always be with me.

Left Hibbing about 11 a.m. under sodden skies. Waved a good-bye to all the dinosaurs, turned on the windshield wipers, put a jazz tape in the stereo, and we were on our way. I could see no reason to sit and drip in the campground. Driving was better.

We took State Route 1 which was again an untraveled road. We could have continued on Route 2 into Duluth, but I didn't want to deal with a city. Instead, we chose driving through some unspoiled north country filled with lakes and wildlife. It was an adequate highway. There were a few small towns, but mostly lakes and beautiful country — iron mountains, white birch trees, and signs warning about moose on the road.

I said to Ink, "Look for a moose." I really wanted to see one of those big, cumbersome beasts, but no luck. One thing I did notice was that every local car had a canoe on top of it. This was canoeing country — waterways everywhere. Since we couldn't spot any moose, we just meandered along looking at all the cars rusted out on the bottom and carrying a canoe on the top.

The sun was out by the time we came to a nice turn-off by a stream, so we pulled in and fixed lunch. It wasn't very warm in spite of the sun having broken through, but Ink took a swim. A couple pulled in while I was eating and we had a pleasant visit. They were staying at a resort in the area. The birds were raucous in this peaceful spot, but there wasn't much traffic. Ink found the stream to her liking — clear and cold.

After drying Ink and wishing the couple a nice vacation, we continued on Route 1. It wasn't a high-speed road and it didn't matter as we were in no hurry. Drove slowly and looked at this wild country. We were within the Boundary Waters Canoe Area. I suspect that in a canoe one could go for miles and miles and miles and surely see some moose. However, we stayed with our home on wheels. Enjoyed the scenery, but never saw a moose.

We finally connected with Route 61, the shore line drive along Lake Superior, about 70 miles northeast of Duluth. What a glorious body of water, grey and cold and strong looking. We were heading north with birches and mountains off to our left and this magnificent lake to our right. I had never seen Lake Superior before. I did remember from geography class that the five Great Lakes bordering the northern region of our nation constitute the largest source of fresh water in the world.

It was a Saturday and the highway was busy. Week-ends are not good for slow moving gypsy caravans. Luckily, it was a four lane road, so I stayed in the right lane with cars buzzing by us. We toodled along grabbing glimpses of the big lake.

Grand Marais was an interesting town with advertisements for nature trails, canoeing, and fishing in a beautiful north country setting. It had a public campground right on the shore of Lake Superior. I realized that I'd better not delay finding a space because there were tons of people pouring into this area for the week-end. I pulled in and, although it looked like carnival time, went into the office where they informed me they had only a few spaces left. This campground could accommodate 300 campers. I made arrangements and was assigned space way down at the far end of the grounds. There was a slight rise on our site which made leveling Tessie easy. Parked up, popped up, and plugged in only to find that the electricity would not work again.

I still hadn't done a thing about this erratic action in the system, should have, but hadn't. I knew we could operate fine on the reserve battery, the only thing I could not do when not plugged into the 120 volts was use the toaster oven, switch the refrigerator from propane, and run my tape deck without batteries. Tessie was having another snit fit so I gave up on plugging in.

There was a man parked facing me. I walked over to him and said, "I just don't understand my electrical system. Once in a while when I plug in, it just won't work. Do you suppose my reserve battery is charging up too much and flips it out? Maybe I'm charging it too much." This lovely man said, "Well, it sure sounds good to me." He didn't know any more about electrical systems that I did. I recognize this now. And, thank God, he didn't or he would have thought I was some kind of nut.

After that episode, Ink and I walked over and took a close look at Lake Superior. It wasn't far from our site. I felt lucky to have found a nice space on Saturday afternoon. I had noticed along the highway that many of the state parks had full signs posted. The shoreline was gravelly, no sand, just big rocks. There were sea gulls floating on the water. Ink had never seen one and she was intrigued with those birds floating around. She had great fun paddling out trying to get close, but they'd fly. They wouldn't let her near them. She'd chase the ones on shore; however, those Jonathan Livingstons can take care of themselves. They flocked around the dump which was not far from our site. The water was steel grey, the shore line interesting. I sat on the rocks while Ink swam and chased gulls.

The people here all looked like Vikings; blonde and red-headed with blue eyes. A handsome group of people and very friendly. There was an interesting pattern to the evenings which I watched for two nights because we stayed through Sunday. From 5 to 6 p.m., it was bar-b-que time. Everyone had a grill and the charcoal fumes filled the air. This was dinner out time. From 6:30 to 7:30 was the paseo. All the campers would walk around the grounds reading license plates and stopping to visit with friends. I had noticed this in Hibbing, too. People seemed to go to the campground for the week-end. It was the social gathering place.

Ink was on her long lead which reached almost to the road, so she was able to con a lot of pats and attention. They'd say to me, "New Mexico. You're from New Mexico?" Some of them, I'm sure, wanted to ask, "Is that a state in the Union?" However, they were kind.

After the paseo, everyone builds a fire. There were large fire pits at each site. You need a fire here in the northland even in the middle of August. Groups would sit by the fire and visit. They were gracious, friendly people, these Minnesotans, who savored being in their parks and enjoyed the beauties of their state.

We had a lovely family parked on the north side of Tessie. They had other relatives in the campground from Duluth. There were cousins, father and mother, a son with his wife and children, and grand-pa. They had two Boston Bull Terriers who weren't sure they liked Ink, but she thought those two small terriers were cute and prevailed on them to be friends. We all visited and I was asked The Question:

"You're traveling all alone?"

"No. I have my dog."

"Oh, gosh, aren't you afraid?"

"Of what? No, we're having a wonderful time."

Ink and I settled in about nine. I wasn't losing sleep over the electrical thing with Tess. Probably should have been, but I bided my time and it all worked out very well. My guides look after me. I have no doubt about that. They were with us every mile of the journey.

Sunday morning I was sitting out at the picnic table still trying to get through my mail packet from Pam. I had been having fun visiting with these lovely people, but I did need to balance my checking and take care of those mundane details. Had all the paperwork spread out under a warm sun. Ink was talking with the bull terriers. The gulls were circling and calling. If one must attend to mundane details, better to do it in a delightful setting.

I was working away when down across the grass came a whirl-wind of a little gal; red-headed and moving right along — directly for me. She greeted me with, "My cousins are next to you and they told me about your traveling all alone. I want to know all about it. I only have a tent right now, but I'd love to see your camper. I want to travel all over the country someday, too, just like you're doing."

Lisa was a nurse in Minneapolis and a delight. She loved to get away from the city and did a lot of tenting. I would guess she was about twenty-five years old, a vivacious young woman. We chatted for a long while. I told her I was finding this traveling the most freedom I had ever had in my life and she should do it, she really needed to do it. I think everyone should make some kind of journey like this. You get connected — connected with the family of man and really connected with yourself. I told her that the campgrounds were safe and secure, the people generally kind and caring, and urged her to make her pilgrimage. We had a lovely visit.

I finished the paperwork at last, had lunch, and then Ink and I strolled the gravelly beach. The weather was pleasant and clear. Made phone calls to Mark and Lois, Pamie telling them I was enjoying every magic minute of the trip. It was another no drive, all loaf kind of Sunday.

In the middle of the afternoon, I hiked up to the restroom for a shower and shampoo. The facilities were sort of barracks type affairs, but this was a big park. The ladies, God bless the ladies. They were out in the wilderness and roughing it, but the hair-dryers were with them. There were always women lined up in that restroom using blow-dryers. We certainly have been conditioned to look our best, even if only for sea gulls. I had my shower with the sound of the hair dryers vibrating throughout the restroom. The water was hot. That was my only requirement — just let there be hot water. It was, and I was grateful. I got out of the restroom quickly since I throw a towel over my head and my hair is on its own. Another bonus in traveling alone.

I had just gotten back to the camper, wasn't even dressed, when the young lads next door came over and said, "We're having a fire tonight. Won't you and Ink please come and join us?" It blew me away. I had planned to write post cards, loaf around, and not even bother to get dressed. But I couldn't resist their smiling faces. After dinner, Ink, on her lead, and I went next door and joined this lovely extended family by the fire. It was easy talk about the heat wave, the Vikings, the state. They asked me about my travels and my state of New Mexico. Lisa was there telling all that she intended to do just what I was doing someday. It was a pleasant evening with good, kind people.

During our conversation, I realized that the license plates on Tessie were a source of confusion for those who liked to read plates. New Mexico provides only one plate which must be displayed on the rear of the vehicle, which, of course, it was. But I had never removed the Arizona plate from the front bumper. I thought it looked spiffy; however, I found some people questioning me about it. Most of them seemed to know vaguely where Arizona was. New Mexico is the missing state in our Union. I spoke with one gal who had grave doubts that New Mexico was part of the United States. She was confused and sure I was from Mexico. We chatted nonetheless and she felt better when I told her I had seen the Vikings on TV in New Mexico.

I didn't stay late at the fire. Bid everyone a fond goodnight, and Ink and I headed home to Tessie. The family mentioned that next morning they were going on north to visit Old Fort William at Thunder Bay. We all wondered if we'd meet again.

It was a good week-end. The people were hospitable, outgoing, and gracious. You appreciate this kindness when you're traveling alone and have only a dog to talk to most of the time. Grand Marais was a nice place, but then I found so many nice places full of nice people on this journey.

Monday morning, August 22, 1988, was cloudy and overcast. I said good-bye to my neighbors. They said they hoped they'd see me again and I felt the same about this friendly family. Could not get in gear and it was almost one before we left the campground. Then, we stopped in the village. It was like a New England fishing town; had the same feel. There were clapboard buildings and lots of little boutiques.

I left a roll of film at a photo developing shop which would have it ready in an hour. I had been snapping rolls of pictures and hadn't seen how the new Olympus was working. Thought perhaps I should get some idea. When I learned the price for 1 hour developing, I opted for only my first roll of 12 exposures. So I had an hour to fritter. Stopped at the post office for instructions on what to do about the extra packet of mail Pam had sent to Chisholm. They gave me a change of address form which I posted immediately. I also called the Chisholm postmaster and asked that the mail be forwarded on to me in North Bay, Ontario, since I wasn't going back to Chisholm.

After I took care of that matter, I walked and looked at this quaint village. I recall I went into Seagull Sam's because I liked the name. I enjoyed looking at all the cold weather clothing — sweaters and heavy duty winter togs. Picked up the film. The camera seemed to be capturing images very well. Never left Grand Marais village until almost three.

# VII. Rainy Days and Muddy Nights on the North Shore

We drove up the highway and it wasn't far until we came to the border crossing into Canada. There was a female customs person on duty.

"Where are you from?" she asked.

"Las Cruces, New Mexico," was my reply.

She just stood there. Finally, she asked, "Is that a town?"

I took off my sunglasses, looked her straight in the eye and said, "Yes. It is a town in the State of New Mexico in the United States of America." That seemed to satisfy her. She smiled and asked to see Ink's vaccination papers. The next question was, "Do you have any firearms with you?"

"My God, no. I certainly do not."

"How long do you plan to be in Canada?"

"I really don't know. I plan to take the Trans-Canadian Highway and meander a bit in your country, and I'm not sure how long the trip will be."

After a few other pleasantries, we were on our way. Still on Route 61 heading north towards the Trans-Canada and Thunder Bay.

It's strange how we create pre-conceived notions. With such a romantic name — Thunder Bay — I had envisioned a tranquil bay with small islands and Lake Superior shimmering in front of me. A quiet, soothing place. It's not a quiet place at all. Thunder Bay is a very large industrial city. Too large, too grey, not my image at all. I did tackle the city since I needed supplies and a cash advance. Got an in-depth view of this northern industrial city with a romantic name.

I learned that it is the largest grain port in the world; over 600 million bushels of grain is shipped each year from this port. Total tonnage shipped in 1987 was over 23 million tons. There

77

are 27 miles of harbor front serviced by 17 grain elevators, five forest product industries, and five petroleum handling facilities. Not romantic at all. It reminded me of Pittsburgh when I was a kid — dirty and grimy and too crowded.

The thoroughfare we were on sucked us straight to the heart of the city. I didn't want to be there, but there we were. I spotted a bank with a parking lot and pulled in. This was an area of dismal brick buildings and railroad tracks. I parked up, told Ink to guard the house. Went into the bank only to find it was not full service. The teller got out a map and gave me directions to the main shopping mall, assuring me there was a full service bank in it and I'd be able to get a cash advance there. On we drove through more congestion. I was finding I didn't like dealing with big cities.

Found the shopping mall after circling a number of blocks. It was a closed arcade; looked like it was ready for winter weather any time of the year, probably needed to be. I had to park on the street. Scooted into the mall, found the bank, and got money. Got back to Tessie quickly and said to Ink, "Let's get out of here!"

There was lots of traffic as we were heading back to the highway. I saw a Safeway store and decided to get supplies while I had the chance. Left Ink to guard the house once again and dashed into the store. In this particular Safeway, there were two aisles of French-labeled foods. I picked up a French canned chicken and turkey stew which looked appetizing, plus the necessary items. Then, back to the Trans-Canadian and on east of romantic Thunder Bay: Canada's third largest port and a community of 120,000 people.

Checked my camper guide. There was a KOA campground a few miles east on Highways 11 and 17 and we decided to spend the night there. En route and right along the side of this heavily trafficked highway, I spotted a big cow moose. She was dark in color and quite ungainly. Of course, there was no place to pull off and take her picture, but I did, at least, see a real, live moose, or moosette. It was exciting and I was delighted to

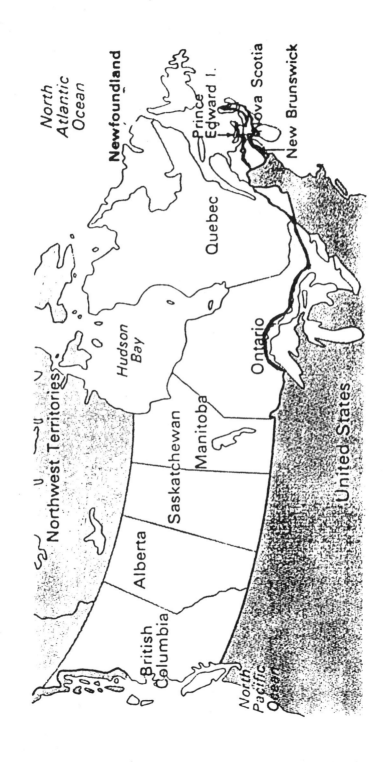

have gotten a close up look.

Pulled into KOA about 5:30 p.m. There was a nice woman in the office who asked me The Question then gave me a space close to the restrooms. Got set up and decided to take Ink for a walk. It was clouding up and looked as if it might rain. As we were heading up the hill, I noticed that across the campground there was a group of motorcyclists. A bunch of men milling around, waving and calling to Ink. I was thinking, what have we here? We had just gotten back to the camper when the office lady came by to see if we were settled in okay.

She asked if I had noticed all the motorcycles and I replied in the affirmative. Of course, I had noticed them. She told me this was a group of policemen doing a caravan together. Once again pre-conceived notions were out the window. No Hell's Angels here, just a group of policemen who fussed over Ink and who were having a fun outing.

We talked briefly with two couples. Californians who thought Ink was beautiful and gave her lots of attention, and British Columbians who were traveling the entire width of their country and hoped to visit Washington, D.C. This wife kept admonishing me not to pick up any hitch-hikers. I assured her I certainly wouldn't do a thing like that.

After dinner inside, Ink and I settled. The weather had gotten worse; cool, windy, and cloudy. Sometime during the night the heavens opened up and dumped. Lots of rain and lots of wind. I woke and was aware that we were having a nasty storm, but Tessie felt snug and warm. Ink was curled up next to me unconcerned about nature's fury. I snuggled up and went back to sleep in our safe little womb.

The Trans-Canadian was not an Interstate as we know them. In many areas it was only a two lane highway: a thin ribbon stretching across the vast reaches of Canada. In the metropolitan areas, the highway was more akin to our interstates. Even on the two lane stretches, there was always a passing lane on the up-grades with signs posted telling how many kilometers to the next one. I was relieved about that since Tessie doesn't hurry and I didn't like to tie up traffic. I always felt self-conscious plodding along in Tess with cars jammed up behind us. There were many trucks (the Canadians call them transports). They are the lifeline of the country along with the water shipping ways.

The Canadians did drive fast. They had vast distances to cover. Like those of us who live in the West where we have wide open spaces, too, they didn't dawdle. When you're in a little 4-cylinder Toyota Chinook, you have no choice, however. There was more traffic than I had encountered in northern Minnesota. Although they drove fast, the Canadians drove adeptly. I was a bit nonplussed at first by the fact that they would come up very close behind me — fast and close. I was thinking, what is this? What's wrong with these drivers? I finally realized they were reading the license plate because they'd pass and wave madly.

It was a welcome gesture from the friendly Ontarians. I was in a foreign country, a long way from home, and I appreciated the waves and smiles. I'm sure New Mexico license plates weren't an everyday occurrence on the north shore of Ontario. I could almost make out the question as they passed and waved, "Where in the world is New Mexico?"

Mileage was posted in kilometers. I knew that a kilometer is 0.62 miles and the easy way for me was to times by 0.6 and come up with a fair estimate of how many miles to the next town. The distance between towns was great. I decided I enjoyed running on the ragged edge for I'd pass a gas station thinking there'd be another just up the way. Not so! There were a few times when Tess was running on fumes, but we always made it to a station.

The directional signs. Oh yes, the green directional signs similar to those in the States with the symbols which everyone was to understand. Except that this well-seasoned traveler looked at them for a number of days not understanding. There was always this question mark on them and I kept thinking, God, they don't know what's there either. It was quite a while before it dawned on me that the question mark meant you could get information.

Then, there were a whole series of roads reading BALL PARK ROAD which seemed a strange name for a road to me. As I drove along and kept observing, there was always a ball park up these roads. It was really quite logical. This was the road to the ball park, but I drove along finding it a strange name. Shades of Canada and the Trans-Canadian highway. It probably was a good thing I traveled only with my dog. There were miles and miles of uninhabited stretches. It was truly frontier country, wide open country with wonderful people who drove up close and fast, then waved a welcome. In this isolated land, it was comforting to know that should I have trouble, there would be help forthcoming from someone on the highway. It was also comforting to know I'd be safe in accepting help. This was not my feeling in the United States: too many crazies in our nation. I often wondered if I would want any one in the States to offer help. You never know who is coming up to your rig and you never can be certain they are there to render aid. Not so in Canada. A good feeling for one traveling alone, but Tessie just purred along and I was happy I didn't have to deal with such a situation. God bless that sturdy little Toyota.

After a night of stormy weather, I woke to find everything dripping and shrouded in fog. It was a grey, gloomy morning; a morning when it lifted my spirits to break out my bright turquoise rain poncho and matching boots. If one must deal with cloudy, gloomy weather, better it should be in a color that gives one a lift.

I took Ink for her walk. Ink doesn't care if it's raining, snowing, hailing, or sleeting, she must have her walk. Perhaps, I should have her take the postal examination. She'd make a great letter carrier if only she could read better. She loves to walk in the rain. She's a water dog. It plays hell with the camper, those big feet all muddied up. Even though I tried to wipe her down, she always hopped into Tessie after a rainy morning walk carrying a ton of mud and dirt. Still, we always had our walkies.

We saw the Californians pulling out and waved goodbye. Talked briefly with the British Columbian couple. Their camper had leaked during the storm and they were in the process of throwing wet bedding into the dryers and mopping up. The kind lady warned me against picking up hitch-hikers again.

It was a slow, foggy morning and we didn't hurry. The police caravan left, suited up in yellow ponchos. I didn't envy them a drive on motorcycles that day. It was a day I'd rather have been curled up by the fire with a good book, but I didn't want to sit and drip in a campground either. Much better to be driving in snug Tessie, so we pulled out around 11 a.m.

It was an challenging driving day. We came again to the shores of Superior. There were low clouds scudding across a steel grey, cold looking lake and lots of fog. Up over some of the rises, it was the proverbial pea soup. I was driving slowly and cautiously while the Ontarians were scooting by me as if there was no fog at all. I was sure they were used to weather like this; however, I at times could not see a thing and there was no way I could drive fast. I didn't feel unduly stressed; just knew I was going to drive according to conditions. Conditions said to me: go slow and easy, you can't see. I had a jazz tape on, Tessie was warm and snug. We made slow progress through the fog layers.

Along the shore of the lake, we saw a sign for a picnic park. These parks are all over Canada and they're neat. No overnight camping is permitted, but for a restful break or a meal, they are wonderful. There's always easy access, picnic tables, and restrooms. They're a lovely place to pull off the highway. We pulled in, I fixed some lunch, put on two more layers of clothing and sat out at a picnic table. The weather was forbidding: cold, windy, and raw. There was something very humbling about being surrounded by nature's fury. I sat there watching clouds and fog drifting over the lake. Everything was grey. It was a landscape full of force and power. I wondered what this shore must be like in November as this was August and it was frigid.

Needless to say, no one else was picnicking that day. We had the picnic park to ourselves until the seagulls discovered us. Ink chased them in and out of the water, having a grand time. The gulls would circle overhead watching to see if I was going to drop a crumb, cawing and cajoling and as grey as the rest of the landscape. While I was brewing a cup of hot tea, I got my birdbook and binoculars out to determine what type of gulls these were. After a glance at the myriad numbers of gulls around North America: large headed, small headed, yellow beaked, black beaked, yellow, pink, or black footed, I gave up and just enjoyed the big beggars.

We spent some lovely time on that bleak shore, then decided to tackle the highway again. Ink was muddy, wet and chilled when she hopped into the camper. The camper would clean up and Ink had had a fun time. She curled up on her pillow ready for a nap. Ink didn't worry about my driving ability, she had faith in me. She, at least, was sure I'd get us safely to our destination. Away we went through more thick fog with the heater on and jazz playing. It was a rather romantic drive — like being the only person on earth.

Our destination for the night was Wawa, Ontario. In this sparsely populated region, we didn't have many choices. I had noted there was another KOA there located on the banks of the Magpie River. Pulled in and answered the usual questions, registered, and was directed to my space. I was driving down the lane slowly when I was greeted by the California and British Columbia couples waving madly. They all told me they had been worried about me and were so relieved that I had arrived safely. We discussed the weather and driving conditions and agreed it had been an interesting day along the North Shore.

It was clearing, so Ink and I took our walk. The weather was still cold and raw. Although I needed a shower, the restrooms were a long way up the lane and I was not in the mood to make the hike. This was the first time I had missed showering two nights in a row. Decided it was another good reason for traveling alone. Ink didn't care how I smelled, so I did a short sponge bath in Tessie.

In spite of not always showering, I did keep a modicum of civilized habits: never went to bed without flossing and brushing my teeth; and, generally, I'd set my table with a placemat and napkin and eat by candlelight in the camper. These little rituals were a way of nurturing myself. This particular evening, I thanked my God doubly for bringing me safely to Wawa after a hard and hazardous driving day. Not many people had waved on the highway this day. It was a day in which you paid attention to driving and nothing else — not even New Mexico plates.

Another rainy morning. The Californians were off early. Spoke with the British Columbians. With a hug and fond good-byes, plus yet another warning not to pick up hitch-hikers, they pulled out also. Ink and I dawdled and doodled, took our walk and pulled onto the highway by eleven.

The Trans-Canadian led us that day through miles and miles of pine forests and white birches. Wide open country, easy driving. I stopped and took a picture of the moose warning: a yellow sign with a big moose on it stating, beware of moose on the highway for the next 10 K. It so intrigued me, I had to have a picture. It was overcast, which seemed to be a way of life on the north shore. This desert rat who wants sunshine 360 days a year wasn't too thrilled with more clouds and gloom. It was a good driving day, however, and we were thankful there was no fog. We tootled along through this vast country. I did make it to a gas station in the middle of nowhere by the skin of my teeth, but it was there when we needed it. Gassed up and kept rolling along, warm and cozy, listening to jazz, and enjoying.

Early in the afternoon, I breezed by a sign which finally registered. It had read, Agawa Provincial Park — Indian Pictographs. I had passed it, but thought, Gee, I don't want to miss that. So we made a turn around and went back to this fascinating provincial park.

There was a notice on the bulletin board that dogs must be on leash. Since it was still cloudy and drippy — another day for my turquoise poncho and boots — I left Ink in the camper. I took my camera and wended my way down a trail that was well marked: down steps and through a lush forest setting with big pine trees, beautiful mosses, and lichen-covered boulders. It was quite pretty in spite of being damp and drippy. A red squirrel sat on the limb of a tree. He made no effort to move as I approached, so I greeted him and took his picture. The forest was still and quiet, there were no people around. I kept going down a series of steps, down and down to the shores of the lake. There were information signs telling of the early Indian tribes and of their love for these waters on the shores of Gitchegumee.

I finally came upon a platform which gave me a start. There were some odd-shaped markings on a boulder that I could see from this platform — ochre and white and two small fish in red. I looked it over and finally determined that what I was to do to see the rock art on around this boulder was to swing myself out on a line hooked into the rock, to rappel across this smooth granite with a thirty degree slope directly into the lake. I was to swing around on the line (for me it would have been with one hand holding my camera) and try not to fall into the lake. There was a life saver on the platform, but there was no one to toss it.

Well, I stood there a while — quite a while — and I looked at that water which was beautiful and clear but cold. I looked at the smooth granite sloping into the lake and thought, I don't need a dunk in that lake. If there had been a boat, I might have attempted rowing around, but I didn't think I should swing out there and make like Tarzan. I stood a while longer and chided myself for being such a chicken. However, there are times when discretion is the greater part of valor. I chickened out and took photos of what was visible from the platform. Sorry I missed the pictographs on the other side of the boulder. I didn't want a cold bath that cold day in that cold water even though I had not showered for two nights.

It was interesting to see that the art the Indians of Canada had left is similar to what the ancient ones had left all over New Mexico. The art here was mainly of fish and sea life, whereas in New Mexico the pictographs show more hunting and camp life.

Before we left Agawa, I checked my guide and found two

camping sites just north of Sault Sainte Marie. I decided to stop at Blueberry Hill because it advertised a restaurant. I felt the need to dine out that evening. We pulled in about 4 p.m. The weather was clearing and we had a site among pine trees which was fairly dry, considering the rain. The natives told me their rains had come late, that they had a hot, dry summer. The drought affected even the north shore of Canada.

We got set up quickly. I could ease Tessie up a small grade and leveled her right away. Popped up, plugged in, and proceeded to take everything out of her. That little camper was filthy. I stripped the seat covers off and hiked to the laundry facilities where I did four loads of wash. Cleaned the camper well, as she was due. Brushed Ink well and tied her. Then went for a hot shower and shampoo. The restrooms were unoccupied and I lingered under that hot stream of water for a long while. I was due, too.

By eight, we all were sparkling and shining. I decided I would avail myself of the restaurant. Ink hopped into the clean camper and settled down on her feather pillow and I walked up for dinner. The only people in the restaurant were local people who worked there: three women and a man. I had lake pike, French fries, and coleslaw — typical restaurant fare — and a piece of blueberry pie. One lady asked me, "Do you like the pie?"

"Oh, yes. It's very good."

"Well, I bake the pies. I live here in the campground."

The cook beamed when I told her I had enjoyed my meal. These people were sitting and chatting about their corn festival and what fun it was. They asked me where I was from and I told them about my travels. I mentioned that I hoped to visit the Maritime Provinces. They offered a wealth of information on what to see and do. People are always delighted when you tell them how much you like their country. I felt enough at ease with these kind folks to ask about the moose signs along the highway. The man explained to me, "Now, you see, they stay back in the bush most of the time, but come April and May when the flies hatch out, the moose do just stand on the highway to escape the pesky things and no amount of persuasion will move those critters. "

I lingered over my coffee and visited with these lovely people: down to earth, friendly, and looking forward to the corn festival. In spite of not being keen on restaurant food, it was a pleasant change and a pleasant evening. Finally said my goodnights and went back to a very clean camper. Ink was clean, I was clean, and Tessie was clean. It was a great feeling after all the mud and grime. Had a wonderful night's sleep. Didn't even dream of falling down the granite boulder into Lake Superior.

Next morning was fairly clear. There were still clouds, but also patches of blue sky. The air felt cool to me; however, I got stirring. Took a run with Ink, did the necessary chores and we were on the highway by 10:30 a.m. We were heading almost directly south towards Sault Ste. Marie. We were barely underway when I noticed that traffic was stopped ahead of us. There were police cars and I thought it must be a roadblock.

As we crept a little closer because the traffic was moving slowly, I noted a large transport in the middle of the road, a pick-up truck over the embankment on its side and all bashed up in the front. When we got up to where the police were next to the transport, there was a dead body in the middle of the road. What a sinking feeling it gave me. Obviously, the accident happened just before we arrived. There was no mistaking the body was dead. It was covered with a shroud and lying in the road. I had a sick feeling in the pit of my stomach. It reminded me that I was a long way from home and what we call life hangs by a tenuous thread.

As we continued on towards Sault Ste. Marie, I turned on the radio and the news gave the details of the accident: A young lad, as I recall in his late twenties, was driving at excessive speed in this section of four lane road. The transport was attempting to turn left into a service station and the lad slammed his pick-up full tilt right into the side of the transport and killed himself. Disturbing, to say the least...

There was a by-pass around the city and I was thankful I didn't have to grapple with traffic. I noticed a Safeway, stopped and picked up some supplies, got back into Tessie and continued on the Trans-Canadian. Still, the pall of that young man's death and the thought of how vulnerable anyone on the highways is, was very much with me.

There was synchronicity on this trip, so much synchronicity. It was still early, not even one o'clock, but I thought, I really don't want to drive today. I'm just not in the mood for driving. This thought had no sooner crossed my mind, when on the right side of the road, I spotted a little green sign reading: St. Joseph's Island — Hilton Beach. I didn't hesitate, I turned off the Trans-Canadian, crossed the bridge over Wilson Channel and found myself in another world.

It was a charming, isolated spot. St. Joseph's is set down in the St. Mary's River which connects Lake Superior and Lake Huron. It's quiet, sparsely populated, covered with stately oaks, maples, and birches, and a riotous profusion of wild flowers.

Route 548, on which I was driving, was a peaceful country road; two lanes winding through this beautiful countryside. I had no idea of where it would lead me, but kept driving and savoring this scenic little island. There were no moose signs; however, there were signs warning of deer on the road. We poked along not knowing what we'd find, but not caring. Came upon a sign reading Hilton Beach Tourist Park, turned in and came to a campsite. It appeared to be a park for fisherman. There were a number of mobile homes lining the driveway into the office.

I stopped and went into the office where a cute young lady assured me that they had space for overnighters down on the spit. I registered, then inquired if there was a bank on the island. The gal gave me instructions on how to get to Richard's Landing which was the populous village on St. Joseph's. I told the gal we'd go over to Richard's Landing before parking up. We headed across the island.

Enroute, we passed a group of log cabins advertised as the Museum. Historic Fort St. Joseph was located on a spit of land overlooking the main channel to Lake Superior. Hay Point, another spit of land, was only a mile from the United States. "The Mountain" on St. Joseph's was all of 1134 feet above sea level. I learned that this charming island had approximately 93,000 acres, and 150 miles of shoreline.

We finally arrived at Richard's Landing after a circuitous route. It was a small, quaint fishing village — rather what I had expected. The main street, which terminated at the waters of St. Joseph Channel, was lined with a few boutiques, a grocery store, a restaurant, an ice cream parlor, and the bank. A sweet village; not many tourists, not many people at all. I got a cash advance, walked around a bit, then headed back to Hilton Beach.

We drove down to the spit of land overlooking the north channel of St. Mary's River and proceeded to park up. This was when I learned that Tessie had a mind of her own. The spit was down the hill from the permanent mobile homes and the office. There were some other small rigs there, mostly fishermen for this area was noted for Lake Huron pike fishing. There was a small lighthouse way up the river, white and gleaming in the sun. I chose my site and was pulling Tessie in facing the bay.

She just wouldn't level. I felt like I had regressed to those first weeks on the road. Kept pulling forward, checking the level, then back and checking the level, but she would not level. I knew I was done-in by that accident; however, she should have settled in. I finally stopped and took stock of this impasse. It was then I realized that I was doing it backwards. If I backed into this site, I'd have a full view of the river and the lighthouse from the back door of the camper. Thought, my God, Tessie knows more about this than I do. Anyhow, I turned her around and backed into the site and she leveled immediately. I began to think my little camper knew more about how she should be parked than I did. And, truly, by this time, Tessie was a personality, an integral part of the gypsy caravan.

We set up and plugged in. It was early, but I knew I didn't want to drive any farther on this day. The air was cool and the beach was rocky, but Ink and I walked a long distance and felt better for it.

Ink tried to get the seagulls to play with her. She'd swim out in the bay just itching to get close of one of the gulls; however, they'd let her get only so near and fly away. It made a good game and Ink enjoyed the sport. I found a weather beaten log on shore and sat and gazed at the lighthouse shimmering in the sun. I sat there and let Nature nurture as she always does. Just sat there feeling happy to be alive in this spot and sheltered from any more driving.

I don't feel there was morbidity on my part. Death is the end process in this game of life, but seeing a dead body stretched out on the road does give one the immediate sense that, indeed, we all are mortal. All the more reason to live each day to its fullest. None of us knows how long we have on this plane. To paraphrase Joseph Campbell: " The underlying fear of the human species is death. Perhaps, it should be of not having lived."

As Ink and I were heading back down the beach, feeling better and in balance, a group of kids joined us. Thank God for kids. They were always ready to visit: friendly and open and good company. Ink did her charm trick and they all patted and fussed over her. We ambled along, the kids telling me about themselves and their summer vacation here on St. Joseph's. I had gotten the impression that the adults at the camp looked askance at a single woman in their midst.

This was an elite club: people who came each year to socialize with friends and to fish. They weren't used to a stranger in their midst. It was a sensing on my part, but I don't think they were comfortable about it. No one spoke to us except the kids. They accept and welcome so much more adeptly than do adults. When do the children stop trusting? What happens and why? Is it the culture, the schools, the parents? I don't know, but I do think we all need to keep a portion of the child in us alive. It does make life much more tolerable. Granted, the world is a sorrowful place, but if you don't have any trust in your fellow man and give a little love, it's not only sorrowful, it's barren.

It was a cool evening and I chose to eat inside. Had an oven dinner which helped take the chill off the camper. Did not make the hike up the hill for a shower. Instead, climbed into my sleeping bag and read a brochure on St. Joseph's. It is the home of a unique stone, a strange, spotted stone which is called a pudding stone. Well, drat, I hadn't looked for pudding stones that day and the article states that they are found nowhere else. Should have picked up a pudding stone. Somehow I was content to have been led to this quiet place. The sounds of the boat motors putting out into the bay for night fishing lulled me to sleep.

We crossed the bridge, leaving serene St. Joseph's Island, and were back on the Trans-Canadian by 10:30 a.m. We were skirting along Lake Huron now, or rather Genevieve Bay which was separated from Lake Huron by a long spit of United States land. Detroit, Michigan, was due south of us at this point. It was again, the merry Trans-Canadian: people waving as they passed, a feeling of camaraderie, not much traffic, wide open country and lots of lakes. The topography had changed slightly. There were not so many birches, not as many trees, more open country. We purred along. There were clouds and intermittent showers, laced with sunshine and blue skies.

When we came to the turn-off for Sudbury, I decided rather than take the gas tank down to fumes, I'd just stop and gas up. Seemed the sensible approach, but not one I had always followed. This morning, I chose to get gas and play it safe. It was a charming town which looked as if it had been there a long time. One of those sturdy towns built to endure the winter weather of this region. Drove down the main street, into the gas station, and filled Tess. Didn't bother to check under the hood because Tessie never needed oil. I always did the under hood inspections when I was at a campsite where I did not feel so subject to scrutiny. I wasn't too adept and always had trouble getting the dip stick for the oil back into the hole. I had more trouble with that damned dip stick. I didn't want anyone watching me struggle with it.

The stop in Sudbury didn't take long and we got back to the highway. I felt some urgency in reaching North Bay before the post office closed. I had requested that mail be sent on from Hibbing and knew if I didn't check on this Friday, I'd be out of luck until Monday. So on we went, enjoying good scenery, good jazz, and feeling in tune with our world.

We arrived in North Bay about 4:30 p.m. It was a bigger town than I had hoped for. After circling around blocks for 15 minutes, I located the post office and went in.

"No, nothing for that name," the clerk said.

"Oh, nuts."

"Do you know we have a postal strike going on in Canada?"

"No. I don't listen to the news or read newspapers very much."

"Well, we're having a strike. Some of the postal workers are out. Mail is moving, but very slowly. If I were you, I wouldn't expect that mail to arrive soon. Don't expect it to come through quickly."

I stood there and wondered if I should stay near North Bay and hope my mail would arrive Monday — or what. It was too early to worry about that now. I thanked the clerk, hopped back into Tessie, checked my guide and read an ad for Dreany Camp Park — rural, wooded flatlands, located on Dreany Lake and only four miles east of town. Sounded good to me.

We followed Route 17 east and had no trouble finding our spot. It had been a rainy day and I was ready to stop. I also had to make an executive decision about mail. Pulled in and went into the office where we did the round of usual questions:

"You're all alone?"

"No. I have my dog."

"Aren't you afraid?"

"Of what?"

The kind lady directed us to a neat site up on a hill overlooking a lush, green meadow, close to the restrooms, and with the lake in the distance. Tessie didn't give me trouble that evening. Obviously, I was parking her the way she wanted. We were parked up, popped up, and plugged in easily and quickly.

There was a camper in the space to the right of us. Ink had hopped out immediately and, when I checked, she was racing around flirting with a fuzzy little dog. I went about my chores of setting up and settling in. The couple next door waved, smiled, and mentioned that their dog, whose name was Chippy, surely did like my Ink. I asked if she was causing any trouble. They told me they were happy to see a playmate for Chippy. They had a fire blazing in the fire ring. By this time they were all outside laughing over the antics of the dogs. I walked over and introduced myself and they extended a warm, friendly greeting. A nice change from the night before.

My neighbors were the LeVert family. John and Bev and their two teenage children Chris and Patricia. They lived in North Bay but had come to the campground for the week-end. John offered me a cup of coffee and a seat by the fire. They were amazed by my solitary travels. John was the extrovert and a great conversationalist. He had a quick and curious mind plus an interest in anthropology. I recall John stating, "God, I can't imagine my mother doing something like you're doing. Just heading out on your own like that. I so admire you. You're really something." Those strokes were welcome and I appreciated this lovely family's hospitality. Knew once again I was happy to be a part of the family of man. This kindness from other campers was more evident in all my travels than were the few isolated instances when I felt like a visitor from another planet.

I mentioned my stop at the post office in North Bay and the LeVerts advised me to forget about getting any mail. They said the strike would continue and that no mail was coming through. After dinner, we all played Yahtzee and visited some more. A beautiful, hospitable gesture from a supportive family. I said my good-nights. Ink and I went into bed about nine-thirty — feeling warm inside and happy to be here.

Woke early. The sun was peeking through fleecy clouds and the birds were chirping happily. Guess they were as happy to see the sun as I. Ink wanted out to see if Chippy was ready for play. I dressed and put her on her lead. Chippy was right there to greet her. I wanted to have toast for breakfast, so got my toaster oven out. Plugged it in and the 120 outlet wasn't working. Thought perhaps the problem was with the oven, so got out the radio and tried it. It didn't work either. Something was wrong with the electrical system again or still. I had cereal instead, feeling totally frustrated, thinking, God, this electricity isn't right. It's starting up again. I don't know, I just don't know. But I did know I had to handle it, or try. So after eating, decided the first thing to check was the converter unit — check the fuses in it. That meant moving the bed, standing on my head, and struggling to remove the fuses. But, I did it and checked them carefully. They looked fine to me. By this time, John and Bev were sitting outside having coffee. I took the fuses over and asked John if they looked all right to him. I explained, "My 120 outlet doesn't seem to be working. I've just pulled these fuses. They look all right to me, but would you mind taking a look at them?"

"Gee, they look great."

Bev offered to walk up and check the master switch for the campground outlets since we had had some wind and rain the night before. She came back saying, "Everything's in order there."

John reaffirmed that the fuses were okay. I said, "Thanks, you two. I don't know what this electrical system is doing, I'm afraid. Ever since the Dakotas, sometimes when I plug her in she works and sometimes she doesn't. I don't understand it at all."

"What did you say?" John asked.

"Well, you know, it's erratic. Sometimes when I plug in it's fine and sometimes I just don't have any 120."

"Boy, that isn't right, Barb. That isn't right at all. Let me come over and take a look. That doesn't sound good to me."

John came over and got into the camper. It's a small camper and two people tramping around in Tessie makes for a large crowd. Of course, Ink had to bounce in and out, too. He took the cover off the 120 outlet first. I think he must have read my mind because he twisted around and said to me, "Now, don't worry, I know what I'm doing here. I just finished re-wiring my entire house." He examined the fittings in the outlet, said they looked a little dirty and worn and he thought he should replace them. He offered to go into town and get new ones.

"John, I don't want you to bother with that."

"No, no, it's no bother. No bother at all. Would you like to ride in with me and see our mall?"

"No, thanks, John. I'll stay and get some of this stuff out of the camper so you have more room."

"I really think we'd better check through this system, Barb. I don't like that going off and on. That's not right."

I was feeling embarrassed by the man's generosity. However, John was determined to do this chore. He had asked me to show him all the guts of Tessie and I was happy to do that.

"I've not had any trouble with this little camper. She's been an absolute gem, you know, except for this damned electricity."

John inspected Tessie carefully. He showed me I had another 120 outlet in the converter panel which I had not known. He asked about the propane tank. I told him it was a devil to get in and out, no way I could do it alone. It was definitely a two-man operation because the tank had to be lowered and taken out from under the fender. It took two men to juggle it back up and into place. He noticed that there was no bolt on the back of the propane tank platform and that bothered him. John went off to town and I weeded out so he'd have more working room.

Bev strolled over to see if she could help.

"I'm really embarrassed to have your husband doing all this for me, Bev."

"Don't worry about it," she said grinning. "It's just the way he is."

She was such a laid-back, lovely gal. Bev was a nurse and not the extrovert her husband was, but a beautiful person, too.

John was back shortly, had the outlets replaced in a few minutes, but still nothing worked.

"We're gonna take this system apart and see what's the matter."

"John, this is your holiday. I can't have you working on my camper. You know, I should have gone to an RV garage and had it checked, but just didn't feel like it. It's not your problem, and I think you've done enough."

"Barb, relax. I just hope someone would do the same for my mother if she was traveling all alone."

"John, believe me, I'd insist my sons lend a helping hand and I know they both would, but I don't think either of them knows any more about electrical systems than I do."

I moved some more things. John insisted I watch what he was doing so that I'd know how to fix anything that went wrong. He assured me that he knew I could handle it. That lad had more faith in me than I had in myself. We checked first on the outside access to the refrigerator. John could see nothing wrong there. We went inside and down under the seats and into the bowels of Tess; kind of tripping over each other and having to coordinate our moves in that small space. When John started checking the main power lines under the seats, he said, "Good God, Barb, just look at this. Nothing is grounded under here! These wires are bare and touching each other. My God, you could have had a fire and burned the whole camper up."

"Lord, I don't understand that, John. You know I had Tessie into an RV place in Cruces before I left. They pulled the whole refrigerator unit out of her. Wouldn't they have noticed this?"

"They might have done it, you know. Just didn't bother to ground everything when they put the unit back in. Anyhow, we're gonna fix it right now. It's no problem to ground all these wires and have it right.

So John started working through the wiring, showing me what to do and explaining the whole system to me. I watched and made some notes and almost believed I could trouble- shoot the system if I had to.

In about two hours, John had that electrical system in A-1 shape. We were all sitting outside eating some lunch and I mused, "Gee, I guess I could have burned up. That's a little scary."

"Yeah, Barb, you could have. But you didn't and it's okay now. Don't worry. I also picked up a bolt for the back of your propane platform and still want to put that on. I don't want that tank falling out. That could be dangerous, too."

This kindness was above and beyond the call of duty in my eyes. How does one ever repay such goodness? John quelled my offers to pay him with, "Hey, I'm glad I was here and able to give you a hand."

I put Tessie back in order, feeling light as a feather. Felt as if I had a whole new lease on life. Although I hadn't dwelt on the electrical problem, it was with me. Now it was fixed and fixed properly. Put Ink on her lead and skipped down for a long, hot shower and shampoo.

By the time I got back, the LeVerts had a roaring fire in the pit. We sat and visited some more. Told them I had decided not to wait until Monday for mail. I had both Ottawa and Montreal to grapple with and felt they'd be easier on Sunday than on a weekday. Said I thought I'd head on down the pike. They agreed that the mail would not come and said they were going home to North Bay to prepare for work on Monday.

Such a delightful encounter this had been for me, I hated to see it come to an end. I asked them if they had ever read *Clan of the Cave Bear* by Jean Auel since they did have an interest in anthropology. They had not, so I filed that piece of information away. Chris shared some of his cartoon drawings with me while Ink and Chippy romped. This lovely, concerned family will always be in my memories and my time with them so fondly remembered. People are so good and so helpful, no matter what our news media would have one believe. The LeVerts were among the best.

It was easy conversation there by the fire, ranging from Bev's and John's views on their government through metaphysics. Stimulating talk and a great exchange of ideas. They agreed with my assessment of the need for the human species to have a connection with nature. We all wondered aloud if there would be anything left of this fragile planet in another century at the rate we humans are wrecking it. Think we could have talked all night; however, we all had a schedule to meet. Bev and John did caution me about traveling in Quebec. I had noticed this view before. The people in Ontario seemed to feel the Quebecers did not like them, did not want them in Quebec, and were unfriendly to them. So they told me to be careful.

I laughed and said I didn't feel this old German broad would have any trouble, but I certainly would be careful and cautious. John retorted, "I don't think you're ever careful and cautious, Barb." We all started to laugh then, agreeing that were I that way, I'd never have set out on this pilgrimage of mine. I enjoyed the bantering and teasing because I knew that's what it was. On that note, we had warm hugs and said our good-nights.

This was the night of the August full moon. I had hoped to see it shining on the campground and the lake. Thought I'd probably bay at it, but the clouds had moved in once again. I had no glimpse of the silver disk that night. Ink and I nestled in, feeling so content and relieved that, at last, the electrical problems were solved. God bless the LeVerts.

We didn't get away from the campground early that Sunday morning. There was visiting back and forth with the LeVerts: a lot of hugs and a lot of strokes. I told John and Bev I'd send a copy of *The Clan of the Cave Bear* and cautioned them to read it before letting Chris and Patti do so. I had no idea whether the sexual passages in *Clan* would bother the LeVerts, but thought they could make the decision as to whether or not they wanted their children reading it. John said, "You know, someday we'd love to do some camping in the Southwestern United States, then go on to California and see Disneyland."

"Any time you come, you'll be welcome at my place."

Again, John told me how great he thought it was that I had the guts to set out on my own. I reminded him that perhaps I was foolhardy and just didn't understand the problem.

All good things must come to an end. After more hugs and

best wishes, Ink and I got it together and pulled out about eleven. It was gloomy and cloudy again, or still. This desert rat was longing for some arid land and sunshine, but it wasn't going to happen that Sunday. We were skirting along the Ottawa River which is the boundary between Ontario and Quebec in this area on Route 17. Lots of lakes and rivers, few towns, and little traffic. The miles ticked by uneventfully. About two, we drove through a town named Renfrew and I thought that name sounded familiar. A little farther down the highway, we passed through Arnprior and it was then that memories flooded back.

I had been in this section of Ontario for big-mouth bass fishing on the Madawaski River years ago — about thirty-five years previously. I hadn't looked at the map that closely, but here I was. What synchronicity! It hadn't changed much, from what I could see as we drove along. There was a big water tank along the highway now but not that much different than it had been years before. Thought, I just keep going in circles, don't I? But then, perhaps we all do.

Just beyond Arnprior, the heavens opened up. It was slow going; raining very hard, very cloudy and foggy. There was no traffic as we splashed through Ottawa. I stayed on the Trans-Canadian and read the directional signs, but caught glimpses of Ottawa as we drove by. This is Canada's capital city and I had hoped to do some sightseeing, but this did not seem the proper day for it, so on we went.

I had found by this time that I tended to tighten up when I had to negotiate large cities, so I'd turn up the jazz, close the windows, set my pace, read the signs, and pay attention to driving. We never had a problem, but I did recognize that cities were not my favorite places. Saw some beautiful buildings as we eased along and knew that would suffice.

I had hoped to get beyond Montreal, but was feeling tired from all the concentration. Instead, pulled into Katawa Campground at exit 79. That was enough rainy day driving for one day. Went a short distance down Limoge Road to the park. It was huge and rocking: lots of people, lots of permanent mobile homes, and lots of cosmetic effects — a pool, putting greens, an artificial lake. They did have a space and we parked up for a night with the sardine effect. In listening to the banter and calling back and forth, I realized that many of these people had been here for the week-end. It was the social life in this section of the country. Many of them were packing up to get back to the city and saying good-byes. There were as many voices speaking French as English.

It was wet, but Ink and I got squared away and went for a walk. At the end of a long lane, we found an open field where she could get a run. No people way back here. The weather was clearing, so I put her on her lead and we did a tour of the camp. All the mobile homes sported little plastic lights on their decks.

I gave Pamie a call to let her know about the postal strike and alert her that, eventually, the packet from North Bay would return to her. It was good to hear her cheery voice. I assured her I was fine and all was going well except for the rain and gloom. We didn't find anyone who cared to visit, so we went back to snug Tessie for dinner and a quiet evening. Surely was a delight plugging Tessie in that evening knowing she'd give me no trouble.

# VIII. Frenchmen and Fleur de Lis

Woke feeling rested after an uneventful night, but the thought of dealing with Montreal was tightening me up. I decided the sooner I dealt with it, the sooner it would be over. Ink and I had our walk as I worked on attitude adjustment. Took a look at the map while I ate breakfast and it didn't help a bit. Saw that I'd need to switch from Canada's Route 40 to Route 20 and also get across the St. Lawrence River. Oh, my God! It had to be tackled, so we left this lackluster park and were on our way to I knew not what — by 10:30 a.m.

It was a divided four lane highway through this more populous section of Canada. There was a lot of traffic and it got more dense the closer to Montreal we drove. I chose a soothing jazz tape, closed the windows against all the noise, and got into a lane that I intended to stay in. Tessie has a small blind spot in spite of side view mirrors. I found it less stressful to roll along in one lane, not having to worry about pulling into a vehicle I could not see. That meant cars were whizzing around me on both sides.

Although the LeVerts had said that people in Quebec were unfriendly, my drive through Montreal proved them wrong. There were Frenchmen going past us on both sides. I was sure we were going to be the cause of a major pile-up on the freeway because they'd turn clear around in their seats to wave and take a look, gesticulating madly and paying no attention to their driving. They realized we were a long way from home and wanted us to feel welcome. It eased my mind that they recognized a stranger and were giving encouragement.

I felt we were causing more than a little havoc on the freeway, but I smiled and waved back, and kept my steady pace.

All was going better than I had anticipated. I relaxed and glanced at this sprawling metropolis and began to think Montreal wasn't that bad. The roadway was well marked and I spotted the connection to Route 20. It went through a tunnel under the river. I really don't like tunnels, they make me claustrophobic, but I gritted my teeth and we were through that old tunnel and out into daylight in a matter of minutes. Best of all, we were on Route 20. The people kept waving and I kept smiling in spite of feeling as if the gypsy caravan was from another planet.

Somewhere in the midst of this melee, a California car went by me pulling a tiny sleeping trailer. A man was driving and he waved. Here was someone from the States. I felt better knowing I'm not the only one up here in French country not knowing where I am or where I'm going. I'm not alone. That encouraging wave from him made me feel so much better. And, we did it! We traversed Montreal with style and grace and found our way.

Rolled up Route 20 in Quebec and congestion was easing. I was looking at the road markers and thinking, what's that little B on the bottom of those signs? Guess my eyesight isn't too sharp either. After more inspection, I discovered it was a fleur de lis at the bottom of the markers. Of course. We were in Quebec and everything was in French. Luckily, the numbers read the same in English or French. We got out of the mash of that metropolitan area and were heading northeast on Route 20 feeling relieved and rather smug.

When I pulled into a gas station along the highway to give Tess a drink, I noticed a small restaurant next to the station. It looked inviting and I decided that I'd treat myself to lunch out: felt I deserved it for having found my way through Montreal. I parked Tessie and told Ink to guard the house. Had a nice lunch while I listened to French-speaking voices all around me. The food was good and I enjoyed the change of pace. Then we headed on up the pike.

Found Quebec to be no driving problem since the major portion of that city was on the opposite shore of the St. Lawrence. We were now going along the south shore of that magnificent river. I would guess it was a half-mile wide in this area, and there were large ships plying the waters of this busy shipping lane. The sun was shining, all was right with our world, and we tootled along enjoying the river views.

I pulled off the highway north of Quebec to check on accommodations for the night. Camping Parc Beaumont on the banks of the St. Lawrence sounded just right. It was early, but I felt getting around both Montreal and Quebec was enough for one day, so decided to stay at Beaumont. Was driving along not paying attention. By the time it registered, I had passed the exit I needed to take to get to the campground. We were still on four lane divided highway and I pulled over onto the shoulder to regroup. There were very few access roads in this area. I thought, my God, if I keep driving up this highway, I'll never find my way back. Sat there for a while then did not do the wise thing but what seemed the most expedient thing to do. There wasn't much traffic, I had this broad shoulder of highway, so I put Tessie in reverse and slowly backed my way down the road when it was clear. It took a while and I did wonder what I'd say to a French patrolman if he should come by. Slowly and cautiously, we got back to the turnoff with no mishaps. My gods do look after me!

Beaumont was definitely a French campground. The brochure they gave me when I registered was written in French and all the signs were in French. It was a lovely setting on an escarpment overlooking the river, and the accommodations were nice: wide sites with hook-ups, picnic tables, fire pits, and lots of grass and trees. I had a panoramic view of the river from my site and no one parked near us. There weren't many people and those who were camping spoke French. They smiled and made me feel welcome, however. Many would stop and pat Ink. She didn't care what language anyone spoke so long as they gave her a bit of attention.

We set up then walked around the park. There was a restaurant, but it was closed. The restroom area, or *bloc sanitaire,* was fascinating. To get to it, we had to cross over a deep ravine filled with glorious wildflowers on a wooden bridge. I stopped and admired the flowers, but Ink wasn't sure she liked standing so far above the ground.

These facilities were set up differently from any I had seen. There was a barracks type building directly in front of the bridge which housed the sinks and toilets, then off to one side was a building with shower stalls. I knew I was going to shower that evening, so we investigated. I opened the door to one of the shower rooms and recognized it hadn't seen much use. There were cobwebs everywhere. All over the fixtures, the windows, the clothes pegs, just everywhere. This was no shower room for one who did not like spiders. I saw no problem except dealing with the webs. Went back to Tessie and got an old towel, then back to the shower room where I batted all the webs down.

I was set for that shower I desperately needed. The weather was sunny and moderate. The view across the river delightful — small farms glistening in the sun up on the green, green hills above the river. I fed Inkus and hooked her up while looking at all the beauty, then headed across the bridge for my shower before I ate and before it got dark. It wasn't much of a shower room, but the water was hot and that was all I needed. Stood there under a hot stream watching the spiders scurrying around, and counted my blessings. Nothing matters as long as the water is hot.

By the time I finished my dinner, it was dark. Ink and I snuggled up, ready for a good night's rest. It was a clear, starlit night here on the bank high above the St. Lawrence. Could see steamers silently gliding on the river with lights winking and blinking in tune with the heavens.

Tuesday morning, we awoke to a brilliant world. The sun was beaming and how that lifted my spirits. Had breakfast at the picnic table watching the ships on the St. Lawrence and listening to the birds singing. Lingered in the sun, finishing my coffee, and checked my map. I didn't bother with detailed maps at all. I had a small Rand McNally atlas and, although the print was hard to read at times, it proved to be perfectly adequate for my meanders. As it was, each time I studied it I discovered more areas that looked inviting than I could possibly cover. This morning was no exception. Route 20 continued along the St. Lawrence and ended above Riviere du Loup where it became Route 132, a solid red lined road which circled the entire Gaspe Peninsula. That really tugged at me, but it was an additional 500 miles. I decided to head instead into northern Maine and see how things were faring in the United States. Besides, I needed cigarettes and they were beastly expensive in Canada.

Thanks to the sunny weather, we were away from Beaumont by 10:30 a.m. Had some waves and smiles from the other campers as we pulled out. My prediction to the LeVerts that I'd have no trouble with the French certainly had come true. They were kind and hospitable to our gypsy caravan.

We had just crossed the bridge over Route 20 and pulled onto the access road when I saw a group of men and a bunch of machinery in the middle of the road. A workman came towards us gesticulating madly and talking rapidly — in French. I stopped and he kept talking away, but I couldn't understand a word he said. Even I could tell there was no getting onto the highway there. Try as I might, I could not decipher the workman's directions.

We turned around, went back across the bridge, then took a lateral road along the river. We were going in the right direction so I didn't worry. Eventually, we saw a road to the right, took it, and found another access road for Route 20. Then it was clear sailing along the St. Lawrence. It was pleasant scenery and pleasant driving. No traffic along here and I could watch the large freighters on that broad river as we breezed along. At Riviere du Loup, we turned inland on Route 185 across a portion of Quebec that was truly quaint; rolling hills, small farm houses, and superlative churches. The steeples looked as if they were shingled in aluminum and they sparkled on this clear, sunny day. It was a medieval landscape — a landscape looking like it had been painted by Pieter Bruegel, the Elder.

Saw a picnic park and thought it would be a good stop for

lunch and Ink's run. The sun was still shining and it was welcomed after all those cloudy, gloomy days on the north shore. We pulled into the park. It was crowded, so I drove up the hill on a dirt road where I knew Ink could do some running and stretching without annoying anyone. I fixed a sandwich and was standing outside soaking up that glorious sunshine when an older man came puffing up the hill saying, "You know, I don't know what I'm doing here. I was born and raised in New York City. Now, my wife is from Quebec and she loves it, but I sometimes wonder what I'm doing here. I find that coming over here to the park and visiting with all the people sure does help. New Mexico plates, huh? Where is that exactly? Are you all alone?"

We talked for a while. He was a nice gentleman who was doing the best he could in an environment quite different from his native New York City. After awhile, this "park ambassador" walked on back to the main parking area to see if anyone else had arrived. I finished lunch, walked up the hill, and was getting ready to leave when here he came again shouting, "Hey, there're some other people from New Mexico down below."

"You've got to be kidding."

"No, really. And I told them you were here."

"We were just getting ready to leave, but I guess I'd better stop and say hello."

We drove down the hill and there was a trailer with New Mexico plates! I parked and got out and was greeted effusively by a delightful couple named Betty and Russell. They were from Rio Rancho, a town on the west mesa just north of Albuquerque. We all hugged each other like long-lost friends; everyone talking at once and all of us agreeing that it was a small, small world.

I mean, how often do you find someone from your home state on the back roads of Quebec? We had a great visit. They were going to take a ferry boat to Newfoundland, then back to the States for more travel in the east. In the course of the conversation, they said, "You know we started out camping in a Toyota Chinook just like yours."

"I intend to start and end in this little Chinook. I really do love her."

Russ advised, "Just have those valves adjusted from time to time and she'll last you forever, especially with the low miles you have on her. Ours was in good shape but we decided we were gonna do some serious traveling and needed more room. We sold it to two retired lady school teachers and they love it."

I told them I felt the primary reason they had stopped making these fine, sturdy machines — just too small for two people over an extended period of time. But, of course, Tessie was perfect for Ink and me as long as she remembered to move when I had to open the refrigerator door. It was nice to see people from home and to talk with Russ and Betty, especially after my time in Quebec where language was a barrier. Told them I was going into Maine, but then planned to do the Maritime Provinces. We bid each other good travels and parted with the hope we'd cross paths again.

# IX. Potato Fields Forever

We entered Maine at Madawaska after crossing the St. John River. The customs officers asked, "What are you bringing in?"
"Just beautiful memories, that's all."

They were two pleasant young men who seemed interested in my views of traveling Canada so we chatted for a while. Madawaska is the northern terminus of U.S. Route 1. which stretches the whole way to the tip of Florida. We traveled south on it in Maine through Caribou and Presque Isle. Romantic names, names I'd heard all my life. I was seeing this section of the Aroostook Valley first hand. I didn't find any campgrounds as we passed through Caribou and Presque Isle. Just south of Presque Isle, however, in the midst of lush, green potato fields I saw a sign reading Neil E. Michaud Campground and knew I wanted to spend a night here. The whole countryside smelled like new potatoes, the fields and mountains were green, and there were trees and flowers everywhere.

I pulled into a drive leading to a farm house with a big barn behind it. Beyond was the campground surrounded by those green potato fields. There was an office sign at the back of the house and I walked across a wooden deck and knocked on the door.

There were no people anywhere — no campers in the park, no one around. I was beginning to think the place was closed when a cute young gal opened the door and a big Dalmatian came bounding out to greet me. Learned that his name was Sam and the gal was the owner's daughter, Julie. She registered me and told me to park where I wanted, explaining that her mother was not at home but would arrive shortly. I pulled into the grounds and had a devil of a time making a choice. Every site was a delight. I finally settled on one with a slight slope so that I could level Tess easily. It was a great site with big pine trees and views of the potato fields and mountains in all directions.

I was set up and starting dinner because I wanted to eat outside and smell the potatoes. Then I heard voices. Looked out and here came Julie and Sam the Dalmatian, accompanied by an attractive woman who introduced herself as Barbara, the owner of the campground. She apologized for bothering me. Said Julie had insisted she come down to meet this woman traveling on her own. She asked if I needed anything, if everything suited me. I told her I was quite comfortable and found the area lovely. She agreed with that, but told me that not many tourists came to the Aroostook Valley, as was evident by the lack of campers.

Barbara and Julie both gave me a few strokes, telling me how courageous they thought I was. I had to tell them I wasn't courageous, just a little crazy. I told them my journey had been a delight, that I had found kindness and good people almost everywhere I had been. Ink, by this time, had vamped Sam and they were dashing around. Barbara said to let them play as no one was here. The dogs played as I talked with these two lovely women. Did have my dinner as the sun was setting, smelling those potatoes. Then I walked up and had a shower with no spiders. It was cooling off rapidly and Ink and I settled in early.

The sun was beaming in when I awoke. It was cool. I put the kettle on for my coffee. That, plus the sun's heat, warmed Tessie quickly. I stretched and lay there rubbing Ink's tummy. The birds were chirping and the whole world smelled green. We'd been on the road for one full month. What a satisfying month it had been. Ink decided she'd better go out and see if her new friend, Sam, was ready to play. I put her on lead since I wasn't ready to keep tabs on her until I had had my jolt of caffeine. I loved starting the day slow and easy this way, sipping my coffee and hugging to myself the fact that I did not have to hurry or worry, just sip my coffee and enjoy.

I opened the curtains to view the potato fields. The sun was brilliant and the sky was New Mexico blue. Noticed a couple of campers down the way. Had no idea when they had arrived, but they were already preparing to pull out. I sat there drinking my coffee, smelling the potatoes, the green and thought, this is a good day to knock off and take care of some things I had been neglecting in the course of my travels. Made the decision that, no, I'd not drive that day. Eventually, got dressed and ate at the picnic table, just soaking up that sunshine. I walked over to the office. Barb was there and I told her, "I believe I'll stay another night if you don't mind. I need to see about a haircut, film developing, laundry, and that kind of stuff. Can I do all that in Presque Isle?"

"Oh, yes. There are markets and a laundromat and some beauty parlors. I'm sure you can take care of all you need to do in town. Glad you're going to stay longer."

She gave me directions for the laundromat and a shop that would take walk-ins for haircuts. Then she smiled and said, "I'm really glad you're staying. Sam thinks that Ink of yours is okay. When those campers leave, just let them play. He needs the exercise. She is such a sweet dog." I agreed with Barbara. Told her that I found Ink the perfect travel companion, in spite of her tendency to jump up and try to kiss everyone. Barb pointed out that I never had to worry about Ink snapping or biting anyone. We both laughed about Ink ever harming anyone. Barb was right, I thought. I had peace of mind knowing that this gentle dog might kiss someone to death, but she'd never be churlish.

I did not bother to secure all things in the camper for the short trip into Presque Isle. In fact, I left a bunch of stuff out on the picnic table. Popping the top, pulling the top down, and securing everything each day was a tiresome chore. However, it was a necessary evil in the plan. I reminded myself often that I'd never have flabby arms with all that up and down pushing I did each day. It seemed a small inconvenience when weighed against all the joy this journey was bringing to me. So I buckled down the top and away we went for a day in town.

On the hill leading into town, we noticed the campus of the University of Maine at Presque Isle. No need to stop and give

Ink a walk this day. A bit farther on there was an IGA market. I marked it as my last stop. Continued on down the main street of this pretty town of approximately 12,000. Barb's directions were good. I found the laundromat with no trouble and lugged in a big bundle of dirty clothes. There was an attendant on duty who said she'd put things into the dryers for me when they had finished washing. Told her I was on my way for a haircut and would return as soon as possible. The laundromat was busy. There was an area with a TV set and chairs for the patrons. A bunch of people were sitting there with some soap blaring at them.

I surely hadn't missed TV in my month of traveling. I'd forgotten how annoying that tube could be — blaring away. Lots of noise but not much substance. A fat old man was plunked down, catching every word as if it were the gospel. I said a fervent prayer to myself that I would never get to a point in my life where I would want to watch TV all day. I firmly believe it softens your brain.

We found our way to the beauty shop — up the street and back a rough dirt driveway. I managed to park, told Ink to guard the house, and went into the shop. The one and only beautician was busy cutting bubble gum out of a little girl's hair. I never learned how this happened but the child had a full head of bubble gun. She was probably about eight years old and seemed nonchalant about the whole affair; however, her mother was distraught and pacing the floor.

I asked if it was possible to get a cut. The beautician told me she'd be happy to cut my hair as soon as she finished with the gum head. She got all the gum out in time. It was an interesting hair-do, but we all agreed that hair does grow. I had enjoyed watching this bit of Americana and didn't mind waiting. Had my hair cut and shampooed and that attention made me feel good. It wasn't a particularly good cut, but the cost was only eight dollars.

Since it seemed that my priorities were directed more to Tessie and Ink in our travels, it was kinda nice to have someone fussing over me for a while. The TV was on in the beauty shop, too. I guess people just turn it on as a matter of habit, but I don't know why they want that constant inundation and intrusion on their thoughts and processes. Perhaps I was more sensitive to this blaring tube because I had been away from it. I found the damned thing annoying.

When I got back to the laundromat, the clothes weren't dry. There were pay phones on the wall, so I made a call to my Mary. Mary Cobbett, a woman very dear to me. In this entire world, only Mary and my Aunt Dora have known me all my life. I'm awestruck to know they both still love me and support me in all my hair-brained schemes. Mary was expecting me and I was looking forward to a visit with her in Pittsburgh, Pennsylvania. I thought I'd better let her know I was closing in and, with luck, would see her soon.

Her first question was, "Child, where are you?" I told her, Presque Isle, Maine, and all was well, that we were having fun and enjoying the gypsy life. Let her know my plans to visit the Maritime Provinces and said I should get to Pittsburgh after Labor Day.

"You're sure everything is all right?" she asked.

"Yes, everything is really fine, my Muthor, and I'll see you sometime after Labor Day." My term of endearment for this woman is "Muthor." She has been like a mother to me for many years. One day we were talking and she suggested, "You know, Barbie, you never did know your mother, since she died when you were so young. I've always felt like you were my own. Why don't you call me Muthor? You can if you want to and I'd like it." So my Mary has been "Muthor" ever since. She's had a great influence on my life and she's a remarkable person.

Loaded the clean clothes into the back of Tessie. I sometimes felt with this laundromat bit that my clothes were dirty before I even put them away, but it was the only solution. Back up Main Street to the IGA market. It was well stocked, but the aisles were narrow. They did have one-day film developing service. Told me if I left the film then, it would be back by five the next evening. Decided I'd better take advantage of this while I had the chance and left film. Did some marketing and headed back to the campground feeling I had accomplished a lot.

The campground was empty when I pulled in except for Barbara on a big tractor mowing the grass. I could relate to Barb's mowing. It was obvious that Barb would rather do the mowing than clean the restrooms, and I'm with her. I had always said I'd rather have someone clean my house and let me do the yard work. As it was, I always did both, but here was a girl after my own heart. The facilities were fine, but not sterile and foo-foo like some. Barb was playing on the tractor, Sam was on his long line. After I parked, I walked down and asked, "Can the pups play for a while?" Barb slowed the tractor and replied, "Oh, great. Can you let him off his line?"

"Sure, no trouble."

"Hey, your hair looks nice. It's pretty short."

"Yeah, I know, but it'll grow. I've had better cuts, but it sure was pleasant having someone coddle me for a bit."

Barb went back to her chores and I released Sam. Sat like a swami on the picnic table watching the dogs play, Barb mow, and smelling the potatoes and new mown grass. All was right with my world, indeed.

After she finished the mowing, Barb came up, took off her gloves, and hopped up beside me on the picnic table. She told me the park was named for her father from whom she and her husband purchased it. She did admit that business was not all that good. I sensed a certain irritation in her that more tourists did not travel northern Maine. As she put it, "Oh, they all go to the coast and it's all jammed up. They don't know what they're missing." I agreed with her assessment of this delightful country.

Julie came home from school about this time and walked down to join us in the warm sun. What a wonderful sisterhood we women have. They told me about another woman who had stayed with them. She came into the campground with a canoe on top of her car. Told them she had just finished canoeing a vast area of northern Maine all by herself; making the portages and lugging that canoe. She told Barb and Julie that what worried her most was whether or not she could handle the canoe all alone: getting it on top of her car and making the portages. She spent time practicing and found that she could do it. Headed out and spent two weeks in the wilderness. She told them it was most satisfying. Ah, yes, we women will stretch ourselves, given the right set of circumstances. There are many pilgrims in the world.

Barb and Julie took their leave and headed up to fix dinner. A couple more campers pulled in. Ink was happy to be on lead after her romp with Sam the Dalmatian. The sun was setting and there were a few clouds on the western horizon glowing pink, orange, and gold. I took a photo just to remind myself that Maine, too, has lovely sunsets. I hiked up to the shop by the campground where there was a public phone and tried to call Samantha in Las Cruces to wish her a happy birthday, but there was no answer. Went back to the camper, took Ink for a walk around the grounds, then we turned in.

I finished Jean Auel's *The Mammoth Hunters* before going to sleep. Her books are well-researched and very informative. Her theories are the latest in the field of anthropology concerning the life styles of our ancient kin (except possibly for the rampant sex life, but it does sell books). Slept well after one full month on the road with no regrets for having followed my inner voice.

I woke quite early. It was another sunny day. That made three in a row, and I wondered if it was not some kind of record here in the northland; however, I was delighted to see old Sol. Had one cup of coffee, put Inkus on lead, and hiked back over to the pay phone to try and ring through to Samantha again. Theo answered and asked immediately, "Barb, when will you be home?" I told her I wasn't sure, but that I'd be back. Wished Samantha a day-late happy birthday and we had a good talk.

Sam said they missed me. I told her I missed them also, but was having fun and enjoying this traveling more than I had ever imagined. We both signed off with love. She and Theo are family to me, but then, aren't we all family?

I was having breakfast at the picnic table when Barb walked down. She told me the temperature had dropped to 42 degrees over night. I asked about check-out time and explained that I could pick up my film after 4:30 p.m. She suggested, "Why don't you just stay another night?" It was a kind invitation; however, I told her I'd better move on before the first snowfall. Since I had to take Tessie down to go into Presque Isle, I felt I might as well drive a bit. She told me to pull out anytime I was ready and to not worry about it. Barb had to leave that morning and I offered to keep an eye on things. So I had the campground all to myself. A loafing, quiet day just waiting until I could pick up my photos.

I did use my time to good advantage. Cleaned Tessie and re-arranged items, got things packed and battened down for travel. Then, I sat out in the sun on the picnic table and did some more nice things for myself: shaved my legs, painted my toe nails — all the while questioning why I was doing it. Guess old habits die hard. I knew Ink didn't care one way or the other, but I felt an obligation to keep a certain amount of civility. Besides, these little pleasures were nurturing. Wrote some postcards and a note to Pamie asking that she forward mail to Mary Cobbett in Pittsburgh. Ink roamed and explored, I soaked up more sunshine. There was no one around. We both enjoyed this free time.

I sat there and thought about my first month of travel, about how beautiful it was, how unstressful it was in so many ways, so many ways inherent in our culture. There were no phones ringing, no TV blaring at me, no demands on my time other than my own. Really, quite a free lifestyle, as free as any I'd ever experienced. This is not to say that I didn't, from time to time, have to struggle against those old habits — linear time, keeping to a schedule, pushing myself — but I was easing off more and more. Reminding myself that, no, I didn't have to hurry, I didn't have to be in a specific place at a specific time, I didn't have to eat unless I was hungry nor stop unless I was tired.

Mentally, I gave myself a little pat, for I was discovering that

I liked being responsible for myself. I liked following an internal locus of control, and I even liked my own company. This has to be the beginning of acquiring maturity and balance, this knowledge that you are responsible for your own well-being and you are responsible to yourself. I decided that I was a fairly self-sufficient person. Yet I knew that I was not alone and without guidance from some power greater than myself. The more I opened to this knowledge, the more guidance I gained. With that last pat, I turned off the profound and headed up for a shower.

I walked over and took a photo of the potato fields next to the campground with the goldenrod in the foreground, the trees and mountains in the background. They had given me so much pleasure. Both Julie and Barb were home before I left and we had a final round of hugs. I thanked those two beautiful women for making my stay so pleasant. They both cautioned me to be careful and take care of myself.

After one last, warm hug, I wended my way back into town. The film had not gotten in, but they said it would be there shortly. I walked across the street and posted mail, and at 5:20 p.m. the photo truck arrived. I took a quick glance at them and was pleased to know I'd have pictures to always remind me of this glorious journey.

# X. The Maritimes: A Lobster Lover's Delight

### New Brunswick

The gypsy caravan was rolling south on U.S. Route 1 again. At Houlton, we turned directly east and crossed the border into New Brunswick after a few miles. There was an interesting customs man at the border station, an older man who asked the usual questions: where I was from, did Ink have her vaccination papers, how long I planned to stay, and finally, "Do you have any guns or weapons?"

"I wouldn't think of carrying such things."

"Well, you won't need them here."

I took this to mean that he was not sure I should be traveling alone in the United States without a weapon, but that I'd be safe and secure in New Brunswick. Our nation has a reputation for violence which it has rightly earned.

It was getting late and the tourist office was closed. We decided on the Kozy Acres campground in Woodstock, located on Trans-Canadian Route 2. The campground was right next to it which made for a night filled with traffic noise. I bought a postcard to send to Scot and Juli as it was the name Scot gave to his bright yellow Datsun. I knew the kids would enjoy a card from Woodstock. It was almost dark before we were parked up and settled. Had a quick dinner, quick walk, and called it a day.

I read the brochure from Kozy Acres as I drank my coffee in the morning. Learned that Woodstock is the oldest incorporated town in New Brunswick, dating to 1856. It has a population of 4800 and is located in the heart of the New Brunswick potato belt. In looking at my map, I discovered that we were now in the

Atlantic time zone, so we had gained an hour. Noted also that Rand McNally lists New Brunswick, Nova Scotia, and Prince Edward Island as the Atlantic Provinces. I had been taught they were the Maritimes; however, that had been eons ago. Perhaps, the recent terminology is Atlantic Provinces.

The map given to me at the office stated that the world's longest covered bridge was just twelve miles up the highway. Decided to forgo the bridge and go back to the charming tourist center. Needed some brochures and information on New Brunswick and these Maritime or Atlantic Provinces. So we headed out about 11 a.m. Atlantic time, which was only 10 a.m. Eastern time, I think.

The information center was architecturally interesting. It was a low, squat wooden and concrete building set into a hill with lots of wooden ramps, walkways, and wide wooden overhangs. The roof was covered with grass, beautifully kept grass. I wondered if there was concrete underneath and who in the world cut that grass. Walked in and discovered New Brunswick hospitality. The ladies at the desk greeted me with, "Good morning. Welcome. May we help you?"

I explained that I had just gotten to New Brunswick and would appreciate any insight on where to travel and what to see. Specifically requested information on the ferry boats to Prince Edward Island. They loaded me up with kindness and information. I also asked where I could mail Scot and Juli's postcard. The gal on the desk offered, "Oh, that's clear back in town. Leave it here with me and I'll post it for you this evening when I go into Woodstock." She mentioned that the postal strike was still on. I wondered if the kids would ever get the card, but paid 46 cents for a stamp and left it with the pleasant lady at the desk.

We finally pulled onto Route 2, heading toward Fredericton driving through the St. John River valley. It is the St. John River which is the commanding feature of this region. It's often referred to as the Rhine of North America and it originates in the northern forests of Maine. It winds its way, here and there harnessed for power and recreation, for over 450 miles through broad, green vistas, lush forests, and rolling farm land to the Bay of Fundy.

New Brunswick itself is one of the oldest settled parts of North America. The early explorers found Maleci and Micmac native communities here. The Acadians, settlers from France, came first and their heritage is still found in the area today. Later, English, Scot, and Irish settlers came, many of them as Loyalists during the American Revolution. The architecture is diverse and well-preserved in many of the towns. There are classic examples of Palladian, Neo-Classical, Gothic revival, second empire, and Queen Anne revival styles throughout New Brunswick.

We drove into a picnic park at Kings Landing Historical Settlement just off the Trans-Canadian. It was a large picnic area with covered shelters, flowers everywhere, great views of the St. John River, and not a soul in sight. I chose a spot overlooking the river, let Ink hop out, and fixed some lunch.

This historical settlement is a meticulous restoration of Loyalist life in New Brunswick between 1820 and 1890. All of the people wear costumes and demonstrate the daily tasks of that era in authentic buildings with furnishings of the period. I did not pay admission to browse within the settlement, but Ink and I did enjoy our lunch break there.

We drove through Fredericton, the capital city of New Brunswick. As you approach the city, there are signs along the highway which read: We've been expecting you! What a sweet welcome. I acknowledged it mentally with: Thank you very much! It's known as the city of stately elms and has a population of about 45,000 people. It was a gracious city with tree-lined streets and historic buildings and homes. There were clapboard houses with square turrets on top, narrow brick churches with brick steeples looking as if they would stand forever. I did not stop in Fredericton, but rather looked as we ambled through. It was a slow-paced, friendly city and people waved to this traveler so far from home.

Just east of Fredericton, the St. John River turns south on its journey to the Bay of Fundy. We continued on east on Route 2. This area was dotted with dairy farms and tranquil herds of cattle. At Sussex, decided to get gas, thinking, don't run on the ragged edge today, Barb. So took the turn into town. I spied a bakery shop on the main street. The lady was standing at the window looking out and didn't appear to have any business. I parked Tessie and walked across the street to the bakery for a few goodies. It smelled yummy. I bought some rolls and muffins and chatted with the lady a few minutes. Then we went on down the main street for a gas stop. I thought I should check the air pressure in my tires and pulled over to the air pump. Well, I walked up and the terminology on this pump was something I had never seen before. It wasn't in pounds per square inch. It was a totally foreign term to me.

I was standing there trying to figure what the terminology meant and feeling a little intimidated by this weird air pump. In fact, I had about decided that the tires were just fine when a young man walked up asking, "You don't understand it?" I had to admit, "No, I really don't." He told me he could convert the foreign terms and asked, "How many pounds do you want in your tires?" I told him and the young man proceeded to check Tessie's tires and fill them. He grinned and said, "Glad to do it, Ma'am." Now that's friendliness.

I wanted to get to the shore on this afternoon, somewhere close to Cape Tormentine where we could catch the ferry to Prince Edward Island. Everything was going smoothly, just rolling along. Until we reached Moncton. I was following the directional signs, I thought, when all of a sudden there were no more. I found myself in downtown Moncton. This was not where I wanted to be, and I hadn't the foggiest notion of how to get out of there. Told Ink we were in the heart of Moncton, and bless her, she didn't say, "Well, you've screwed up again, haven't you?"

Ink and I agreed we might as well relax and view the city since we were hopelessly lost. The downtown area was beautiful:

wide streets lined with sidewalk cafes, trees and flowers, posh
shoppes, and elegant brick buildings. It was very nice, but I kept
thinking this is not where I should or want to be.

In searching for signs to lead me out of the fair city, I began
to realize that it was a tourist mecca. There were signs for the
Magnetic Mountain where your car would roll up the hill with
no power; signs for Magic Mountain Water Park with four giant
water slides; signs directing me to Bore Park; lots and lots of
directions for tourist attractions, but nothing to give me a clue on
how to get out of downtown Moncton.

We kept going in what I hoped was the right direction,
praying fervently that Tessie wouldn't be sucked up the Magnetic
Hill. Eventually, we were back on the highway. I still don't
know how we found it, or did it find us? The traffic was heavy.
It was evening commuter time by now. I decided to get to
Shediac, the lobster capital of the world, and hang it up for the
day. As we were driving into town, I spotted a roadside
restaurant advertising lobster to go. Hung a sharp right and
picked up a gorgeous lobster wrapped in brown paper. Checked
my guide while we were off the road and found that Parlee
Provincial Park was in Shediac.

The directions were easy and we were at the park in minutes.
I was glad, because I knew I couldn't wait long to eat that
sumptuous lobster. It was a large park with camping sites far
from the water, but it was adequate. Set a record that evening in
setting up. My mouth was watering for lobster. Stuck it into the
oven, put a cup of butter on top to melt, ran Ink around the
park, then sat down at the picnic table and attacked my gourmet
meal. Lobster, that is, real lobster from cold, northern waters
with chelates, is manna from heaven for me.

I had packed a pair of lobster cracks (thank you, my guides)
and I waded into that lobster with gusto. By the time I finished,
I had butter rolling down my chin, down my arms, all over
myself. But what a treat!

It was getting dark and clouds were beginning to roll in,
along with mosquitoes. They were large and had voracious

appetites. Put Ink on her lead and we took a more leisurely stroll now that my tummy was full of lobster. I then hooked her up and went for a shower. Did not stay outside for fear the mosquitoes would devour me, but hopped into Tessie, read a while, and slept well.

In the morning, we were once again in the rain mode. It was cloudy, windy, and raining hard. Consequently, we were ready to leave by 10 a.m. Stopped at the office to inquire about the beach. The night before, I had read that it was one of the finest salt water beaches in New Brunswick and it had the warmest waters north of the Carolinas. I didn't want to take a swim that morning, but I did want to see it. The gal gave me directions.

At the beach area, I met another gal in a booth entrance since it was a fee area. I pulled up and explained that I was interested in driving along and looking at the beach. The gal waved me through saying, "Do enjoy looking. There'll be no fee for that." So in the rain and clouds, we drove slowly along Parlee Beach: lots of low sand dunes and sea oats, not many breakers. It did remind me of beaches in the eastern United States; however, I did not get out to check the water temperature. On this grey morning, there were no swimmers, surfers, or even sea gulls in sight. We waved to the young lady as we left, found our way out of the "lobster capital of the world," and headed towards Cape Tormentine, New Brunswick, to board the auto ferry run by Marine Atlantic for a trip across Northumberland Strait to Borden on Price Edward Island, more commonly referred to as PEI here in the Atlantic Provinces.

I had been wise enough to read some of the information from the tourist center near Woodstock. Noted that at this time of the year, the ferries ran about every hour. That relieved me of any need to make a schedule, so we meandered, enjoying the countryside. About an hour out of Shediac, the clouds dissipated and the sun came beaming through. By the time we arrived at the ferry terminal, it was a sparkling day.

Although there was no ferry boat in sight, traffic was cued up to purchase tickets for the crossing. We pulled into a line and I discovered another redeeming feature of this 18 foot Chinook. Because she was small and had only one set of tires all around, Tessie came under the same fee schedule as cars. I hadn't even thought of that aspect of my travels before. After paying fees, we moved up into the waiting line. That really brought home the fact that Tessie was a little one. We were swallowed up by the big camping rigs, long trailers, and huge transports which surrounded us. I patted Tess and told her she might be small, but she was sturdy and loved.

Once we were parked amongst the giant rigs, there was nothing to do but wait for the ferry to arrive. I walked over to the terminal building and looked around while I drank a cup of hot chocolate. Browsed in the gift shop, then went back and took Ink for a short walk on lead. There was a grassy area with picnic tables overlooking the water.

As Ink and I were strolling there, the ferry came plying its stately way across the strait. I was putting Ink up when a group of young girls walked by. All of them raised their arms and saluted me with, "Way to go, Lady." It was touching and pleasant. Evidently the feminist movement is world-wide.

I felt a bit apprehensive about pulling onto this big boat rocking up and down, but I was committed. Tessie, after my pep talk, moved with dignity beside all those huge vehicles. The parking attendants were helpful, and we settled into our space on the ferry for the ride across to PEI. I sat in the camper and read the fee schedule: Automobiles, Auto Trailers, Campers, Motor Homes, Vans up to and including 20 feet - $6.25: over 20 feet to 30 feet - $9.40; over 30 feet - $12.50. Tess went for $6.25 plus my passenger fare of $2.40 for a total of $8.65. Seemed a reasonable price for a boat ride of approximately 45 minutes. I had a little trouble with the schedule until I discovered one side was written in English and the other in French. I had grabbed it with the French side up and thought, how am I supposed to read this thing?

The ferry still hadn't gotten underway, so I read an article on linking Price Edward Island to the mainland by means of a tunnel, bridge, or causeway. When PEI reluctantly agreed to join Canada in confederation in 1873, it was with the promise that the federal government would provide them with year-round transportation between PEI and the rest of Canada — and it still hasn't come about.

Public Works Canada is studying the possibility of linking Cape Tormentine and Borden, replacing the existing ferry service. A bridge or a tunnel are the two options being considered. For the present, the year-round ferry service is operated by Marine Atlantic. It costs the government approximately 25 million dollars in operating subsidies each year, plus the replacing of old ferry boats. The number of cars and trucks using the service has been steadily increasing at a rate of from 2 to 3 percent a year. This increase results in crossing delays, especially during the summer tourist season. In winter, the delays are due to bad weather.

Early in 1988, the islanders voted on a ballot asking: Are you in favor of a fixed link crossing between Price Edward and New Brunswick? Yes or No? Voter turnout was almost 65% of the eligible voters. And, 60% were in favor. It is possible that the ferry boats will become a relic of the past. I was glad they were still running and delighted with the crossing. It was a typical ferry boat with vehicles jammed into the hull, and decks for walking and viewing up top.

Although Ink had never been on a boat, she takes all things in stride. It was rather dark and she curled up on her feather pillow ready for a nap. She seemed comfortable and we were underway, so I went hopping around the ferry boat, taking a look and exploring. I hadn't been on a ferry since I was a kid, but found it still held the same fascination for me.

When I arrived on deck, there was my cheering section. I talked with the young ladies and learned that they were students at the University of New Brunswick on their way to PEI for the Labor Day weekend. They were a delightful group who made me feel like some kind of adventurous explorer. They did exclaim over the fact that I was traveling alone, but they didn't ask if I was afraid. They recognized that I was enjoying my aloneness and my travels. In response to their questions, I told them a little about my trip thus far. They all said, "We'd love to do what you're doing." My advice was — "Do it!" After chatting with these supportive young women, I walked the decks, took some photos, and by that time we were pulling into Borden.

## Prince Edward Island

Tessie eased her way off the ferry boat among all those big rigs and transports with style and grace. We did, however, pull over and let the herd of traffic go by. I wasn't in a hurry — didn't even know where we were going. So, we sat by the side of the road and looked. Prince Edward is a picture perfect island: neat and well-kept with pink soil. It's a warm pink color and very fertile, one of the few fertile places in the Maritimes. After the traffic thinned, we turned left onto the highway and shortly were in the town of Summerside. Saw a large shopping mall with good parking and pulled in for a look. For me, the most beautiful thing in all the markets in this region were the lobster tanks brimming with live, succulent lobsters. Bought another one for dinner and a few items, then went back to the camper where I checked my guide. Read an ad for a park on the shores of Malpeque Bay which sounded inviting.

We drove northeast from town and down a country lane edged with potato fields which looked even greener contrasting with the pink, pink soil. There were immaculately kept farms, cows grazing contentedly in jade green fields, and the sun was warm. It seemed a perfect place to be.

Pulled into Raynor's Camping and Trailer Park about 3:30 p.m. knowing it was early, but not feeling the need to drive any farther that day. They gave us a space in a grassy field with huge old trees not far from the restrooms and only a short walk over to the bay. As soon as we set up, we walked down to the shore of Malpeque Bay which is noted for its oyster and lobster beds.

Ink decided she should take a swim. The tide was out and she plunged into the water full tilt. Shore birds flew off in every direction as this big black dog galloped across the beach. When she hit that water, I could see her shudder. It was so cold it took her breath away. She didn't swim long. When we got back to Tessie, I put the kettle on and give my chilled dog a good rubdown with a heavy towel. She was cold. We snuggled up together in the sunshine beaming into Tessie and took a little snooze. I think both of us had forgotten how far north we were on the continent.

The park was relatively uninhabited — very few campers on this holiday weekend. I put the lobster into the oven. Ink and I were warmed up and took an evening stroll around the grounds. We met a gentleman from Maine who told me they had been coming to this area for many years. He was concerned that the waters were becoming polluted in the Bay and the oyster and lobster beds were diminishing. We agreed that this small planet was being stressed to its limit. As he was taking his leave, he said, "Be sure and tell your husband I said hello." More preconceived notions. I merely smiled and said, "Why, thank you very much." I never found the need to advertise that I was traveling alone and, as with this pleasant man, many people assume you're with someone. I preferred to let that assumption stand.

With sunset came a steep drop in temperatures. I was happy to munch out on lobster inside snug little Tess that evening. Ink hopped in early and snuggled up next to me while I read more literature on PEI — think she was still chilled from her swim. I turned off the lights and curled around that black body, happy to feel Ink's warmth. This picture perfect island must be formidable in the winter and populated by hardy souls. I slept that night of September 3 in a pair of heavy sweats and woolen socks and was not all that warm.

I woke up freezing. It was cold. That's another wonderful feature about my Tessie; I don't even have to get out of the sleeping bag to put the kettle on. Can reach over and light the burner while still in bed. Once the stove is lit, the chill dissipates rapidly in such a small space. The sun was rising over the potato field, the bay was sparkling, and the camper warmed nicely. I sat huddled in my sleeping bag drinking my coffee and thinking, winters must be something here. However, the higher the sun rose, the warmer it became. I drank my coffee gazing out on all the pristine beauty and decided it wasn't all that cold.

Ink had met a local dog and they were racing around in the meadow under the trees. I fixed breakfast, put on a jacket over my sweats and sat at the picnic table in the sun. A couple from British Columbia strolled past with an ancient collie. Ink greeted them. She and the collie had a sniff, but no romp. We all agreed this was a charming island.

I put Ink on lead and went over to the restroom where a woman told me the temperature had dropped to 38 degrees the previous night — and this was early September. I showered and shampooed. The water was hot, thank God. It was a perfect day on this perfect island: clear azure skies, brilliant sunshine, and crisp air. It was a day for exploring. We left the campground about 11 a.m., not knowing where we would go, but sure that we couldn't go too far on an island. It didn't matter if we got lost for we wanted to take a long look at this beautiful spot.

We headed in a westerly direction on a good highway with no traffic, skirting the outer boundaries of Summerside. The first town was Miscouche where I marveled at the church as we rolled by. This was the heart of the Tyne Valley. It was lush country; cows munching in fields which stretched down to the water's edge. I decided this seemed too much like interstate driving. With my preference for pike-shunning, when we came upon a narrow country lane, I looked at Ink and said, "What do you think, shall we see what's down there? No need to worry, my gal, when we come to water, we know we have to go in another direction, okay?" Ink, ever the perfect travel companion, looked at me as if to say, "Sounds good to me."

I have no idea where we were. We puttered along on lovely peaceful country lanes. There was no traffic, so I could gawk and look to my heart's content. Somewhere in this area, I saw a sign reading Belmont Provincial Park by a dirt road and turned in. We eased along and came to a beautiful park area with a playground, an incredibly pink sand beach, open green fields filled with wildflowers, pavilions for picnicking, and not a soul there.

I pulled way up into a high field with twisted pines on the rim of the hill overlooking the water and parked. Ink and I roamed for a long while wondering why there were no people. It was Labor Day week-end, but evidently the season is over on PEI before Labor Day. With the morning temperature being only 38 degrees, I guess only hardy souls and fools like me come this late in the season. We found it wonderful not to be hassled with traffic and people.

Ink and I scrambled over the hills; I stopping to marvel at the scenic views and she happy to run and explore. Had I been a more seasoned traveler, I would have stayed in this solitary, lovely setting overnight. Instead, we pressed on to see more of the island. It was as we were leaving Belmont that I took jazz tapes out of the deck and put on Vivaldi's *Four Seasons.* This was an island for Vivaldi!

Got back to the paved country lane and turned left to wander through still more glorious countryside. It was a champagne sort of day and I had that sense of well-being that comes when one is seeking one's bliss. We were lost, by culture's definition; however, I felt very centered here on this snug little island. Not lost at all, but rather, found.

As we continued down the road, we arrived back in Miscouche. We had done a circle tour and were coming back to the main highway. This small country road ran directly in front of the church I had noticed. I took this to mean I was to have a closer look at the church, so pulled into the empty parking area and got out. It was a white, wooden structure trimmed in black with twin steeples in front. The front of the church was at least three stories high with the steeples soaring higher still. At the rear corners were small steeples similar to those up front. Prince Edward Island is noted for its churches and I saw many. This one was truly elegant. I walked the grounds and took photos.

We were again on the main highway, but after a few miles, I turned down another country lane and before long found myself in Cavendish where I played the tourist role to the hilt. Cavendish is the site of the house that Lucy Maude Montgomery used as her setting for Anne of Green Gables.

It was beginning to get cloudy and cool. I knew Ink would be comfortable, so I pulled into the parking area along with many other tourists and went to see this abode.

Lucy Maude Montgomery was born in New London, Prince Edward Island, on November 30, 1874, just one year after the island had entered the confederation of Canada. In 1908, her first novel, Anne, put Prince Edward on the literary maps of the world. Maude, as she liked to be called, died in 1942. She had published over twenty books, hundreds of short stories and poems and her name was known far beyond the English-speaking world. It was *Anne of Green Gables* that I knew and loved best. The house was once the home of cousins of Maude, and she used this area as a setting for her story. Some people say that many of the traits that we remember from that red-headed, freckle-faced Anne were traits of Maude Montgomery's also.

I walked over to the bungalow set amid lovely flower gardens. It was a white, wooden house with dark green trim, not a large structure. The rooms were furnished to depict the period setting of the novel. Anne's room upstairs was sparsely but comfortably furnished. The feature that hit me was the lowness of the ceilings. They were very low which, of course, was an efficient means of conserving heat in that cold climate. In spite of tourists rushing past me, I took my time in this cozy bungalow. Walked across the parking lot to the restrooms and then into the gift shop and tea room. I bought a copy of *Anne of Green Gables* to take to Theo. It was nice that I could buy this gift at its setting and I knew Theo would love *Anne*. Even though there were lots of people milling about, the setting still retained the tranquility of the by-gone time of which Maude wrote so well. I did play tourist to the hilt here. Even bought myself a sweat shirt with Prince Edward Island emblazoned across the front, feeling that once in a while one should get into the swing of tourism.

After the touristy junket, we drove over more hills and dales, past more scenic farms, and were in Prince Edward National Park. It is a small coastal strip along the Gulf of St. Lawrence. We ambled along looking at pink sand dunes, pink sandstone cliffs, and the sea. Pulled into a parking lot overlooking the beach, which was deserted, so Ink and I took a beach walk. She did not go swimming. I knew the water was not warm enough for me, but the Gulf was lovely. We had a nice stroll then headed on down the road. I hadn't the foggiest idea of where we were. It was clouding up even more and I thought perhaps we should find a place to spend the night. Checked the guide, still shunning the provincial parks — not the wise camper yet.

In doing the drive along the Cavendish section of PEI National Park, we came to a dead end so had to backtrack and find another means of getting inland. Eventually found ourselves on Route 6. I had read of a campground that I thought had to be close. It was 14 miles west of Mt. Stewart and called Winterbay Tent and Trailer Park. The weather had turned grey and gloomy. We kept on and, sure enough, I spotted a sign and pulled in, thinking, my God, Winterbay. I was cold last night in Summerside. I may freeze solid tonight.

Skirted my way around some deep puddles in the driveway. There was a friendly woman behind the desk in the office which was also a store. This woman said, "Aye, you're traveling all alone?" I did my usual, "No. I have my dog." But there was no, "Aren't you afraid?" follow up here. She just said, "Aye, you're the brave one and so far from home." I smiled and told her I certainly was, but I loved her charming island. She told me she didn't think it very charming in the winter. As we talked, her niece came into the store; a cute gal of 19. Her aunt called to her to come and meet this woman who was traveling all alone. There was more socializing and telling them of my travels thus far. These two women were supportive and encouraging. This pilgrim welcomed their warmth and friendship.

I finally drove across a grassy field and got parked up in the space they had assigned me. It was good; surrounded by big trees, with a view of the bay, and within sight of the laundry and restroom facilities. It was only about 5:30 p.m. and I decided to do a load of wash. I was walking across the field when the niece joined me, wanted to know more about New Mexico and desert country. She told me with great pride, "I'm going to Ontario this fall." The campground is closed for the winter and rightly so I think. I told her I had had a wonderful time in Ontario and thought it was great that she was going.

"Yeah, it'll be nice to get off this island."

"But it's so beautiful and peaceful."

"Oh, it's just the island."

She stayed and visited while I did my laundry. A vivacious girl who was living in all this serenity and longing to get away from it. We humans are never satisfied, are we?

After laundry, Ink and I walked. We met a lady who was from the island. It was obvious the islanders dread the cold, harsh winters. I commented on the beauty of Prince Edward and she agreed, but added, "It's getting cool already and winter will be here soon and winter is bad." She told me that when the weather is really stormy, the ferry boats are unable to run and the island has no link to the outside world. She recalls times when supplies run short and there's not much selection in the stores. She tossed her head, smiled, and said, "Aye, but we always make it." A hardy group, these islanders. Hardy and gracious.

Even though this was Winterbay, it was warmer than the area of Summerside. The clouds were thick, which tends to hold the heat in, but it seemed a misnomer. We still snuggled fairly early after a glorious day of exploring the back roads and by-ways of this island which some people call a million acre farm. It is Canada's smallest province: only 140 miles in length, but it affords many unique places for sightseeing. Thought, yes, it is a fertile little island and with all the succulent seafood in the waters surrounding it, one could almost live from the sea and the land. Curled close to Ink, pleased with our day of meandering on PEI, and slept well, as usual.

Woke to windy, rainy weather. It wasn't cold, but it was overcast and not a pleasant morning. Even Ink refused to go out and check the campground. I drank my coffee while I checked ferry boat schedules. Found that we would not have to backtrack and I never like to do that. With luck, and if I could find my way to Wood Islands, we could catch the Northumberland ferry which would take us to Caribou, Nova Scotia. I noted that schedules changed after Labor Day and crossings were infrequent. I decided we had better catch a boat on this Labor Day. That was an error in judgement on my part. We slowly got ourselves ready in the rain and left Winterset about 11 a.m.

Clouds were scudding across the bay, the windshield wipers were swishing, and rain was falling heavily. Not a day for exuberance, but one on which I preferred to drive. I thought we were heading for PEI's capital city, but we never did get to Charlottetown. Instead, we were once again on country lanes. We poked along in a southeasterly direction through still more green farmlands dotted with lovely coves and bays. My intention to see Charlottetown was good even though I preferred not to grapple with cities. and, on this rainy morning, I was spared.

The weather was clearing when I saw we were in the Belfast area on Route 207. I knew I had read something about this historic area, so pulled over to check. St. John's Church at Belfast is billed as the oldest one still active on the island, and it was just ahead. I stopped and viewed another immaculate white church set on a grassy hill in a grove of maples. The church was surrounded by an intriguing cemetery, but the wind was up and it was damp, so I didn't walk and read tombstones. Decided to leave that for another time.

Everywhere on this prim island were inviting country inns and quaint bed-and-breakfast establishments. I thought I'd like my kids to come here for a summer vacation. It was that kind of island.

Pulled back onto the road, meandering along, not knowing where we were and not caring. I knew we needed gasoline; however, we came down over a hill and found ourselves at the boat dock at Wood Islands. I hadn't noticed all that many people on the island. I think they were all parked in line right here waiting for the ferry to Nova Scotia. It was jammed. We were there and I felt committed, so we queued up with the rest of the vehicles. It developed into a three hour wait. The weather cleared and the sun broke out. I felt better about making the crossing. Although there was a fast food stand, I hopped into Tessie and brewed a cup of tea and fixed some cheese and crackers. I watched the people milling around as I ate. Everyone was in good humor; not at all upset about the long wait. It was a holiday week-end and was to be expected.

I was closing the door of the camper when a wren-like lady came up to me smiling and saying, "Aye, lass, you're a long way from home, aren't you now?" Melvina worked for the Tourism Department of PEI. She suggested, "Well, you're gonna have a bit of a wait. Why don't I interview you?" Sounded good to me and I was able to say from the heart, "I loved your island." She asked about my traveling alone and I answered, "No problem. It's been a wonderful experience and PEI has been a high point for me."

After talking for quite a while, we parted friends with the promise that next time I was on the island, I'd give Melvina a call and we'd have a lobster dinner together. I sat and read while Ink snoozed. Eventually, we did make the crossing and got to Nova Scotia about 6 p.m.

## Nova Scotia

We pulled off the road and waited for the disembarking traffic to speed by, then set out, not knowing where we were once again. Somehow, we got off onto a dirt road and were hopelessly lost. We needed gas desperately and I thought, this may be the night we camp by the side of the road. Not only were there no signs of habitation, no cars had passed us for what seemed like miles. I thought, Oh, my God, we're in the wilderness for sure. Kept laughing and driving. Ink always intuitively knew when I was unsettled. She had hopped into the passenger seat and was nuzzling my armpit. I patted her and told her not to worry, laughing, but wondering where in hell we must be. The gas gauge had been on empty for a half-hour. I knew we had better keep going until we ran out of gas or found a station, whichever came first. Felt I had pressed my luck too far this time. I patted Tessie, too, and told her we were looking for a station and encouraged her to hang in there. We came around a bend in the dirt road and there was a gas station. Whee! There it sat right on the side of a paved highway. Who could ask for more?

I don't remember what brand of gas it was. They could have charged me $50 a gallon and I would have paid gladly. A young lady came out to pump the gas — they still pump gas for you in Canada — and I meant it when I said to her, "Boy, am I glad to see you!" Tessie took 15.6 gallons of gas that evening. She has a 16 gallon tank. I had pushed my luck, but all ended well. I asked the girl if there might be a campground close and she told me, "Sure. Just down the road, not more than 3 kilometers is the provincial park. It's on the left side and there's a sign."

Saw the sign reading Salt Springs Provincial Park just as she said. We pulled into the office, registered, and were directed down another dirt road to the sites. It was dusk by this time and as we drove down the hill I was taken aback by a large cemetery to our left. Curved around the cemetery and on down the hill to a large, open camp site: not many campers and no restrooms and showers, but lovely. I had noted this tendency of our species to huddle together, and it surely was apparent here. There were only seven campers in this large site and all were parked right up on top of each other. I didn't want to be too far away, but could see no need to contribute to the sardine effect, so we drove on down the lane and took a space by the river. I could see the other campers and also the cemetery, but we had some space.

It was getting dark and the parks in the Maritimes had no

overhead lights. Evidently, they see no need to waste electricity in that manner. I preferred it because the night skies were so brilliant. Ink was outside on her lead and I was fixing dinner when I heard this strange moan. Thought, oh, oh, the spirits from the cemetery are up and about. Heard it again, and at the same time heard Ink's lead hitting the bumper.

I stepped outside and said, "Hello?" Heard a quivery female voice return my greeting and a gal stepped into the light from the camper. She had been walking down the road to the outhouse when Ink decided to greet her. She couldn't see that black animal in the dark and had let out this weird moan. We both had a great laugh when I told her I had been fixing dinner, wondering if the spirits in the cemetery roamed around after dark, when I heard her moan. We laughed even harder because she told me she had been thinking the same thing walking down that dark road when Ink nosed her leg.

We settled in shortly after dinner cleanup as it had been a wearing day. I thanked my God for leading me well once again and bringing me to this peaceful park. If the spirits did roam, I slept too soundly to hear them.

I woke early. The sun was shining and while I drank my coffee I studied the map of Nova Scotia. It was time to find out just where we were. Nova Scotia is billed as the festival province of Canada and has an area of 21,420 square miles. I discovered that Salt Springs Provincial Park was off Route 104 about 11 miles west of New Glasgow. The map was marked with designations for different scenic tours on Nova Scotia such as: The Marine Trail, The Sunrise Trail, the Fleur de Lis Trail. I had been told that Halifax, Nova Scotia's capital, was lovely. It appeared there was lots to see and do. As I drank my coffee and studied the map, what beckoned me was The Cabot Trail around Cape Breton Island, yet another island. Decided to head east and north and do Cabot Trail. Put Halifax on hold. The roads were well-marked, for which I was grateful. I did not need another hopelessly lost excursion this day.

Ink had her romp. There were a few people out and about.

The cemetery monuments were sitting stolidly in the sun over on their knoll. Once I made the decision about what I wished to see, I got Tessie secured and we left Salt River about 10 a.m. It was great being on a major highway as I didn't feel like dealing with dirt roads that morning. We drove east through more delightful countryside. At Antigonish, as we were rolling along this major thoroughfare, I saw a large shopping complex off to my left. One building had a sign reading Souby's Super Market. Thought it might be wise to pick up a few supplies, so pulled in.

It was a well-stocked market with lots of goodies. The produce was the only thing not to my liking for it was cold climes produce: cabbages, turnips, parsnips, lots of potatoes, but no citrus, no avocados. There was broccoli; however, it was $1.69 per pound. Produce aside, the cheeses and the seafood more than made up for a lack of my produce favorites. I stood like a kid in a candy shop at the seafood counter, overwhelmed by the variety and abundance of all those sea creatures. There was a lobster tank. The fish man seemed to enjoy my delight with all the fish he had on display. Everything looked sumptuous; however, I chose another lobster from this cornucopia. He plopped it into the microwave, wrapped it, and said, "I hope you'll enjoy it." No matter what the day brought, I'd have another heavenly dinner that evening. The lobster cost $5.95 a pound.

Got back to Tessie and Ink, stashed the lobster in the refrigerator and drove on up Route 105. Had to cross the Canso Causeway which spans the Strait of Canso and joins Nova Scotia to Cape Breton Island. The causeway and the soaring bridge across the Strait were impressive. Driving across the water and then over the high bridge gave me a queasy feeling. It was almost as bad as going through tunnels except I could see all the boats and sea birds, but I do feel a little vertigo on high spans. We took it slow and easy. In no time were on terra firma again.

## Cape Breton Island
Here on Cape Breton the routes were marked with picture

signs for the different scenic drives. We turned off 105 and followed the Ceilidh Trail along St. George's Bay on the west side of the island. It was called on my map the most spectular drive in North America and it was impressive. We drove up and over high capes and headlands with views of the sea, flocks of sheep on the hillsides, and verdant green country. We were climbing steadily and intersected the Cabot Trail at Belle Cote, a small seaside town which had directional signs to the beach. Drove down a dirt road and pulled over for Ink to take a run. Had to take some pictures here for the coastline was magnificent; great breakers rolling in for miles along the deserted beaches and green mountains in the background. The sun was shining but the air was very cool. So we didn't tarry long, but proceeded on north on the Cabot Trail driving along the coast. It was good highway and there was little traffic.

It reminded me of scenes of Hawaii — cliffs dropping greenly into the sea below and glimpses of inviting, sheltered coves. We chugged uphill, stopping often to enjoy the vistas and arrived at Cape Breton Highlands National Park. Continued on up the coast, but soon turned inland and across the northern portion of the island. My pass entitled me to camp within the park, but the wind was blowing hard and cold so I kept driving, still listening to Vivaldi and enjoying Tessie's warmth.

It was about 30 miles across the island. We came out on the Atlantic side on a high bluff with a breath-taking view. Stopped at a look-out and took more pictures. The road was winding along the coastline way down below us and the Atlantic was covered in white caps. Had just gotten back on the road to ease our way down the mountain — the mountains in this region were about 1500 feet in elevation — when up the road chugged the red and black Mercedes bus I had seen in Kadoka or its twin. I doubt, however, if there are two buses quite like this one in the entire world. I was tempted to turn around and intercept it to see if the Germans were still traveling, but thought better of it on this twisty decline.

I hoped to spend the night at Ingonish Provincial Park, so

continued south. When we arrived, there was a closed sign posted. That was a disappointment, but we were still on Cabot Trail skirting the sea and I was sure we'd find accommodations. We drove through quaint fishing villages with descriptive names like Wreck Cove, French River, and Breton Cove. Found a campground at Indian Brook. Pulled in and registered for a space with electricity, thinking about that lobster I had tucked away. They weren't busy and gave me my choice of sites, so we parked down on the shore with the door opening to a view of the calm bay. I plugged in the toaster oven, put a cup of butter to melt on top, and plopped the lobster in to warm.

Ink and I then took a walk along the shore. It was rocky, but the water was calm in this sheltered cove. There were some small islands out in the bay and the headland stretched for miles off to the right. The wind was not blowing and it was comfortable. The bay was beginning to reflect pink and lavender from the setting sun which had sunk behind the mountains. I sat at the picnic table munching on lobster, watching the bay become more lavender and thought, this must be heaven, it's too cool for hell.

There was a group of bikers tenting in the woods not far from us and Ink went over to say hello. The kids fussed over this black, wiggly dog and walked over to talk with me on this perfect evening. They were from New Hampshire — three fellows and two girls — and were biking all of Cape Breton Island. Sturdy kids! The girls told me they were longing for a bath tub, and how I could relate to that. They had been on bikes for ten days but they all agreed it was an exhilarating experience.

It was dark before I went into Tessie. I sat there at the picnic table, drinking my tea and gazing over the bay. Ink was curled up by my feet, the bikers had a roaring fire at their site. Way down the headland, some lights twinkled. I heard a lone bird calling and the soft sighing of the waves hitting the shore. It was tranquil and good for the soul. I felt so blessed to be making this journey. Said my thanks to my God and ended another beautiful day.

It was a cool night there on the bay, but the sun was beaming into Tessie and sparkling on the waters when I woke. The camper warmed quickly as I sat drinking my coffee. Noticed the bikers were breaking camp, packing up tents and equipment and getting themselves ready for another day on their bikes. Felt I, too, should get myself moving. The restrooms weren't much so I didn't take a shower, knowing my dog didn't care how I smelled. Another thing that endeared Ink to me — I discovered she didn't like lobster. I'm very selfish when it comes to sharing lobster with anyone or anything. So I offered her a bit grudgingly. We have owned dogs who love to munch on lobster shells; however, Ink didn't want a thing to do with lobster. I was grateful I didn't have to share my delicacy with her.

Ink was roaming around. No one required that she be on leash all the time here in the Maritimes. A more relaxed attitude than in the States where she was always getting into trouble for not being tied. She bounced over to say good morning to the bikers. I started securing Tess: did dishes, put everything in its place, unplugged and unpopped. We were ready to leave about 10 a.m. Saw the gal bikers coming from the restrooms and we hugged with wishes all around for a safe trip. I don't know why I worried about the kids because I'd pull over to look at a lovely view and they'd pass me. They were making good time. It was nice to have their company that morning along the Trail as we continued south skirting St. Ann's Bay. (It's at St. Ann's that the Highland Scots have their Gaelic College, the only Gaelic college in this hemisphere.)

At the tip of St. Ann's Bay, we joined the major highway then drove through Baddeck where there's a national historic park in honor of Alexander Graham Bell who summered here. This was the culmination of the 184 mile loop which was the Cabot Trail and we were back on Route 105. We crossed the Canso Straits with more confidence.

### Nova Scotia Again

I pulled into Souby's in Antigonish, scooted in, greeted my

fish man with, "I'll have another one of your succulent lobsters, please." He looked at me quizzically and asked, "Don't you like any other seafood?"

"Oh, I love all seafood, but I can't get lobster like this in the Southwest part of the United States. I'm trying to get my fill while I can. So, please do another one for me."

I chose a neat, little fellow which the fish man popped into the microwave and wrapped. I was off and running with visions of another gourmet dinner that evening.

We continued on the Trans-Canadian through New Glasgow and arrived at Truro about 3 p.m. Found a bank and got a cash advance, then pulled into a commercial park on the outskirts of town. It was early, but I needed to do some housekeeping chores. Here, too, the heavy tourist season was over. The lad at the office directed me up the hill with, "Just choose a spot that's to your liking."

We drove up and found a good site not too far from the restrooms, but not close to any of the few campers. I stripped Tessie down and gathered up all the dirty clothes. It was a good hike down to the laundry facilities. The lad had said Ink could run so long as she didn't disturb anyone. We made four trips up and down the hill; lugging laundry, checking washers and dryers, getting some good exercise. Got Tessie all scrubbed up. By this time, Ink had had plenty of exercise, so I put her on lead and I went over to scrub myself. Showered and shampooed under a strong jet of hot water, humming and happy for life's little pleasures.

I sat at the picnic table and pigged out on my lobster while I watched the sunset. Ink and I did a turn around the grounds before dark. Then I snuggled up and did some reading about the Tidal Bore. I remembered from geography class that the Bay of Fundy has the highest tides in the world. In reading, I found the reason for this is that the tide water enters the Bay of Fundy at its widest point and comes in just like it does elsewhere in the world, but the farther up the Bay it travels, the more it changes. The water literally piles up as it moves up this funnel shaped bay. It's squeezed by the ever-narrowing sides and the constant shallowing of the bottom forcing the water higher up the shore. The long length of the Bay is another reason the tides are so high. When the lower tide runs out, it collides with the incoming high tide combining forces to make an even higher wave coming in. This combination of wave forces is called resonance and the length and depth of the basin determines its particular rhythm.

The water in the Bay of Fundy rocks from one end to the other in time with the water in the Atlantic Ocean. These tides, which occur every 12 hours and 30 minutes, move an incredible one hundred billion tons of briny water up the shores of the Bay of Fundy. The onslaught is estimated to nearly equal the 24 hour flow of all the rivers in the world. In Truro, I had noticed signs everywhere exclaiming, See the Tidal Bore. When I was in the office while doing my laundry, I noticed a schedule for the tides. I asked the lad at the desk about the Tidal Bore and he said, "You must see it. The tide flows right up the Salmon River in Truro and there's a great place to view it." Thereupon, he gave me instructions and jotted down the times of the tide for the next morning, September 8. After all this reading, I decided I'd better go and see this phenomenon before I left the area.

Woke early and didn't fool around that morning. I had my schedule in hand and the Tidal Bore was to come streaming up the Salmon River at Truro at 11:27 a.m. I surely didn't want to miss it. We retraced our steps, the manager's directions were detailed and I found my way to a lovely view area. There was a charming country inn with adequate parking. A large crowd of people were standing on the banks of the river waiting for the Tidal Bore.

It was cool and Ink didn't mind guarding the camper. I walked across lush grass down to the bank and noticed immediately how wide the mud flats were in relation to the amount of water in the river. It made a sweeping turn just down from the view site. There was a large sand bar covered with gulls. It was a wide river bed. I talked with two ladies, one from Truro and the other her guest from the U.S. whom she had brought out to see the Tidal Bore. I took some pictures of the river flat while I was waiting. Everyone was standing around, chatting and waiting.

Finally, someone yelled, "Here she comes!" Yes, indeed, here it came — this small ripple in the stream rolling up the river. I stood there thinking, my God, is this all there is? I realized I had been expecting a humongous surfing-type wave. This was not that much — just a small ripple. Then I had to consider how far it had come and what force could bring this amount of water upstream. The mud flats were covered with water in a short time and that wide river bed was full from shore to shore; however, it wasn't what I had expected.

I wanted a huge wave roaring up the river, but I didn't dare say anything. There were hometown people here and I knew asking if that was all there was to the Tidal Bore would not be kindly received. I did take pictures and I did see it. I thought it was appropriately named. In retrospect, it was a sunny morning, I had an opportunity to visit with nice people, the setting was lovely. After all, I wasn't in any hurry, and I can always boast that I saw the Tidal Bore.

As we were heading back to the highway, I told Ink she had not missed much. We streaked across Nova Scotia, heading back to New Brunswick. It had dawned on me that I told my Mary I'd get to Pittsburgh shortly after Labor Day and here we were still tooling around the Maritimes. It was already September 8 and it was time to be heading south and back to the States.

At Amherst, we stopped for gas. Right next to the station was an inviting cafe, so I decided to lunch out. It was a cozy place and smelled delicious. A friendly waitress took my order for a bowl of clam chowder and a piece of apple pie. I didn't eat out often, so I enjoyed it even more when I found a spot with good food and good company.

### New Brunswick Again

I wanted to tour the Southeast Shore of New Brunswick, wanted to see more of the Bay of Fundy. I studied my maps when I got back to Tessie and noticed that our route was taking us directly toward Moncton. It looked as if I could avoid most of the city, however, and head south along Route 114 to Hopewell Cape. I don't know what went wrong, but, once again, we ended up in downtown Moncton. I felt I was learning more about Moncton than I really wanted to know. Still couldn't find any directional signs, but, as with the first go-around, kept driving and, sure enough, managed to find my way out of that impossible maze again. It was a beautiful city but seemed to set my itinerary back a few hours each time I got near it.

Finally found route 114 which ran along the bay. The full force of those tides was so evident all along this area. It was one of tide-carved rock formations, rugged coastlines, vast mud flats, and the muddy, roiling waters of the Bay. When we got to Hopewell Cape, I parked and got out to look around. This Cape is noted for its flower pot rocks. Discovered there was a large clock mounted on a billboard at the top of a sturdy wooden staircase leading down to the beach and a schedule for the tides.

Shazam! I was in luck because the tide was out. I went down the stairs — stories and stories of steps — to the beach proper which at this time had no water on it. The flower pot rocks were fantastic monoliths rising from the beach floor to a height of approximately 50 feet. They were named flower pots because on the very top there was soil enough to support trees and vegetation. The remainder of the rocks were smooth and sterile from the tidal waters which crept over them when the tides came in. They did look like flower pots on a grand scale. It was an interesting shore; lots of seaweed, small tidal pools, erosion patterns from the force of the tides.

I walked, looked, and took pictures, all the while realizing I was on the bottom of the sea. I marveled over this tremendous force and knew I wouldn't want to be on this beach with the tide coming in. Took comfort in knowing there was a warning siren up at the billboard. Climbed back up the stairway leisurely, but did wonder how fast I'd have to run up those stairs to beat the incoming tide.

It was early evening, so we wandered down the road and spent the night at Fundy National Park. This park was established in 1948 to preserve a part of Canada's natural and cultural heritage. It encompasses 206 square kilometers and represents a sample of the upper Bay of Fundy shoreline with its spectacular tides and moist, coastal forest of spruce and fir. The park ranger directed me to site #48 which had electricity in Chignecto North campground. It was a short drive to the turn off from Route 114. We found ourselves in a beautiful forest setting — white birches and thick evergreens. There was no one near us. That evening I built a fire in the fire pit to warm me as I ate outside in a jewel of a setting.

Ink and I took a walk at dusk, but hopped into Tessie early as there were no lights. It had been an exciting day: Tidal Bores, flower pot rocks, and Moncton re-visited.

Woke to a chill in the air. Before I stirred from my sleeping bag, while I drank my coffee, I wrote in my journal: How to express this joyful feeling? Sun is shining. It's warm. Birds muttering, insects flying, not another human in view. Little chipmunk skittered across the road. I feel so in harmony with nature and myself — a part of all that is. So filled with delight at being here. Hate to get back on the road, but must head south. Love the Maritime provinces. Think a summer on PEI would be heavenly. Loved New Brunswick, Nova Scotia, and Cape Breton. Feel satiated with beauty and good food. What a sense of well-being!

Ink was outside on her lead while I was dressing. Felt her pull against the bumper, looked out and saw a handsome German Shorthaired Pointer who had come to call. Ink was giving him her full-vamp treatment. I hopped out to talk with him, too. About this time, a young couple walked up, asking, "Is our dog disturbing you?"

"Not in the least. Glad to see him. He is handsome and Ink always loves to meet new friends."

"Gee, are you from New Mexico?"

"Indeed, we are."

"We're from near Denver, but we're living now in New Hampshire."

"Wow, that's a change. How do you like it?"

The kids went into a lengthy dissertation on New Hampshire living, stating that you must be hardy to survive. They were there only to complete Master's work and were renting an old farm house which they claimed they could not heat as it was cold and damp. Said they were getting that Master's and going to California as soon as possible.

I asked them if they got this horrible feeling of being hemmed in by the eastern mountains. I was born and raised in Pennsylvania but, after living in the Southwest, whenever I go back there I feel I've got to push those little hills away so that I can see. I get claustrophobic.

The kids agreed, "God, you're right. You can't see!"

"No, there are just no vistas. I think that's why I've enjoyed the Maritimes. At least, you have the ocean and great distances to view."

We all agreed that in the West if you can't see for fifty miles there's something wrong. Once you get used to those vast distances, it's hard to cope with close little hills. We chatted a while longer. The kids wished me safe journeying and I wished them luck with the Master's work and hopes for getting back West soon. Fixed breakfast and sat in the sun at the picnic table. It was an outside morning.

As I ate, a lady strolled up and greeted me with, "We're just down the way. How are you this morning?" I asked her to join me for a cup of coffee and some conversation. She and her husband were from New Jersey and were going back home after two weeks of camping. She said, "You know each time we head out, it's harder to go back home. I think I prefer being on the road." I agreed. This life was as close to total freedom as I had ever come. We hugged and said good-bye since we had to get ready to leave this delightful place. I thought about spending another night, but Mary was expecting me.

At Fundy National there were no Ranger Ricks driving

around. They request that, when you vacate your space, you drop your stub into the box at the gate. Then they know it's empty. I had pulled over to do that when a camper with New Brunswick plates pulled up behind me. It was an older couple and the lady rolled down her window and yelled, "Aye, lass, you're a long way from home now, aren't you?"

"That I am, but I've really loved it here in the Maritimes."

"Oh, you like it then?"

"Sure do! But today I'm heading back to the States."

"Well, you know, I have a sister living in Aztec."

"You're kidding."

"No. I've been there." I could tell from the inflection that this pert little woman wondered why anyone would live in that desert country.

"And you like it here, eh?"

I never had to fudge about my liking the Maritimes. Told her about the wonderful time Ink and I had had; about eating lobsters, about the ferry to PEI, about all the delights I had experienced in her country.

She beamed and asked, "You're not afraid then?"

"No. I have my dog and she's the perfect travel companion. We've not had any problems, just fun."

She reached over and patted me on the arm with, "Aye, lass, you have pluck! God be with you."

We took Route 114 within the provincial park traveling through the Caledonia Highlands; great stands of birch and evergreens, deep ravines, untouched country, then picked up the Trans-Canada heading south. Had to go through St. John's, but there was a by-pass and it wasn't like Moncton. Here at St. John's, the St. John's River meets the Bay of Fundy. When the tides come in, they actually force the water to flow up river, creating the reversing falls rapids. Now, I didn't bother to go and see it. I had seen the Tidal Bore. The river is affected as far up as Fredericton. You never lose sight of it and you're always aware of the force of this great bay and its tides.

I had read more about the tide in the information paper the

ranger had given me. It stated there's no giant wave that sweeps across the beach and crashes on the shore. On the contrary, the murky water creeps slowly but steadily over the flats, rising in places at the pace of a leisurely walk. After six and one quarter hours, the beach is totally covered, then six and one quarter hours later, it's exposed once more. I guess I could have climbed up those stairs at the flower pot beach and managed to stay ahead of the tide.

We had passed through St. John's and were driving down the coast toward Maine. We were almost to the mouth of the Bay of Fundy when I noticed a picnic park high on a cliff overlooking the Bay. It was a lovely park with neat grey and white shelters, restroom facilities, and lots of parking, so in we pulled. I was reluctant to leave the Maritimes. Ink roamed flower-filled meadows while I ate and looked at the beach far below. Watched a small fishing boat bobbing on the waves of the Bay. We doodled and dawdled at this park called New River. We finally drove on and arrived at Calais, Maine. Had no trouble with customs, don't even remember a conversation there. The world was different in Maine.

# XI. Narrow Roads, White Church Steeples and Slow Going

Calais was a scenic town: big wooden houses with widow's walks on the tops and yards full of maple trees. I really wanted some pictures of those houses; however, there was no place to park. The roads were narrow and the drivers not especially courteous. I had to get a cash advance and so parked in the bank lot. Ran across the street to the drug store for toothpaste. After the gracious hospitality of the Maritimes, I found these down-Mainers a bit dour, a little reluctant to give you any service at all. I did get cash. In the drug store, I finally walked over to a cashier with my toothpaste and she condescended to take my money. I was thinking of heading back to New Brunswick. Outside of town, I saw a sign for Campobello Island, New Brunswick. I had always thought Campobello was in the United States, but it isn't. It's just over a hump-backed bridge. I went back to New Brunswick, of course.

Crossed over the bridge and was on Campobello Island, New Brunswick, heading toward the Roosevelt Campobello International Park which is a unique example of countries' cooperation. It comprises 2600 acres and was established as a joint memorial by Canada and the United States. Here are the cottage and the grounds of the Roosevelt family. I went into the visitor's center and they gave me a map and directions to the "cottage." This "cottage," which was the summer vacation spot of the Roosevelts, had 34 rooms. I walked across the grounds and viewed this huge red cottage sitting in the middle of grounds planted with dahlias and pinks.

Inside, I was free to wander around and look at the rooms. Most of the furnishings were used by the family. Wallpapers,

149

curtains, and rugs are the originals or reproductions provided by the Park Commission. There are many reminders of FDR and his family: his crib, the large frame chair used to carry the handicapped President, the family telescope, a collection of canes, and a megaphone for hailing boats off-shore or latecomers for family meals. The kitchen, laundry, ice house, windmill, and water tank tell their own stories of life and work in these summer "cottages."

I walked through gardens and landscaping of the Roosevelt era on wooded paths, through fields with vistas of islands and shores of Passamaquoddy and Cobscook Bays in New Brunswick and Maine. Then visited the Hubbard cottage. This rambling white house with a large veranda is the last Victorian style summer residence in the Park area. I spent a long time poking around and walking the grounds thinking that my staunch Republican grandfather was probably rolling over in his grave. However, I truly enjoyed seeing the lifestyles of another era and these mind-boggling "cottages." Since I was in the vicinity, why not?

Learned that Herring Cove Provincial Park was a short distance from the Campobello Park. I had another night in New Brunswick in an unlit, serene setting. We never got to the campground until after six, but it was uncrowded. Parked up, had a long walk, and turned in early to the mutterings of birds settling for the night also.

When we awoke, the world was misty grey. The fog was heavy and it was sprinkling. Everything was grey, but it was warm. I was beginning to feel stressed about getting to Pittsburgh and thought we'd better roll. Ink and I took a quick walk in the still mist. Left the campground before 10 a.m. after a quick breakfast with no lingering over coffee. This time we were leaving New Brunswick for certain. Headed down Route 1 into southern Maine.

It was Saturday and there was lots of traffic. The roads were narrow and jammed up. At Ellsworth, we turned left and drove a loop through Acadia National Park and Bar Harbor. Another error in judgment on my part. Traffic was bumper-to-bumper in some areas, creeping past scads of touristy commercial stands. Lobster was selling for $6.95 per pound and I was glad I had had my fill. Acadia was scenery similar to the Maritimes, but with masses of humanity. Drove and glanced, but did not stop. Bar Harbor was a tourist trap. However, it was there and I took a quick look.

Back to Ellsworth, through Bangor, and onto Route 2. I was determined to get across Maine. I had forgotten how different eastern driving is. Not the wide open spaces of the west, but rather small towns every few miles. Scenic small towns, but a stop light on every corner and slow going. It was tedious, but I kept rolling along looking at neat white steepled churches and small towns. The weather had cleared and it was sunny and scenic, but tedious. We did make it to New Hampshire where we hung it up at a commercial park near Gorham.

It was the weekend and I was back in the United States. The park was jammed and well-lighted. We had a narrow space up the hill from a railroad track. It had been a hard driving day and I was out of sorts. I did manage to find an area where Ink could take a small run, then retreated to Tessie, fixed dinner, and crawled into bed for some reading, no socializing. It seemed a noisy place after the serenity of the Maritimes.

Awoke early after a night of listening to trains rumbling by on the tracks down below our site. Still feeling out of sorts and questioning whether I really liked "civilization." Put Ink on her lead and had my coffee. Decided, since I had to deal with civilization, I'd take advantage of the showers. I hiked up to the ladies' room where the sound of hair dryers was going great guns. I had seen nothing posted, nor had I read my ad sheet from the campground hosts carefully, so I was dismayed and disgusted to find that a shower cost fifty cents. The spaces were not cheap at this park. An additional charge for a shower really dinged me and, of course, I had no money with me. It was the principle, not the fifty cents. I went back to the camper, had a quick breakfast, and said, "Inkus, we have to get out of here."

We were pulling out when I noticed a phone booth and thought I'd better check in with Mary and Mark and Lois. I knew a chat with loved ones would get me over my tiff quickly. With Mark and Lois it was, "Oh, Mom, where are you?" I filled them in on my meanderings in the Maritimes and assured them all was going well and the gypsy caravan was *en route* to Pennsylvania. Then called my Mary. She was concerned as I knew she would be. Told her I was on my way and would get there by the evening of the 14th. I felt badly about worrying Mary, but learned that adhering to a schedule was not conducive to enjoyable traveling. I was pressing and trying to hurry. This is not good, especially in the eastern regions of the country.

I told Mary I would be stopping at the cemetery before I came on to visit her; the Old Dutch Cemetery near Sandy Lake, Pennsylvania, where my parents and many relatives are buried. I knew I had to spend some time there. Mary had offered to drive up with me, but this was a solitary duty. I needed some time alone there. We signed off with love and see you soon, God willing.

Turned onto Route 2, heading west and feeling better. We were winding through the White Mountains, the home of Mt. Washington, the highest peak in all of the northeast. It wasn't a day for sightseeing and I rolled by many ski areas, many signs for wonderful sounding places like Franconia Notch and Covered Bridge; gritting my teeth and driving. Here again, we were routed through scenic little towns, many scenic little towns with the ever-present white church steeple and traffic signals on each corner. I was beginning to think I'd not get to Pennsylvania in a week. I was trying to drive too fast and I wasn't enjoying fully the beauty of the Granite State. Setting a schedule was not good. It stressed me.

Just after we crossed the Connecticut River, a few miles into Vermont, we came to Interstate 91 going south. I had checked my map and knew I needed to get farther south. Here was the perfect means. It was one of the prettiest Interstates I'd ever traveled — rolling over hills, skirting the Connecticut River, cutting through massive granite outcroppings. Fast, easy driving for a change.

Pulled into a rest area to fix lunch. There were picnic tables. I tied Ink at the table and sat down to eat. This was nothing like the picnic parks in the Maritimes. It was close to the Interstate, crowded and noisy. I was securing Tessie and getting ready to roll on. Had the back door of the camper open. Ink was still tied to the table with a worried look as if asking, "You're not gonna leave me here, are you?" Was going over to get Ink when a red VW camper pulling a trailer with a motorcycle on it pulled up behind Tessie. A young lad got out: bare-footed, in cut-offs with a water bottle in his hand; tall and tan and young and handsome. He greeted me with, "Hi, you're a long way from home." I grinned and said, "You are, too. You're from California, aren't you?" He looked surprised as there was no license plate on the front of his camper.

"Yeah, I am. From near L.A. How'd you know?"

I explained I had raised my sons in California and there's no mistaking a California youth. This lad looked like my Scot. California kids always look so tan and lean and healthy no matter where they turn up. My next question for him was, "What's a nice boy like you doing in a place like this?" He came over and we sat down at the picnic table. His name was Bob. He had made the trip cross-country to reestablish ties with a brother living in Boston. He had been touring around while in the area. I asked, "What do you think about the East?"

"God, why is everyone so up tight?"

"I don't know, I really don't know, but it does seem to be par for the course here in the northeast."

We visited for quite a while. I sensed a need in this young man to talk even more. There was some questioning on his part about where I planned to spend the night. I had no idea, but was tempted to suggest that we camp in the same area and visit some more. He commented that he had enjoyed the trip but found it lonely at times and wished he could share his experiences with someone. I knew this was a plea for help. This lad desperately wanted to talk, but, somehow, I didn't want to get involved. I needed to get to Pittsburgh and I shined him on. Said my good-byes and wished him good journeying, and he did likewise. As we were heading on down the Interstate, Bob passed me and again I sensed that I should give this lonely lad some time and sit and visit this evening. It would probably be comforting for both of us. But I didn't do it.

Kept rolling south. Didn't mind the traffic that much, just turned the jazz louder. At Brattleboro, we once more headed west. This road led through Bennington, Vermont. I was curious about the town and the college. Bennington is the most expensive college in the nation and I wanted to see it. In 1988, the tuition, fees, and room and board ran $17,990. That's a lot of money for an education. I had no intention of spending that amount but thought I should try and discern what made it so expensive as I drove by.

We were traveling through the Green Mountains now. Bennington was a sumptuous town. It looked like what we all expect a college town to be: tree-lined streets, good shops, and expensive restaurants. The campus, off to my left, was filled with solid, blue-blood brick buildings. It was an interesting glance at an expensive college nestled in a posh town.

Shortly, we were in upper New York State. It was late afternoon and I knew I should seek a place for the night. Here on the backroads, I felt we were in the middle of nowhere. Checked the guide. There was a state park at Grafton Lakes. I never did see a sign nor did I ever find it. We continued south and, when I found a spot to pull off this narrow country road, rechecked my guide. Found a listing for the Alps Campground in Averill Park.

It was 6 p.m. by now. I was on the proper route, according to the guide, so kept driving, but no campground. I turned around, thinking I had missed it. I drove up and back along this stretch of road three times and still found no campground. It was almost dark and I was weary. I didn't panic since we had a full tank of gas, food and shelter at our disposal. But this was a narrow road, no shoulders, no place to pull off. I had visions of driving all night and that didn't please me.

I stopped at a convenience store and the clerk had no idea of where the campground was. Luckily, an older man had heard my questions and told me it was on up the road. He said, "Just keep going. You'll start up the hill and over on the left you'll see a sign. You just haven't gone far enough. Just keep going." Away we went, back down the road for the fourth time. Ink was asking if we were gonna eat that evening. I didn't like driving on unknown, twisty country lanes in the dark, but we continued for what seemed like eons.

Said to Ink, "My gal, we may have to park in a school ground tonight or whatever 'cause I don't think we're gonna find the campground. Don't worry. We'll be okay, I think." I had given up any hope of finding this elusive park when I spotted a dingy, unlit sign beside a dirt road for the Alps Campground.

We eased up the rutted dirt road and came to a bunch of barracks-type buildings. I saw an office sign; however, there wasn't even a light on. I followed the road around past mobile homes, trikes, and bicycles lying helter-skelter, but no sign of people. I thought, well, at last I have come to the tenement district — it was scuzzy, a cluttered-up mess. I was able to discern a spot with a slight rise and pulled Tess in knowing I couldn't go any farther. About this time, here came an old beat-up pick-up truck. I heard a voice ask, "You want to camp here tonight?"

I felt like saying, "No, I just pulled in to admire the view," but it was no time for levity. The voice said, "I opened the office. Come on down and register." I drove back down the road past more scrungy mobile homes and trash. Went into the office, feeling like I had had it for this day. The voice had a body. He looked just like Mickey Rooney with tattoos. Told him all I needed was the space, no electricity, no water, just a spot off the road. I was about to leave when he said, "I sure hope the State Police don't stop you."

"Why would they do that?"

"Well, ya know, you've got an Arizona plate on the front of your rig and New Mexico on the back."

"Yeah, I know that. What's the problem?"

"Well, I don't think that's legal."

I was testy and tired. Looked at Mickey and told him I really didn't think I'd worry about it nor should he. Left the office, parked Tess, fed Ink, and fixed myself a cup of tea. I had no appetite by this time, just wanted to stretch out. Closed things down and snuggled next to Ink. I had to ask myself if the day might have been less unsettling if I had followed my inclination to play Good Samaritan to that lost, lonely young man from California.

We slept well in the tenement district. I always felt secure in my womb Tessie and I was thankful we were off the highway. I recall waking partially during the night and hearing an airplane flying over. I had not heard that sound for three weeks; didn't hear planes in Canada. Welcome back to civilization.

When I awoke, found that daylight didn't help the looks of this campground one bit. Beggars can't be choosers, however. As I put the kettle on, I saw a big mutt come running down between sites through trikes and trash. Let Ink out, since I didn't think anyone would mind. Ink thought this was a great and glorious place. The pup was as playful as she and they went dashing around having a great romp. I let them play as I got myself together slowly — feeling the effects of the previous day's stresses. I never did grapple with the restrooms at this park. I was sure it wasn't worth the walk, having seen the way the grounds were kept. Did a quick scrub in Tess and got ready to leave, assuring myself that today would be better. When I called Ink, she was as dirty as the campground, but happy for such a great play session.

We were back on the narrow country road by 10 a.m. Followed a maze of country roads, but knew we were traveling in the right general direction. In about a half-hour, we came to the New York State Thruway heading straight south. Scooted down it until we caught a road west through the Catskills. This was better driving for me and I was regaining my balance. The Catskills are delightful eastern type mountains. Everything was green, green with a small dot of color from a tree starting to turn. I had to tell myself no, no pictures of fall foliage yet. It will get better.

When we got to Oneonta, I made a gas stop, then went into a market for supplies. This market had a whole section of meat cuts for a single person. Not big packages, but rather one pork chop, one filet, one meat patty. I thought it was a marvelous idea; wish more markets would stock this way. Unfortunately, much of the sales in the country is still geared to daddy, mommy, and the two kids and it's not an accurate picture. There are lots of singles in our nation and this packaging geared to them was exceptionally fine. I picked up a beef patty for one and a thick pork chop for one. What a progressive market. I'd love to see more of this around the nation.

At Oneonta, we got onto another Interstate. I was hitting the main roads, but needed to make some time and distance. Went southwest on Interstate 88. Don't know why I shunned the Interstates so much. You could sit and relax, no dealing with narrow roads and losing your way, just roll along. That's exactly what we did, rolled along the Interstate southwest from Oneonta through Binghamton and Endicott. At Waverly, we entered my native state of Pennsylvania. Da Da.

# XII. The Long Trek down Memory Lane

It wasn't late, but I decided to spend the night in Towanda on the banks of the Susquehanna River. This was home territory and I thought Ink should have a swim in the "Susky-hanna," as my Papa always called it. Pulled into a pleasant campground and was welcomed by a charming woman. Her TLC was appreciated after my experiences of the past few days. She made me feel so comfortable, saying, "I think you're so brave. Now, if my husband and I can help with anything, you just feel free to call on us." She registered me and directed me to my site down the hill by the river.

It was a lovely camp; a large open meadow with few campers. Got parked up, popped up and plugged in. Took Ink and we headed down to the river where she had a swim. Everything was incredibly green, even the easy-flowing Susquehanna was green: a lazy, green river which Ink and I enjoyed. Got dirty clothes together and went across the meadow to the laundry. While they were washing and drying, cleaned Tess and brushed Ink. Prepared that big, single pork chop and ate outside.

There was an older woman staying at this campground who followed me around. She was having a difficult time dealing with the fact that I was traveling all alone and enjoying it immensely. It didn't fit into her world view at all. Yet, she was intrigued. My heart went out to this woman. Her only topic of conversation was her husband and what he had done. I never heard her say one thing about her life. Although I wanted to ask, "But what about you? What have you done? What has your life been?" I knew this would throw her for a loop. She was from a different generation.

I thought how lucky I was to be living in an age where, even

158

though at times you were considered an oddity to be traveling alone, at least you had the freedom to do it. You didn't have to disguise yourself as a man, which was the routine in the early days of our history. This woman went out of her way to talk with me. She was down on the river bank, she came to the laundry room, and followed me to the restroom. I sensed she was trying to reconcile this lifestyle of mine with what she had been taught was the norm.

The dryer was very slow and the clothes still weren't dry even after I had finished dinner and listened to the birds. It was dusk and the lazy Susquehanna was glowing in the sunset. I had cleaned Tess and Ink and now it was time to clean me. I checked the dryer again and my robe and gown were still damp. I put another quarter in and went for a shower. This was a secure, quiet campground, so when I finished showering, I looked around carefully, saw no one, and made a dash for the dryer and my robe in nothing but my towel and turquoise boots. If the little woman had seen that, she would have written me off as crazy, I'm sure.

Everything was dry and I donned my robe and gown in the laundry room then strolled across the meadow feeling smug and clean.

I woke fairly early. The sun was beaming and I felt no need to hurry away from this comfortable campground. Took Ink over and she had another swim. Took a photo of her on the bank, thinking I surely did have a slew of pictures of Ink in water. Went back to Tessie and rubbed Ink down well then put her on lead to dry while I ate breakfast outside.

The owner was mowing on a big tractor and the air was heavy with the scent of new-mown grass. Slowly got ready while I savored the calls of birds and the tranquility of the setting. Encountered the little woman at the restroom and we talked a bit, or attempted to, coming as we were from two different worlds. Stopped and said good-bye to the campground owner and complimented her on the immaculately kept facilities. She gave me a warm hug and said, "God be with you. Have a safe journey."

It was 11 a.m. before we turned west on Route 6 to wander across northern Pennsylvania. These were place names I remembered from my childhood: Tioga, Coudersport, the Grand Canyon of Pennsylvania. We stopped somewhere in the Allegheny National Forest for a picnic lunch. There was no one at the site and Ink could run. I sat and gazed at these green hills with a few spikes of brilliant color. The trees were beginning to turn. Looked at all that foliage I had grown up with — mountain laurel, rhododendrons, maples, oaks, and evergreens — plants that love the acidic soil of the east and won't tolerate the alkalinity of the Southwest. Rolled on leisurely through rolling hills dotted with neat farms and cattle in the fields.

When we got to Corry, it was only five p.m., but I was ready to stop. I knew we'd make it on to Pittsburgh the next day. It was only about 115 miles south and, even with the stop at the cemetery, I knew I'd get to Mary's on schedule. Pulled into another charming green campground relatively free of people. The owner here was a bear of a man, a huge man. He was wearing shorts and a pair of hiking boots with a sleeveless T-shirt and he was muscled. He apologized for his appearance, explaining that he was doing repairs before the winter weather set in. I registered, and he asked, "There's just you and a dog?"

"Yeah, just me and my dog."

"Well, you know, we're not busy. Is your dog well mannered?"

I assured him that Ink was one fine animal with not a mean bone in her chubby body and that she did listen well.

"Then don't tie her up, okay? As long as she doesn't disturb anyone, let her have a little fun."

My heart went out to this big, kind man who understood that dogs need to be free to explore and run, too. We had stayed at a few parks where I was sure the rules and regulations were backwards: the dogs should have been running and the kids should have been tied.

We parked up on a grassy site and had dinner outside. There

was a small pond across the grounds in which a blue heron was wading. I hadn't expected to see a blue heron in northern Pennsylvania, but there he was in all his glory. I watched his antics while I ate.

We took a long walk at dusk. Talked with a cute lady riding a three-wheeled trike. She lived in a mobile home here and said she loved it. Ink and I wrapped it up early. I knew I had a big day coming up. Thought I'd better have a good night's rest for the trek down memory lane tomorrow. So it was into the sleeping bag with Joseph Campbell's *Myths to Live By*. Lights were off by nine and we slept well.

When Ink and I awoke, I put her out on her lead. With Ink, I watch her as she sees more than I do. She has a sixth sense. We always agreed on campgrounds. Ink was more open-minded about some than I. There were a few in which she didn't seem comfortable, however, and in those I wasn't comfortable either. I learned to watch this dog because she never missed a thing. On this particular morning, the back door was open and the sun was shining in as I was having my coffee. Ink was staring intently, sitting and staring over at the pond. I looked out to see what she was watching. There was a doe and two fawns down at the pond having a drink of water. There was mist on the pond and the deer looked so peaceful and beautiful. What a nice omen with which to start what I knew was going to be a full day.

We were *en route* by 10:30 a.m. Followed Route 6 on west until we got to Route 19 leading south. We were heading for a small cemetery here in western Pennsylvania in the middle of Amish country that had a lot of memories for me. There was a sign on the left side of the road directing me to Sandy Lake. I drove into Sandy Lake trying to recall how many years it had been since I had visited this area. Seventeen, I believe, yes, seventeen years since I had been anywhere near here, but nothing changes much.

In Sandy Lake, I was like a homing pigeon. I drove north again to a town called Mt. Lebanon, came to a road to the right which I knew was it and turned down this tree-shaded country lane. As I was turning a curve, there was an almost physical tug to look down the lane. There was the stark, simple white church where my Mother's body had been viewed for the last time. I kept driving; had no desire to go to the church. After all these years, I can still remember how very dead she looked lying in the harsh daylight of that church.

I wondered how far into the cemetery I'd be able to drive, since the road leading up to our plots had always been horrid. There was a big new sign at the entrance. It was no longer called the Old Dutch Cemetery, but Mt. Lebanon Cemetery. I pulled in and the road up to our burial plots had been paved. Things do change after all. I could drive clear to the top of the hill in Tessie. It all looked, except for the massive growth of foliage, as it had always looked. A quiet little cemetery spread over the hills and nestled under the trees. Almost everyone in that cemetery was related to me on my maternal side.

I let Ink out and we walked across the hill to my parents' graves. Waves of emotion were welling up as I walked over and sat down between the two ground markers. I sat and cried for a while. By the time I was twenty-three, both my parents were dead. I suppose all of us question why? Why did they go so soon? Mama died in 1941 when I was just ten years old. Then, Papa died in 1954.

Needless to say, I've often wondered what kind of turns my life might have taken had they lived longer. My immediate family certainly lacked longevity genes. My mother was only 48 and both my brother and father died at 57. This has been another reason for my refusing to defer pleasure too long. You never know when this tenuous thread called life will be severed. To paraphrase my mentor, Joseph Campbell: The underlying fear of the human species is death. Perhaps what we should all fear is not having lived. With the gene pool I was drawing on, I felt I'd better go for it while I could.

I sat there and shed quite a few tears, perhaps of relief for getting here, perhaps of sadness, possibly of self-pity. I started looking around this pleasant knoll and still more memories came flooding back. The cypress and rhododendron that I had watched my father plant after Mom's death had grown so large I could hardly see the headstone that read Henning. The cemetery is miles from anywhere and there's no one to make annual trips to care for the graves.

I fixed lunch. Had a bagel with cream cheese and some fruit juice while I sat on the graves and talked to these two parents who had been gone so long. I thanked them both for what they had given me. Somehow, thanks to them, I had survived all that life threw at me and still found it a good experience, but not always easy. Life is a learning process, unfortunately we don't have any choice over the lessons we must learn.

Somewhere, I evolved a philosophy that has carried me through. I feel that my parents gave me a lot of strength and security, plus a good sense of humor and the ability to laugh at myself. Life is sorrowful and difficult, but one's perception is the important thing. For me it's exhilarating and worthwhile. I can't change the world, I can only change myself; however, if each of us were to work on that — an acceptance of different views and love in spite of differences, this world might become a better place. I hoped they weren't unhappy with how I had handled my life.

Ink and I walked and read tombstones. Up on the knoll with Papa and Mom are my maternal grandparents and the graves of both their parents. There were three generations of my sons' forebears on this hill. I thought, my boys are never gonna see this place, never. I must take some pictures, not with morbidity, but for the family history. It should be done.

It was impossible to see the headstones with all the growth of rhododendron. I didn't have pruning shears with me, but I had a pair of scissors, so I spent time clearing away the rampant growth. I worked lovingly there among tombstones of people who had been special and had done much to shape my life and views. The groundstones of my parents were covered with grass. When I trimmed my mother's it read: Effa B. Dean wife of C.A. Henning. I said out loud, "Oh, Mom, you were more than C.A.

Henning's wife. You were a woman in your own right."

It had taken me a long time to acknowledge that possibly my Mom wasn't happy to have me come along when my brother was almost eleven. She was very active in Eastern Star and other clubs and it had to have been a burden for her. I was with Aunt Clara and Aunt Dora much of the time and Mary seemed to care for me more than did my Mother. I was an active, noisy kid and my mother wasn't well.

What a blow my father's loss of his dairy company in the depression must have been for her. My understanding is that we lived high on the hog until Papa lost everything. Then the move away from her family clear across Pennsylvania to Huntingdon where my father arranged to take over a restaurant from Mom's Uncle Harry. I was only six and I escaped all the trauma. I do remember that all we owned was packed into the car we drove to Huntingdon, and we all lived in one big room in a boarding house.

The whole family worked in that diner to make ends meet; Mom, Dad, and my brother Bill. For me, it was an exciting adventure, but it couldn't have been for my mother. I cleaned her stone and talked a bit to this woman I never knew well.

Then I trimmed Papa's stone. I was always my father's child. Even when Mom was alive, it was my father that I always turned to. I said, "Oh, Pop, you may not have done everything right, but you did the best you knew how. Left with a ten year old daughter who was incorrigible couldn't have been easy. I thank you for it, my father, I thank you very much." Went ahead clearing and cutting and got the headstones visible.

My father was such a human man, or I perceived him that way. He was a man very in touch with his feelings, which is a rarity in our culture. I'm afraid I grew up thinking all men were that way and that you could talk with them the way I could talk with my father. He was father, mother, sister, brother, and friend to me and to many people. Everyone brought their problems to my Dad and he always listened with empathy and always, in some way, tried to help.

I don't know how the decision to bury Mother in the Old Dutch Cemetery was made, but he had to buy a burial plot. Papa bought three lots up on this hill each of which would hold eight bodies. I don't know what he had in mind; however, there's lots of room on the hill for lots of bodies. There was a period when older relatives died and my Aunt Clara would call asking, "Barbie, is there room in the plot for Uncle Quay, for Uncle Mac, for Grand-pa and Grand-ma?" I'd always tell her to plunk them in there on that lovely hillside.

At one time Aunt Dora and Uncle Els wrote asking about buying two spaces thinking they should be buried in Pennsylvania. I told them to feel free to use some of that hill. It was the way my expansive father did things.

My Grand-ma, Ina Barbara Rupert, for whom I was named, was special to me. I lived with her for a time after mother's death. She was a quiet little Dutch woman who had had nine children, seven of whom reached adulthood. Then she had a grandchild to care for. Grand-ma was from a different generation, one in which the cult of true motherhood had not been fashionable. My mother was the oldest daughter. Both Aunt Clara and Aunt Dora remember her as the one who took care of them. Grand-ma never said much, never imposed any restrictions on my coming and going — just let me roam and explore and gave me a lot of freedom. It was a Huckleberry Finn kind of existence, and I think it was good for me. She never spoke of my mother's death. In fact, no one spoke of it. I desperately needed to talk about it; however, I was left to grapple with that problem on my own. I have always treasured my aunts' assessment that I am very much like that sweet woman for whom I was named.

I did take pictures of all the tombstones for the family record, and also because I knew I'd never be in that cemetery again. There's certainly space for me, but even my brother is not buried there nor is my Aunt Clara. Still the Old Dutch Cemetery is chock full of kinfolk.

I spent quality time there on that hill I'd been going to most of my life. It was an emotional catharsis making my peace with my relatives. I left the cemetery happy for the opportunity to say good-bye and let it rest. I had not known my mother well, but this visit helped me view her as a woman who handled a lot of adversity with style and grace. My Papa, whom I knew full-well had many faults, but who was always there for me when I needed him, I thanked doubly. He gave me his zest for living, his insatiable curiosity, his child-like wonder, and his good, common sense. Who could ask for more?

We took the back road south to Grove City where I had lived with my Grandparents. Drove down Broad Street which had not changed much in all these years. Got back to Route 19 and rolled on south for a visit with my Mary.

Route 19 is a busy highway leading directly into Pittsburgh. Mary had suggested that I go through Liberty Tunnel and climb the hill to Dravosburg. But, smart ass me decided I didn't want to deal with a tunnel, downtown Pittsburgh, and all that traffic. I'd go another way — and, indeed, I did. I don't know where we were. Pittsburgh was Moncton re-visited. There's something about river towns that throws my guidance system into a tailspin. We headed cross country over hill and dale and horrid roads, but eventually got to Mary's.

I was on a wretched, narrow road. There were no shoulders, ragged edges and I was driving cautiously. Cars were stacking up behind me and, at first, I was pulling off when I could to let them pass, since everyone seemed to be in a big hurry. It wasn't safe pulling off on these jagged edges and it was jolting for Tessie. Not only that, these drivers went roaring by with not so much as a thank you, go to hell, or drop dead. Nothing!

I pulled over three times and finally said to myself, hold it. This is a way of life here. Let them jam up. I'm not pulling off and placing myself and my camper in jeopardy again. I did have quite a caravan behind me from time to time; however, staying on the road seemed the expedient thing to do. Pulling off onto the miserable shoulders stressed me and I didn't like it so I didn't do it. The drivers were not pleasant. All seemed preoccupied and rushed. No one waved to greet a traveler who was a long way from home. Pretty much every man for himself. I knew if I was to survive, I had to join the club, so I drove on the road and ignored the line behind me.

We finally came to an area that seemed familiar along the Monongahela River and I kept rolling. That intuitive sense perked me to stop at a phone booth and call Mary. I felt I was not far from my destination. It was about 4:30 p.m. and Mary answered with, "Child, where are you?" When I gave her coordinates, she laughed and said, "Lord, you're almost here!"

"Yeah, I had a feeling I was close, my Mary."

"You just stay put. I'll be right down and lead you home."

In less than fifteen minutes, this wonderful woman arrived. We hugged and kissed and giggled. It was so good to see her. I requested that she not drive as fast as the locals. We set off slow and easy to Mary's cute house on the hill overlooking the river. It felt so good to be there. In spite of loving the travels, there is a certain amount of stress in finding your way each day. Now I was snug and secure here with this woman who meant so much to me. It was nice to park up and not have to drive, just visit and have fun.

We pulled up in front of the house and had a conference on where I should park Tessie. Mary mentioned that she was allergic to dog hair and preferred that Ink stay outside. That simplified things for me. I knew there was a large pad behind the house where the garage access was. Mary's house is one story in front and then drops down the hill with the garage on ground level in back. I suggested we take a look and see if I could park Tess down back and still leave room for Mary to pull her car in and out of the garage. There was all kinds of space for little Tess.

"Okay! This is great and I'll just stay in the camper with Ink. I couldn't leave Ink alone. We've been together too long and I just couldn't leave her. All we need is a plug-in for electricity and we'll be fine."

I pulled Tessie down and Mary threw a power line out the

bathroom window. Leveled Tess, plugged in and popped up. It was a beautiful campsite with a magnificent river view. Mary was taken aback by my decision to stay in the camper, but for anyone who has never camped it is difficult to understand that you have everything you need at your fingertips. To move into a house is more work than it's worth. Besides, there was no way I'd leave my faithful travel companion to sleep alone. So here we were in a lovely site with the greatest camp hostess in the world.

We had dinner and lots of talk. I took a long soak in the tub and begged off early as I did feel tired. Was settling into Tess with Mary leaning out the window asking, "Are you sure you're all right?" and me yelling back, "God, I'm wonderful. This is a super campsite. I'll see you in the morning, my Muthor. Don't worry about me. I'll have my coffee here in Tess. You just yell when you're up and about and ready for company."

I noticed that Ink was working her magic on Mary. Somehow she ended up in the kitchen getting sumptuous handouts from dinner. Mary said, "She's really beautiful." I agreed and added that she was sweet and loving, too. Think Ink and I could have moved inside with no argument from Mary; however, it was infinitely easier to stay in Tess. We settled in there in Pittsburgh after a satisfying but emotionally draining day trekking down memory lane.

I spent four laid-back, leisurely, loving days right there parked up behind Mary's house. Would have my coffee in the morning watching the barges on the Monongahela and enjoying the view of the valley. The air quality in Pittsburgh is much improved since I was a kid. The steel mills are no longer belching fumes, which makes it a depressed employment area, but there's no longer a grey pall hanging over the valley and it actually sparkles.

Mary is a repository of stories about my family. She had known my father and mother, my aunts and my grandparents before I was born and has known me all my life. We share a common bond in having had to learn early on that each of us is responsible for how we cope and deal with this world. Mary was literally shoved through the window of an orphanage when she was seven years old. I was left pretty much to my own devices when I was ten.

Perhaps you learn that if you're going to survive, you might as well be positive and look at this world humorously. All of us create our own reality. Both Mary and I have chosen one in which we look at life, commenting from time to time: The whole thing is crazy. But we cope with it and see the humor. Mary has had adversity in her life, but has never lost her zest for living. That's a special sort of person.

At 54, Mary decided to go into nursing. Her husband was retired, her sons grown and this dauntless woman went for new experiences and adventures. She told me that all her neighbors told her she was crazy, she couldn't do that.

I knew the constraints well because that's just what I was told when I decided to set out on a solitary trip in a camper. Here, too, both Mary and I learned to listen to our inner voices and go against the norm in seeking what was right for us. She graduated with honors from nursing school in Pennsylvania.

The days were filled with fun and games. We whizzed around in Mary's car. I didn't have to take Tess down and I didn't have to drive. Ink endeared herself to the whole neighborhood. It's established and quiet with neighbors who have known each other for many years, have a supportive network, and are involved with each other. This is becoming rare in our country. Everyone relies on Mary. She's that kind of person and always has been.

We went to the mall where I found *Clan of the Cave Bear* to send to the LeVerts, got Mary new walking shoes, and giggled at the antics of all the people. Mary has always been an astute observer of the species and can mimic anyone. She kept me in stitches with her stories. Got Tessie into Mary's mechanic for a checkup and an oil change. Got caught up on lots of things that I didn't handle when driving every day. Mary's older son, Bill, was there for the week-end and we renewed friendships. I cooked Mexican food for dinner Saturday night, at Mary's request. It was good to be there and was a reason for my journey. I needed to touch base not only with the dead, but the living. Especially this woman who has been so much a part of my life. Called Mark and Lois to let them know I was getting close, but did not set any estimated time of arrival in Tennessee. I still had more trekking here in Pennsylvania. I'd learned the hard way not to schedule myself, not after breaking my butt to get to Mary's on time. Let Pamie know that her mail packet had arrived. Did call my sister-in-law in State College, saying I would be there sometime that coming week for a visit with the Henning clan, but did not give a specific date. Finally, called friends whom I'd met in Oaxaca, Mexico, who lived in the Pittsburgh area and found that they wanted me to come and see them. I was flattered that they were willing to make time in their hectic schedule for me. Sturge is a potter and Dorothy is a clothes designer and the two of them work long, hard hours so that they can escape to Oaxaca for a few months each winter.

I think Mary would have agreed to my parking out back forever, but there was this need in me to get on with the journey and she understood. We had loved and laughed and had such fun together. Ink, by this time, was going everywhere in the car with us, was in the house whenever she wanted, was eating morsels of tasty food from Mary, and telling me she thought we should stay right there. We both agreed it was a tremendous campground. But on Monday, September 19, we said our good-byes and left Mary's about 2 p.m.

She had assured me it was an easy drive to Oakdale where I was to spend the night with Sturge and Dorothy. Pittsburgh worked its charm again and I got hopelessly lost. Kept passing the same landmarks, going around in circles until I found a major route which eventually led me to Oakdale. Called, and Sturge led me to their beautiful home out in the country where he has his pottery studio and Dorothy her sewing room. Spent a delightful evening with these gracious people. I am blessed to have good friends and good people who have surrounded me in this life.

It was raining when I woke that Tuesday morning. Dorothy and Sturge were up and about because they have a schedule to meet, yet they were kind about my imposition on their time. We had breakfast and more wonderful conversation, but I knew that the best thing I could do was to go on my way and let these busy people get back to their projects. The primary question was when are you coming to Oaxaca for Christmas again? I told them I was certain it would not be this year as I didn't expect to get back to New Mexico until around the first of December. I would be confronted with looking for housing and getting settled as I was planning to finish my degree work in the Spring semester. We breakfasted and they fussed over Ink some more. I loaded her into Tessie, however, and we got under way about 11 a.m. after fond hugs.

Luckily, it was only a short distance over to Route 22 which would take me through Pittsburgh and on east. Route 22. Oh, my God, I'd certainly traveled that road often when I was a kid. More times than I care to remember. My father's business took him from Huntingdon to Butler to Altoona to State College. It seemed I was loaded into the car much too often for what I considered a dull, long journey. On this day in 1988, it was a different trip down memory lane.

I have to admit that the mountains didn't seem as big, the hills up and down them didn't seem as high, and the trip didn't seem as long and tedious. Because this portion of Pennsylvania is relatively free of huge urban centers, there is still abundant wildlife, lots of birds, and good trout streams. It's lovely country where man and nature seem to have achieved a balance. Then, too, it was home territory.

I was delighted to find a by-pass around Altoona: happy I didn't have to deal with any city at all on this day of travel. I stopped for gasoline, then headed northeast toward State College. When I drove into Tyrone, I knew I had to visit Grier. The Grier School just outside of Tyrone was home to me during my high school years. Here again, I was a homing pigeon — took the road along the river, then wound up the drive to school as if I'd never been away.

This small boarding school was founded in 1851 as The Mountain Female Seminary by the Grier family and is still owned and directed by the Griers. It has a special place in my heart. My father and I cut a deal: I'd go to Grier and he'd buy me a horse. Papa had re-married and his wife did not become a mother for me. In fact, she couldn't stand me. It was a difficult situation all around; difficult for my father, difficult for my step-mother, and difficult for me. So Papa suggested enrolling me at Grier and buying me a horse. I was crazy about horses and it sounded like a good deal.

I was spending more time with my brother Bill and Ginny in State College than at my father's home. We checked into it and, although Papa got a lot of flak from Aunt Clara, Aunt Dora, my Mary, and Ginny — they all thought it was awful to send me away to a boarding school — I went to Grier. Looking back, it was the best thing that happened to me in my teens.

At Grier, we were expected to achieve academically and athletically. And I did, although I never considered myself one of the brains. Classes were small and stimulating and I learned to think for myself. Grier gave me the freedom to question theories and ideas, to make choices on what I accepted or rejected, to evolve in my own way. I know Papa didn't think he'd have to buy me a horse, but I held the man to the deal. I had my own mare, Heels Up, and she was my best friend.

I wound up the hill past Old Main and the Grier's residence and pulled into visitor's parking overlooking the courtyard. It all looked comfortably the same and, in that moment, I regressed forty years. I walked slowly across the veranda and into the office. When I queried the receptionist about who was now headmaster at Grier, she replied, "Dr. Douglas Grier." That brought me up short.

"Dougy," now addressed as Dr. Douglas Grier, was seven years old when I graduated. Thought to myself, God, you're getting old, woman. I asked if I might see Dr. Grier and explained that I was an alumna. I was ushered into Doug's office and noted that he looked very much like his father, T.C. Grier, who was headmaster when I was at school. We chatted easily. I found that Doug had matured nicely. I used discretion in not telling him that I remembered him as a small tad who turned somersaults on the lawn during graduation ceremonies. He very graciously told me to feel free to roam and look and to make myself at home. I asked him about his mother, Solveig, and what a pleasant bonus to learn that she was here at Grier. Doug and I walked together down across the lawn and caught Solveig as she was leaving for Tyrone.

She remembered me well, even the fact that I was one of the seniors who petitioned for Jimmy LaRosa to become our riding master. Solveig had been an ally in that endeavor and Jim was head of the riding school for years. He still lives at Grier. We talked a long while, catching up on forty years. Solveig told me she spent most of her time in Florida now and that she did have a problem with her back. To me, she was still as beautiful and with it as she had been forty years before.

I went back to the main buildings and walked through the halls. The sounds hadn't changed — a cacophony of sounds from the rooms — jazz and classical music, talk and laughter. Climbed the stairs of Old Main to my room. I took a lot of guff at Grier because I had the only totally private room in the entire school, M-25, and I would not move from it in spite of the pressure put on me. I needed my space even then, my privacy. I needed the freedom to close the door and know I could be alone. I've always had that need.

I knocked on the door. A cute gal greeted me with, "Sure. Come on in and look around." Now there was a bath and roommates, there were phones, and the girls were allowed to eat in their rooms. Things do change; many more creature comforts. I had chosen the complete privacy of M-25 over having a bath of my own. All of us in Old Main shared a communal bath with three tub enclosures and three toilets, but each room had its own sink. The door out to my veranda, which was really the porch roof over the entrance to Old Main, had been changed to a window. I thought I wouldn't like that. I had loved sitting out there among the trees when I was at Grier.

Went down to study hall, then through the library and the living room. It all looked great. Stopped at the camper and let Ink out telling her I had always been in trouble over dogs when I was at school, so I might as well be now. The two of us walked the grounds. There was a new computer building. Doug told me the music buildings were no longer used for that purpose, but they looked the same. Strolled through the village of Birmingham and down to the stables. Spoke with some of the girls while they fussed over Ink. I asked them how they liked Grier and got the same response I would have given: a sort of shrug and, "Oh, it's okay." I told these young ladies that I understood fully, but I assured them that over the years their memories of Grier would become very precious.

At length, I decided that we had better be on our way. I had told Ginny that I would probably arrive that evening, but not to worry if I didn't show until Wednesday. Ginny has known me a long time and realizes that I run on my own schedule. We were ready to pull out when a lad on a bicycle coasted up to Tessie. He was teaching Spanish at Grier. A male teacher, yet! In my day, we had a male riding master and Mr. Dayton, the art and drama coach. That was it. Grier is getting progressive. As is the case in small communities, he had heard that I was visiting and that I had been traveling the country. He commented on my traveling alone. I laughed and told him Grier turned out independent girls even forty years before. I left Grier with my heart filled. It had been home to me and still felt familiar and comfortable. I'm glad Papa and I cut the deal; feel I got the better of it.

Took another familiar road down the Nittany Valley and got to State College about five. I had not been there since my brother's death eleven years before, but had no trouble finding the house. Ginny was sitting out front on the swing and it was good to see her. She accepted my decision to stay in the camper easily. I parked up in the drive and proceeded to renew ties with the Henning clan, my brother's family. Bill and Ginny had four children. I have three nephews and, finally, a niece. Now there's a great batch of grand-nephews and grand-nieces coming along. Chuck, my oldest nephew, was born while I was at Grier and I had the pleasure of watching him develop when he was a baby. Did not see the other kids as much, as I had moved to Albuquerque; however, I made trips to Pennsylvania from time to time. Bill and Howd, the younger sons, still live in State College, as does Cathy, my niece. Since Ginny had to have a section for Cathy, she chose to have it on April 4; therefore, Cathy and I share the same birthdate. The times I did see the Henning children were fraught with trauma. Bill called for me to bail him out when Ginny had her first nervous breakdown. I came from Albuquerque and took over the household when Cathy was five months old. When Bill had a serious automobile accident, we were living in New Jersey. Ginny was also in the hospital again. I took my two sons and went to the rescue. That Christmas of 1963, I had six children, Bill in one hospital, Ginny in another, but we managed some semblance of celebrating the holiday season. I spent a day with her therapist, suggesting that if Gin were ever to regain her footing, it would be while Bill was flat on his back.

I think Ginny always realized that she had an ally in me. I used to tell her I'd shoot my brother if he were my husband. Ginny is a gentler soul; however, his carousing and drinking caused her to seek shelter intermittently in the hospital for a period of about five years. She was home for Christmas with all of us. I left for New Jersey with my husband and children after seeing that Ginny had help and support. She has not been in the hospital since. My brother eventually lost his business, his home, and a leg to alcoholism and it was instrumental in his early death.

It had been eleven years since I had seen the Hennings, and there again, at the stressful time of my brother's death. This visit was under normal conditions and the family was functioning well. Ginny and I had time for reminiscences and quiet talks.

Visited all the children at their homes. Ginny took me to the new mall and we ate Italian. Patti and Howd invited me out for lunch and to tour their dental lab. Ginny, Ink, and I had a delightful dinner with Cathy and Terry at their home down the valley in Penn's Furnace. Their dog, Emily, and Ink had fun together. The family was kind and gracious to me and the visit was satisfying. It's always good to see the gene field expanding and know there is continuity.

I'm now the repository of the oral family history, the one who has the stories of my father and the kids' father to relate to them. Know I've always been something of a mystery to Ginny and the kids. They were interested in my travels, but I knew they could't relate to someone just heading out as I had done. The Hennings have lived in State College all their lives. They go to the same place each summer for vacation. They enjoy the tried and true and have no desire to seek out the new and unknown. I told them all every family should have at least one "gypsy aunt."

Knowing the old Spanish proverb that states that after three days guests and fish start to smell, and believing it, I made plans to leave State College and my loving relatives on Saturday. I had called Chuck, my oldest nephew, in Burke, Virginia. He, Carol, and the children were expecting me to stay with them for a few days. Told Chuck I'd probably arrive on Sunday, but not to worry about me. So it was hugs and good-byes to the Henning clan and away by 11 a.m. with good memories.

Followed back roads through this section of central Pennsylvania past neat patchwork fields interspersed with orchards. The foliage was beginning to turn with a scarlet tree here and there among all the green. I had decided to visit Gettysburg which is southwest of State College. The nature of the topography in this area of Pennsylvania negates a direct route. There's a whole series of mountain chains, all part of the Alleghenys, which flow in a northeasterly direction. The roads follow the valleys between the mountains: a whole series of mountains with great names: Tussey Mountain, Jack's Mountain,

Blacklog Mountain, Shade Mountain, and Tuscarora Mountain.

I eventually traveled on Routes 322 and 22, skirted Harrisburg, then made a turn over to Carlisle to catch Route 34, a scenic road going directly south into Gettysburg. Stopped at Hollabaugh Brothers fruit farm — open from July till November and located in Adams County a mile north of Biglerville. It was early for harvesting, but there were baskets of apples and pumpkins, jellies and jams, and heavenly smells. Bought a few Nittany apples, then wandered into Gettysburg.

We arrived early on this Saturday afternoon. It is one our great National Parks, I guess. It all depends on how you view National Parks dedicated to war; however, it is an historic site in our nation. The town has become a tourist trap. Flea markets and vendors everywhere. I drove around but did not stop. Probably my perspective of southern Maine and now Gettysburg was colored by the weekend bargain seekers. I had begun to think that everything was for sale, that the diffusion of goods in this nation is carried out totally through flea markets and garage sales.

Since I needed nothing in the way of treasures nor did I have room for them, I did not join the throngs. I did want to drive through the battlefield. We parked up at a campground named appropriately Artillery Ridge, less than a mile from it. The campground played on the theme. Streets for spaces were named Musket Run, North Confederate Avenue, Rifle Fire Road, Rebel Hill. It wasn't crowded and our site on Musket Run was fairly private and close to the restrooms.

Clouds were building up and it was spitting rain when Ink and I got back from our walk, so we settled in early. I read about all that was available for the tourist here in the area. There was a wax museum, a Lincoln Train plus model train displays, a game farm, General Lee's headquarters, the Gettysburg Battle Theatre — just something for everyone. All I wanted to do was drive through the battlefield which is six miles by seven miles in size and surrounds and encompasses the town. The battlefield is where two mighty armies locked in mortal combat over the fate of our nation. Lay and listen to the spatter of rain on Tessie's roof. I had enjoyed my visit with the Hennings, but appreciated a night of solitude here at Gettysburg in the rain. Sunday morning it was still raining. Everything looked soggy, grey, and gloomy and we didn't get an early start. We meandered through portions of the battlefield viewing marble monuments, cannons and stacks of cannon balls, and statues of fallen heroes. It was very quiet and very somber. The gloomy day seemed an appropriate backdrop to this battlefield where so many young men were killed. There was no one around and Ink and I hiked in the mist and read markers. Then we meandered down narrow lanes glistening in the rain; leaves scudding along the ground and clouds scudding overhead. A perfect day for touring this burial ground and contemplating why wars are necessary and why man, or perhaps governments, still use this archaic method of solving differences. It was depressing, but wars are depressing for me. They seem so senseless.

# XIII. Criss-Crossing
# the Old Dominion State

Got out of the cemetery and caught a road leading to Interstate 81. This was no day for pike-shunning, but rather to hop through a number of states easily. On 81, we breezed past Hagerstown, Maryland, Martinsburg, West Virginia, and into Virginia. The rain had stopped, but it was overcast. I pulled into a tourist information center, parked up and had lunch, then availed myself of information on how to get to Burke from the girls at the desk. Got a map of Virginia, went to the restroom, and pushed on.

At Front Royal, we headed east toward Burke and the Washington area. This was Sunday afternoon. We kept rolling along, no problem. But the closer we got to the D.C. megalopolis, the more traffic jammed up — everyone was heading back into town for Monday's work. I said, "Ink, I think we need to get off this Interstate before we get sucked right into the nation's capital." Ink never argued with me. Just wherever we went, there we were. I had a detailed Virginia map and it looked as if there were all kinds of back roads that would lead us to Burke. We turned south off the Interstate. Drove slowly through more rolling hills, narrow curvy roads, pretty country and got to Burke, or what I assumed was Burke, Virginia.

We were in Suburbia, Anywhere, USA. It's amazing how homogenized the housing in this nation has become. I drove past tracts that could have been in California, Arizona, or Massachusetts. I knew I'd not find Chuck and Carol's house in this sprawling suburban scene, but I was fairly certain that this was the proper town — tho' I had not seen a sign. I was driving up a wide boulevard when I saw a jogger and pulled over. Hated

179

to break his pace, but I needed to know if I was in Burke, and if there was a public phone booth close by. He looked startled when I asked him those questions, but was kind and told me that two blocks on up the street I'd come to a large shopping mall with phones and, yes, this was Burke.

Found the mall and called the Hennings. Carol said that I was not far from their house and she'd be right over to direct me on the final leg. I described Tessie and said I'd look for her. She arrived shortly and led me to their home and another visit with family. I was grateful for the assistance because I'd never have made it through the maze of cul de sacs. It was an area of large tract homes, neatly manicured lawns. It seemed to me like Irvine East. They wouldn't hear of my sleeping in Tessie, just pulling up and camping. For that matter, there was no level spot available, so I packed up some necessities and moved into the family room along with Ink. Closed Tess down and gave her a rest here in Burke.

Chuck was cooking dinner. Bill and Melissa, the kids, had changed radically since the last time I had seen them. It's always the kids who make us aware of how the years are speeding by. Chuck and Carol were more entwined in my life than the others of the Henning family. They had visited us in Irvine when they were *en route* to a tour of duty in Hawaii. When the tour was finished, we again had the pleasure of their company plus two little ones. Melissa was three. Bill was only three months old.

Now Melissa was twelve and Bill was nine. It was a whole new ball game. They had a sturdy dog built much like Ink named Barclay. Ink and Barclay hit it off immediately. Old Aunt Barb moved into the house and acted like a civilized person. I did feel I was imposing for there was an estrangement between Chuck and Carol. I noticed that they didn't stay in the same room with each other. Although I had great and meaningful conversations with each of them, it was never with the two of them.

On Monday, Chuck and the kids had left before I stirred. Chuck is a Lt. Colonel now and doing his time in D.C. Carol is working on an MBA to augment her nursing degree. Knowing the rigors of studies and families, I told her to do what she had to do and I'd take care of myself. While she studied, I did some laundry, had a hot shower and shampoo. Ink and Barclay buddied around the yard which was fenced. It was a laid-back day. When Bill and Melissa got home from school, they insisted I come with them to riding lessons at the old Mount Vernon stables. Here was another common thread, I was crazy about horses, Cathy was crazy about horses, and now we had Melissa crazy about horses. I watched the lessons and jumped every jump with the kids. It was a treat to be around the stables and horses.

After dinner Tuesday night, I called through to my son Scot in California. Chuck and Carol had hosted Scot in Hawaii when he decided to take a summer vacation there. He stayed with them and had a great time. Chuck and Carol didn't put any parental restraints on him and he was free to wander and explore. I knew Chuck and Scot would enjoy chatting for a few minutes. Besides, I was happy to check in with my son.

Chuck had asked to see the pictures I had taken of the trip. I brought in my small atlas, since I had marked routes I'd taken and stops I'd made. We looked through the photos as I showed him locations on the map. Chuck finally asked incredulously, "Barb, is this the only map you have? Don't you have a more detailed map with you?" I grinned at him and replied, "Chuck, how can I be lost when I don't know where I'm going? That's the only map I need. It shows me north, south, east, and west and that's all that's important when you're meandering."

He shook his head unbelievingly. I realized that he planned a trip from point A to point B and there was no flexibility once he had made his decision. People miss so much doing that, but it is the way most people travel.

Wednesday, Carol and I went to Washington. Carol had suggested taking the new subway. We drove over to the station which was lovely, open and inviting, but there was no place to park. We drove round and round looking for a space to park the car, but there wasn't one space available. What a frustration and what a lack of planning!

Carol, undaunted, drove into Washington. It was a short, fast trip. I had not been in our nation's capital in almost forty years. We walked around the Jefferson Monument, drove by the strong statue on a point of land overlooking the Potomac River called Awakening. Parked the car in a garage downtown and had lunch at a sidewalk cafe. Did a quick walk-through of the National Gallery, the Air and Space Museum, and the Museum of Natural History, where I read with interest that the Ghost Ranch is designated a world treasure area for *Coelophysis,* one of the oldest dinosaurs in the world.

We didn't have time for in depth viewing and I said to Carol, "Boy, I could spend a month just nosing around the Natural History Museum, you know." Carol invited me to come and stay with them and do just that anytime I wished. I looked longingly at the Smithsonian, but knew it would have to wait.

Our nation's capital is a repository of information and a beautiful city. Even though I had heard of the numbers of street people in D.C., I was still shocked. They were in evidence everywhere; urinating off curbs, huddled in cardboard boxes, plunked down on the grass looking poor and lost. This was not true in Rome when I was there in May of 1988. I had to question how a nation that bills itself as humane and prosperous could allow this misery, but I came up with no answers. It was an enlightening afternoon and we were back in Burke by the time Melissa and Bill got home from school.

I told the family at dinner that evening that I thought I should be on my way the next morning. Chuck was able to take the following afternoon off work, however, and invited Carol and me for a cruise on their boat and a chance to see Washington from the river. I couldn't pass up an opportunity like that. Besides, Ink and Barclay had become close buddies and were having a ball. We stayed another day. Called Mark and Lois that evening and let them know Mom's whereabouts and that I was slowly making my way south.

Thursday morning, Carol and I drove over to the marina to meet Chuck for our river cruise. I apologized to Carol for taking her from her studies, but she assured me that our talks were more important to her well-being than classes. They have a nifty outboard cruiser. Chuck seems to have inherited his Grandfather's love of the water and boating. My father kept a cruiser on the Allegheny River and I remember some fun times on that boat.

It was cloudy, but we had a lovely float down the Potomac past Mt. Vernon, the War College, clear into the Tidal Basin with views of the Washington Monument in the background. We drifted by the back side of the Pentagon, which Chuck told me was the more attractive side, and on past the JFK Center for the Performing Arts. One would not suspect, drifting on the Potomac, that all those street people were lying around. We ate a picnic lunch rocking on the boat and looking around. I was glad I had consented to stay for this outing.

At dinner, I promised the Hennings I definitely was on my way tomorrow morning. Chuck asked where I was going. I replied with a grin, "South, Honey. I'm getting anxious to see my chickies in Tennessee, so it'll be south." He asked if I had ever been to Assateague Island where the wild horses are and I told him no. Chuck said, "Barb, you should go that way. It's a great area."

I thought, why not? Might as well see it while I'm here. Said to the family. "Okay, I'll do that." I think it gave Chuck a feeling of comfort that I was setting off with a destination in mind.

I was sitting in bed that evening when Bill came in and sat down beside me. Bill is more quiet than Melissa, or it could be that he finds it hard to compete with her garrulousness. This evening, he asked, "Barb, you're my great aunt?"

"Yes. I'm your daddy's aunt and your great aunt."

He gave me a big smile and said, "You really are great!"

Who could ask for a nicer compliment? And, I had found them really great, too. I grieved for Chuck and Carol and the impasse in their relationship. My heart went out to both of them and to the kids who sensed deeply that all was not well with their parents; however, it was a problem I had to leave with them, one they would have to solve.

I had said my good-byes to Chuck on Thursday night, but the kids hopped in for final hugs early Friday morning before leaving for school. Carol and I ate breakfast together. She thanked me for giving her more insight into the Henning family. I reminded her that the perspective was only mine; each of us sees others only through our own eyes. She gave me a small volume to take with me, saying it had helped her and she was sure I'd enjoy reading it. Then, she led me over to a shopping center where we hugged and said our good-byes.

After our parting, I took care of business — a cash advance, gasoline for Tessie — and we were on our way. The gypsy caravan was rolling and it felt good to be back on the road again. In spite of Chuck's telling me to follow Route 95 around the D.C. area then take the road to Annapolis, cross the bay at the bridge and it's a short hop to Chincoteague, I guess I was preoccupied and not paying attention. We were on Route 95, rolling along with the jazz blaring, when I saw a sign for Fredericksburg.

That didn't seem right, so I pulled off the road and looked at the map. We were heading directly south on 95, not toward Annapolis and the bridge at all. I thought, oh, my God, Chuck would flip if he could see me now. By this time, I wanted to see the refuge and those wild ponies. Drove farther south, caught a lateral over to Route 301 and headed northeast. The meandering was with us again. It was a good mistake for we saw a portion of Virginia that was quiet and definitely below the Mason-Dixon line. Stopped in the town of Port Royal for a sandwich, then crossed the Rappahannock River. Drove a few more miles and then crossed a toll bridge over the Potomac and were in Maryland. I paid attention and did connect with Route 50 where we took another toll bridge over Chesapeake Bay. We were on the correct road after a pleasant detour.

Because of our circuitous route and long detour, it was getting late. The sun was beginning to set in the Bay and I thought, I'm not going to make it to Chincoteague tonight. Checked the camper guide and read an ad for a fishing campground right on Chesapeake Bay at Nanticoke. We turned onto a country road leading to Nanticoke. It was flat country dotted with large trees.

Drove through a small village called Bivalve; neat, two-story wooden houses painted white and surrounded by hollyhocks and vegetable gardens. A scene from yesteryear. The sun was low in the west and the countryside was bathed in a luminous golden light. We got to Nanticoke about 6:30 p.m. and found the campground a scene from yesteryear, too. The office was in an old wooden building which also housed a general store. An old dog was lying by the doorway.

A kind man registered me and directed us to a grassy site under a large tree. The old dog had come out to investigate. He and Ink had a romp as there were no restrictions on dogs being free, so long as they were well-mannered and friendly.

It was a warm evening here on the eastern shore of Maryland. I sat at the picnic table and watched a copper-colored sky while Ink and the old dog visited. There were muffled sounds of small boats chugging out to the bay and soft voices of people over at the dock. It was a kindly site far from the beaten path.

I was sure the Hennings had never seen this section of Maryland on their trips to Chincoteague and was thankful that I didn't have to rush from point A to point B, but could check out all the secluded areas in between.

Turned in early. It felt good to be back in my little womb Tessie. I read the volume Carol had given me. There was one sentence that grabbed me: Fear is the absence of love. I lay and rolled that around. This journey had to be filled with love since I did not feel any fear.

It was October 1, 1988. I seemed to find myself in fascinating places at the beginning of a new month. On the first of

September, I was in Woodstock, New Brunswick. This particular day, we were in Nanticoke enroute to Assateague Island Seashore. It was a slow and easy morning, no hurry. Was having breakfast at the picnic table when old dog came over. Ink and he sniffed and greeted. While the dogs had a tussle, I did the dishes, got Tessie in shape for traveling, and got ready to leave. We drove back over the winding road. As we passed through the village of Bivalve again I thought that little town could tell some fascinating stories.

When we got to Salisbury, we headed south and back into Virginia, then turned east and arrived at Chincoteague about 1:30 p.m. I drove down the main street lined with clapboard buildings and boutiques. It was a resort town, but the season was coming to an end. There weren't great hordes of tourists, even though it was a Saturday. Drove south to the end of Main Street and turned around. Went back north to Bridge Road and a campground which was close to the Refuge. It was early, but I pulled into the campground and made reservations. It was a large complex, and not crowded at all. We had a site down by the fish pond and close to the tent area. It was wooded, no one parked close, and it looked fine. I gave Ink a run and fixed some lunch, but did not pop Tess as we were on our way to Assateague Island to see the wild ponies.

Got our pass to re-enter the campground — this was for the protection of the patrons — then took Bridge Road and crossed to Chincoteague Island. We stopped at the Ranger Station and met with a set-back. I pulled up to the window and, of course, Ink leaned out to give her greeting to the rangerette who said, "I'm sorry, no dogs are allowed in the refuge. No dogs allowed at all."

"But my dog has traveled with me all over the States and Canada and I have no place to leave her. This camper is our home. What can I do?"

"There's a kennel just down the road."

"Gee. I'm gonna have to think about this."

We circled around the booth and headed back across the

bridge. I didn't see the kennel, but I knew I didn't want to leave Ink in one anyhow. We drove back to the campground and pulled into our site. I was sitting trying to collect my thoughts and fighting disappointment. There were two women from Pennsylvania parked up the way from my site in a tent camper. They walked down and said, "Boy, you're a long way from home."

"Yes, in a way, but Pennsylvania was my birth state and I've just visited family there."

"You're traveling all alone?"

"No. I have my dog. She's a great travel companion, but we've just been turned back from seeing the wild ponies because of her. They won't allow dogs in the refuge and I don't know what to do."

These sweet ladies asked, "Why don't you tie her by this tree? We're going to be here all afternoon and we'll keep an eye on her. You just go and see the refuge."

I had never left my Inkus. I had driven a long way and really wanted to see the refuge, but wasn't sure I wanted to leave my dog.

"You're sure you wouldn't mind? I'd really like to see it."

"Not at all."

I had a long talk with Ink, explaining that I was going to be gone for a while, but I'd be back. Felt awful as I was going to be driving away with her home and everything. I put her feather pillow and water under the tree and explained to this great dog of mine that I'd be back shortly. The ladies waved and yelled, "Now don't you worry. We'll keep an eye on Ink." I drove out of the campground once again, touched by the goodness of the people I kept meeting on this trip.

The refuge was magnificent. The ponies were grazing in a meadow right beside the roadside. The firemen from Chincoteague swim them across the bay each July and auction some of them off to raise funds for the fire company and to help care for the herd. They're large, handsome ponies, well-proportioned, with fine heads. Not the Roman-nosed, crude heads of many of the Mustangs in the southwest, but refined, good heads. One group of five ponies contained three pintos, a buckskin, and a bay; good looking stock. They were standing knee-deep in meadows that looked like they could support a much larger herd. This refuge is lush with grasses, wildflowers, pines and evergreens.

There was a circle drive around the island with views of a scenic lighthouse, heavily forested sections, meadows and grasslands. I did the circle which was only about five miles and did not take long. I decided to drive it one more time. And how serendipitous. As I was rounding a corner, I saw a group of people standing by the roadway. I pulled off to see what they were looking at. There was a dainty doe with two fawns down in a hummock of grass just off the roadside. The babies lay there and didn't move at all, just looked curiously at all the people. I was able to walk up close and get some pictures of the doe and her two fawns. I have no idea of the species, but they had black and white ears and were diminutive. Seeing those gentle deer helped me understand the regulation against dogs at the refuge — even nice dogs like Ink.

I headed back to the campground, knowing Inkus would be wondering where her Mother and her home had gone without her. Ink was wiggling from tip to toe as I drove into our site. I sat down and hugged her and told her I'd never leave her for long. I did tell her the refuge was no place for a dog, but I was happy to have seen it.

The Pennsylvania ladies walked down and told me that Ink had been very good. They said, "You know she just stayed on her pillow there, but she never stopped looking down the road for you." I thanked the ladies for their kindness and concern. We all laughed about what poor Ink must have thought when I drove away without her. Ink takes everything in stride but was overjoyed to have me back. We went for a long walk. I told Ink I didn't think I'd have to leave her like that again as I gave her a few extra hugs and pats.

Put Ink on her lead while I hopped into Tessie to start dinner.

Was getting our meal underway when I heard Ink give her special cry that means come over here and pat me. About that time, I heard a woman's voice say, "Well, there's a big dog here, but I don't see anyone else."

I hopped out and noticed another Toyota Chinook parked on the road in front of my space. There was a woman standing over by Ink and I said, "Hi." She responded, "Hi. We saw your Chinook and thought we'd stop and say hello and see how you like it. You're from Arizona?" They were reading my front license plate. No. I hadn't taken it off.

I explained to them that Tessie was from Arizona originally, but we were really from New Mexico. We started comparing our Chinooks. There is a brotherhood among Chinook owners. When we passed on the highways, it was common practice to wave and blink lights. We all realize we have a sturdy, reliable machine under us. These friendly people were the Weavers from near Harrisburg.

They were curious about my Chinook and my travels. We had a great visit. I invited them in to check out my Tessie and then walked over to look at their Chinook which was arranged differently. We all agreed that we loved our little campers. The Weavers had 104,000 miles on their Chinook and it was still going strong. They commented on my bravery in heading out all alone. I told them it had been a beautiful experience with no problems and I was grateful for my reliable machine. They both laughed and said, "With all the more miles that Toyota has on her, she should last you the rest of your life." After a few more pleasantries, the Weavers bade me good travels and went on their way.

In the morning, Ink and I walked around the grounds. I talked with the Pennsylvania women and they asked if I really had to leave. I told them I felt the need to head on down the highway since I was getting anxious to see my kids in Tennessee. I thanked them again for their help in watching Ink.

Got squared away and pulled out about 10:30 a.m. When we connected with Route 13, we drove south along the east shore of

Virginia heading for the Chesapeake Bay Bridge and Tunnel complex. We were ambling down this narrow peninsula — a spit of land jutting between the Atlantic Ocean and Chesapeake Bay — and I thought, I've been down this road before. It had to have been this road. My father had a passion for ferry boats. We would travel miles out of our way so that we could ride a ferry. He thought it was one of man's greatest inventions.

During World War II, my brother was stationed in Smyrna, Tennessee, at the Army Air Force Base where he was an instructor in B-24s. When we'd go to see him, it was never in a straight line but via the Chesapeake ferry. We'd detour clear out to this peninsula so we could ride the ferry and eat soft-shelled crabs. Those big, top-heavy ferries lumbering across the Bay were an experience. Here I was meandering over the same route.

I remember one morning when the ferry was rolling so heavily that all you'd see was the bay waters and then the sky. Papa thought it was great as he sat in the restaurant on board eating fried eggs and ham. Most of the passengers were holding on for dear life and looking slightly green.

This was a road I'd traveled before! Now there were bridges and tunnels spanning the Bay. I had to laugh at myself. For a person who hates tunnels and high bridges, I had certainly chosen an inappropriate route. I'm sure Papa would have preferred a boat. I thought I should have a look at this marvel of engineering, so on we rolled.

The Chesapeake Bay Bridge and Tunnel complex opened on April 15, 1964. It took three years and six months to build the crossing. The shore-to-shore length of tunnels and bridges is 17.6 miles. No tax money was used in the building of this complex. We paid our toll willingly and took our chances.

We climbed first up the Fishermen Inlet Bridge: 110 feet horizontal clearance and a 40 foot vertical clearance. Followed the causeway along the North Channel Bridge which had 311 feet horizontal clearance and a 75 foot vertical clearance. Then it was the Chesapeake Channel Tunnel — 5,420 feet long. I get stifled down in those things; however, there wasn't much traffic and Tessie didn't seem to mind rolling under a huge body of water.

Came up out of that hole to another span of causeway and then down again in the Thimble Shoal Tunnel — 5,738 feet long and 90 feet below sea level. There are also four man-made islands rising thirty feet above the water along the route. As we emerged from this tunnel, there was one of these islands which housed a parking lot, gift shop, and long dock extending out into the Bay. I parked up and got out to walk around. I was feeling dizzy after dealing with tunnels and water. I walked and took some photos, breathed deeply of the fresh salt air, felt firm land under my feet, and, in no time, was ready to tackle the final portion.

It was a fascinating trip and we made it with style and grace. Ink found it disconcerting to look out and see the seagulls flying beside us looking in at her, but she seemed to have faith in my ability to get us across this span. I had placed my faith in Tessie and she purred along in her stately fashion.

We reached dry land in the Norfolk area. I thought about going to Virginia Beach, but remembered the conversation with the Weavers. They had urged me to take the drive along the James River to view all the old plantation houses. That seemed the way to go, so we hung a right. We found our way through Norfolk, crossed another big bridge, breezed through Newport News. Turned off the Interstate and wandered through Williamsburg. Here again, we hit it at the wrong time, a Sunday, and there were wall-to-wall people. I couldn't find a spot to park up Tess easily, but we drove around this historical city. In trying to find the road along the James River — the directional signs were non-existent — we kept driving and seeing more of Williamsburg. After going in circles, looking at stately brick buildings and tourists, I negotiated the traffic jams and found my way to state route #5 and headed northwest along the north bank of the James River.

There were lovely old plantations all along the route. Well preserved large houses rimmed with magnolia trees and set amidst acres of gardens. Most of them were open to the public for a fee. We pulled into Sherwood Forest Plantation where I could park Tess under a shady canopy of old oaks. I let Ink out since there were no people around. Evidently, they were all in Williamsburg. We walked through a forest toward the main house on a soft, dirt pathway lined with logs. When we came to the main drive, I did put Ink on her lead even though there was no sign of habitation or people.

Sherwood Forest was the home of President John Tyler. It is considered the longest frame house in America. It's 300 feet long, was built about 1730, altered and renovated by President Tyler in 1844. It still looks much as it did when Tyler left the White House in 1845 and came home to the plantation. Since that time, the plantation has been continuously occupied by members of the Tyler family and has been a working plantation for over 240 years. All of the original 1600 acres are still in the Tyler name.

There are over eighty varieties of century old trees in the gardens, 37 of which are not indigenous to the area but that have thrived with TLC. We walked up the carriage road to the entrance and then clear around the house. We did not go in as there are admission fees now to visit the interiors of these magnificent plantations and I was sure Ink would not be welcomed. We walked through the gardens in back of the house admiring old, old cedars, tulip poplars, magnolias, and a fine specimen of a ginkgo tree brought to America from the Orient by Admiral Perry in the mid-19th century when Tyler re-opened the trade route to the Far East.

The house was a long structure with sturdy brick chimneys at both ends of the middle three story section and again at both ends of the two story sections. The mid-section was three stories high with the top story dormered on the roof line and the brick chimneys rising above the dormers. On each side of the mid-section are two story wings with dormers and brick chimneys, and finally each wing is terminated by a one story section — a long structure all of white clapboard. It was well built and made to last, as it has. Ink and I ambled around the grounds and enjoyed the quietness and beauty.

We continued our drive along the James River. Stopped and viewed Evelyton from the sweeping drive leading back to this huge brick house. Noticed that the admission fee was $11.00 here, and was glad I wasn't devoted to historical plantations. We turned down a dirt road to Westover Church. There was no one here either and Ink and I ambled once again. This was an austere brick church, not even a steeple. There was a narrow brick walk leading to the entry door between privet hedges. It was small, sturdy and charming.

The afternoon was slipping by and I thought we'd better stop gawking and gazing and be on our way. I was glad the Weavers had suggested this tour, as was often the case. Someone in a campground would ask if I had seen thus and so and say, "Oh, you really should see it." I was usually happy I took those suggestions. I saw some sights I might otherwise have missed.

Came off Route 5 somewhere in the Hopewell area. The guide listed a state forest with camping facilities not far from where we were. This was just south of Richmond and we did have some traffic. It was late afternoon and the clouds were becoming thicker. We found our way to Pocahontas State Park and it was a glorious setting, lots of oak trees and hilly terrain. By this time, it was very cloudy; and starting to rain.

We pulled up to the Ranger Station, but there was not a soul there. I decided they must come by to collect later in the evening. All the parks seem to have a different routine, each bent on creating its own little entity. Anyhow, we drove on into this forest and made a turn around one site which didn't look inviting. There were no campers anywhere and I was beginning to wonder if the park was open. I knew I was going no farther that night as we headed up another dirt road. It was raining hard. We came to a great area with restroom facilities, a large, open site with plenty of parking spaces. There was no one here either. It looked like a fine place to spend the night. I backed Tessie into a sloping space between some huge oaks. Ink hopped out and started exploring in the rain. I knew we'd have a heap of mud in the camper, but she certainly wasn't going to disturb anyone. Popped the top and started to prepare dinner. We didn't have electricity as this was a primitive site, but no problem.

I was in Tessie when, all of a sudden, I heard this zing, zang, zap on her roof. The war was starting! It didn't take me long to determine what the noise was. With the rain and the breeze, the oaks were dropping acorns at a prodigious rate and they sounded like bullets hitting the roof. I sat and laughed out loud. It was like cooking in the midst of a battlefield.

It was getting dark. I was putting Ink on her lead when I heard an engine growling slowly up the road. Told Ink I guessed we were going to have company for the night. A pick-up pulling a large trailer pulled in — slowly and hesitantly. It was a couple from North Carolina, an older man and his wife. They stopped to ask me if the site was open. I told them I hadn't the foggiest, but I planned to spend the night. The man said, "Well, I don't want to back this trailer into one of those spaces." I suggested, "There's no one here at all. Why don't you just pull up to that upper level and park straight out. What difference can it make? And, it's sure easier."

The North Carolina couple did just that and I was happy to have someone around on this rainy evening. Ink hopped into Tessie. I donned my poncho and boots and hiked up to the restroom for a shower. It was sparkling clean and there were spacious stalls. I was quite alone, so I sang and splashed and spent a long time under a stream of hot water. When I got back to Tess, Ink was all curled up. We fell asleep to the sound of acorn bullets thunking on the roof. We were snug and cozy and it was a good sleeping night there at Pocahontas State Park.

There was still light, gentle rain when we woke. Acorns still falling, but not much else happening in the old campground. Ink was out exploring and getting muddy. I got myself together and was heading for the restroom when I saw my North Carolina neighbor. She was walking across the way, a plaid umbrella over her head. We exchanged greetings and she came over to me and asked, "Young lady, are you alone?"

"No. I have my dog."

"Law, aren't you the brave one! You know, we were so tired when we came in here last night that I didn't think much about it, but we got parked up and I said, "You know Harold, I don't... I think she's alone over there."

"Oh, I have Ink and we manage very well."

"You just come right along with me. I've got to have Harold meet you."

We walked up to the trailer together. I learned that her name was Lottie and she and Harold were retired, loved to travel, had four children, were *en route* to Richmond to see one son and his family, plus more.

Lottie yelled, "Harold, I want you to come on out here and meet this little woman traveling all by herself all over this country." We all visited in the rain. These gracious people kept telling me how brave I was. It was a welcome boost to my ego, in spite of the fact that I didn't feel brave at all, just delighted and blessed to be able to do this journey.

Lottie hugged me to her warm and ample bosom and said, "You just are something else." I explained that I was going for a visit with my children in Tennessee and had seen family in Pennsylvania and Washington. That seemed to ease their concerns about my being alone — I was going to see family. They were a warm, loving couple. I realized again that our country is filled with good and kind people and wondered why we never hear of them in the news.

Harold was anxious to get started, so we said our good-byes. I think Lottie would have visited all day, but he loaded her in. I waved them a fond farewell then got about getting the gypsy caravan together.

It was almost 11 a.m before we pulled out. I still had not seen a ranger, and when we left the park there was still no one at the gate. I blew a kiss and thanked them for a free night in the rain with the acorns banging on the roof. I didn't know what else to do.

On that rainy, quiet morning, we meandered on small county roads. It was misty and closed in, pleasant driving. We came to Route 360 and followed it for a short distance to Route 460. This would not be the most direct route, but I knew I must see Appomattox Court House National Historic Park. There wasn't much traffic, just clouds and mist, green country, hills and farms. My favorite kind of driving day; Tessie purring along, jazz playing in time to the windshield wipers, everything snug, cozy and warm. Ink was snoozing on her feather pillow. All was right with our world as we chugged along the back roads of Virginia.

We did visit Appomattox Court House. More huge battlefields attesting to the great number of lives lost during our Civil War. I always seemed to tour these memorials on a cloudy, gloomy day which seemed appropriate. There's a saying in our family: "Happy the bride the sun shines on. Happy the corpse the rain falls on." I thought of it as I drove past all the graves in the rain.

We pulled into a parking area devoid of cars. It was still spitting rain. I put my poncho on and took Ink out for a run. Put her into the camper with the explanation, "I'm gonna go and look at this historic site for a few minutes, my gal. You guard the house." Walked up to the village of Appomattox Court House which has been restored to its Civil War appearance: red brick buildings connected by red brick walkways. With the rain-washed sheen, the contrast between that red brick and the green, green grass was vivid.

I walked around this quaint, quiet village reading signs and taking some photos. It was so hushed I could almost imagine the ghosts of Lee and Grant meeting there to end a devastating period in our history. I spent time gazing at the house in which General Lee surrendered his Army of Northern Virginia to General Grant and the Army of the Potomac and mourned for all the young men who gave their lives so that our nation might survive undivided.

Went back to Ink and Tessie. There was no one in the

parking lot, so I fixed lunch and ate there. Then it was on across Virginia, heading west on Route 460. Passed through Lynchburg and before we reached Roanoke, we were able to get on the Blue Ridge Parkway. It was a nice run that afternoon. The Parkway was a meandering road through the mountains. On this day the mists and clouds were hanging down in the valleys and the tops of the hills looked like islands in a sea of whipped cream. It was one of those romantic days when we felt we were all alone with Mother Nature. There was no way to hurry on this winding road and I had no desire to. We stopped at a number of pull-outs and enjoyed the surrealistic views of green hills, grey mists, and scudding clouds. We ambled along and about 5 p.m. came to Fancy Gap. Loved the name — Fancy Gap.

The Trail Inn Family Campground was at Fancy Gap. I wanted to do some laundry and clean Tessie, so decided to spend the night. We were directed down to a site on Doe Trail Loop across from the playground which Ink commandeered as her own. We parked up, popped up, and plugged in early and I did household chores. The rain had stopped and the trips back and forth to the laundry facilities were more pleasant without it. Threw dinner in the oven while I was tending to chores. After dinner, Ink and I took a long walk around the grounds. I put her up and went to call the kids since I knew I'd be able to make it to Kingston the next day.

Lois answered and said that Mark was away on a business trip but she was delighted I'd be there tomorrow. We cut the phone conversation short, agreeing we'd have time to visit when I got in. I told Lois I'd probably be there before she was home from work and I'd take care of dinner. Assured her that I could find my way to the house and was looking forward to the visit.

As I was going by the office after making my call, I looked in the window. There was a group of people sitting around eating ice cream cones. One lady smiled and waved me in. I stepped into the office. The group was campers spending time at this campground, most of them from the Virginia area with that soft, lilting accent. The lady who waved was in charge of the office that evening. Her name was Barbara, too, and she was related to the owners. She was there on vacation giving them a little help with the chores.

Barbara asked if I'd like an ice cream cone and that sounded good. She scooped up a big cone for me and I joined the rest of the group and visited. They seemed astonished that I had traveled so far and especially alone. I answered the old familiar questions. They were fine people and we all sat and ate ice cream and had a pleasant chat. They laughed when I told them about my experience with the bullet acorns at Pocahontas. They told this neophyte desert rat that anyone in Virginia knows better than to park up under oak trees in the rain.

Wandered back to Tessie. Settled in for the night, telling Ink that tomorrow we'd be at her dog cousin's house. Didn't bother going for a shower either since I could take a hot soak in the tub at the kids' house. Had a wonderful night's rest knowing that tomorrow would bring us to Tennessee and a visit with my children.

We woke early. I was excited about getting to the kids. Inkus had her run, I ate, did dishes, and got Tess in shape for travel. Barbara, the office gal, came by and we chatted a bit. Still and all, I was on my way by 10 a.m. that morning, ready to see my chickies. Leaving Fancy Gap, I got smart and headed north on a good road. No more Blue Ridge Parkway. Went north and caught Interstate 81. It was clear sailing through the last section of Virginia. I had enjoyed my wandering in the state immensely. Had meandered Virginia almost as long as I had meandered Colorado.

# XIV. TLC in Tennessee

We took Interstate 81 heading southwest and crossed the border at Bristol, Tennessee. We were on our way. The Interstate driving was easy, boring, and noisy with big trucks whizzing by constantly. This section of Tennessee was wide open country and we could breeze along on all four cylinders. Tessie seemed most happy going about 55 and I never pushed her. At times, however, I felt we were the slowest caravan on any Interstate in the nation. Tennessee reminds me of Pennsylvania with more openness. It's the same green mountains, the same flora and fauna, but not as closed and hemmed in. You can see more distant horizons. We rolled along enjoying the scenery.

Had no problem negotiating Knoxville. Although the children work in Oak Ridge, they live in a small, lake community with a mailing address in Kingston. Lois had said, "Oh, Mom, you know where you get off the Interstate. I'm sure you can find the house." I was sure it would be no problem and we turned off where I knew we should. I had been to visit the kids at Christmas in 1986 and had helped them move to this delightful area from Oak Ridge. We drove across neat farmland; horses and cows in the fields, lots of water and trees. I knew I was in the right area, but do you think I could find the turnoff to the lake? No, of course not. We chugged round and round little country lanes until I said, "Ink, I can't find the kid's place coming from this direction. I've got to get to the Oak Ridge highway and approach this problem from that direction. I know I can find the turnoff that way."

It took a while to find the Oak Ridge road, but eventually we wandered onto it. Drove down it until I was certain it was the one, then turned around, came back, and from this approach recognized landmarks and made the turnoff easily. Found my way to the kid's house in Merriweather Acres. We pulled into the yard about 4:30 p.m.

The only one to greet us was Socorro, Mark's German Shepherd. Ink hopped right out and worked her charms on "big pup." He thought this black wiggly dog was okay. While the dogs got acquainted and played, I parked Tessie up. Ink refused to let Socorro come into the camper. He was curious about this little house on wheels and really wanted to check it out; however, Ink would hop in and sit at the door and absolutely refuse to let him come into her house.

Lois had told me where to find a key and I went inside, since I had told her I'd get dinner started. I knew my little girl would be home before too long so flapped on a skillet and got dinner underway. Walked around and played with the dogs. I knew it was going to be a time to relax, to forget traveling and finding my way. It was a time for enjoying my kids and the beauty of the lake and being together. I said a special thank you to my guides for bringing me to this safe and loving haven.

Lois pulled in about 5:30 p.m. There were lots of hugs and giggles while we put dinner together and jabbered away. We stumbled over each other as we talked and shared. I condescended to sleeping in the house and did take that long, leisurely soak in the tub. Socorro and Ink were hitting it off well. Ink didn't mind at all that Socorro had to be alpha dog. She'd just wag her tail at him and do her thing.

That evening I didn't bother getting Tessie settled in. Lois had to be off to work early, so we went to bed at a reasonable hour. I told Lois I'd relish a quiet day at the lake with the dogs and would not drive anywhere, that I'd get my possessions moved into the house and doodle around. It was nitey, nite with, "Oh, Mom, we're so glad you're here."

"It's wonderful to be here, my honey."

As Ink and I snuggled in, I felt so thankful to be here, so thankful to have come so far so safely and joyously.

Lois had gone before I started moving the next morning. I got out and parked Tessie on a level spot up above the house and shut her down. Moved all my stuff inside and talked with Socorro and Ink as they ran back and forth with me. About noon, Lois came home feeling lousy with a cold. We sat and visited some more while caring for Lois's cold. Mark called that evening, checking to see if I had gotten there and to let us know he'd be home the next evening.

Lois took the next day off and nursed her cold. I went out and cleaned Tessie well. Markus arrived home about 6:30 p.m. How wonderful to see this handsome son of mine! This one is very like me. We laugh about it at times, but both recognize that we are alike. He and Lois always understood my desire to make this journey. They were supportive and encouraging; never made me feel like I must be crazy to do such a thing. It was always, "Go for it, Mom." Since I was fighting cultural norms, this wonderful, loving input was comforting.

The days settled into an easy routine there at the lake. The dogs and I would walk and enjoy the beauty. I got chores done that I had had on hold. Put all the photos into an album after labeling them. Would usually fix dinner. Cooking standing up was a treat after Tessie. Just floating, sumptuous days of not having to make decisions. The kids entertained me, treated me royally, and they made the decisions.

On the 9th, Lois entered a biathlon; biking and running. Mark and I drove over to the finish site to cheer her on. She finished first in her class, of course. Mark and I had some quality visiting time. I treasure my relationship with these two young adults.

That Sunday afternoon, I called my Aunt Dora in Ft. Lauderdale to let her know I would eventually get there. Loved not making any decisions. The kids took care of everything; making plans and entertaining me. Lois said that afternoon, "Mom, tomorrow is Columbus Day, and I don't have to work so I've planned an outing for the two of us. How would you like to go to historic Rugby?" It sounded super to me as I was happy to float.

Monday morning, Mark went to work and Lois and I went to Rugby. Ink thought it was great to stay and help Socorro guard the house and didn't mind being left at home with her handsome friend. Lois drove. It was relaxing to sit and look at the mountain scenery and not have to read signs and find my way. This Rugby was in the Tennessee Cumberlands. I had already been in Rugby, North Dakota, the geographic center of North America. The circles just kept turning.

This village was an interesting social experiment. Rugby was founded in 1880 by the English author and social reformer Thomas Hughes. Hughes was the author of *Tom Brown's School Days* and *Tom Brown at Oxford*. Hughes was attempting to solve a problem unique to the young sons of the English gentry. The law of the period excluded them from inheritance and class pressures kept them from entering any but a few socially acceptable professions in England. So Hughes decided to start this colony in America where these young men's energies and abilities could be directed to manual trades and agricultural endeavors. He stressed that Rugby was not meant to be exclusively English, that private ownership of the land and freedom of religion and expression would prevail.

The village flourished and foundered for a decade, reaching a peak population of around 450 in 1884. These early years were marked by adversity. The first winter was the most severe in a quarter century. During the summer, drought and typhoid fever struck, killing seven of the colonists. They attempted to establish a tomato canning factory and a pottery business, neither of which succeeded. Very few of the colonists made even a modest living. After the turn of the century, with many of the original colonists gone, Rugby was a small community of some 125 residents.

The *Chattanooga Times* editorialized about Rugby in 1823 and suggested that the buildings and landmarks of the original Rugby settlement should be restored and maintained. Today's Rugby is a neighborhood determined to protect its greatest asset, its rural historic identity. Seventeen of the original buildings are on the National Register of Historic Places. They are beautiful;

restored and repainted in magnificent pastel shades of pink and brown with solid architectural detail.

We toured the church and walked the dirt lanes of this scenic village. The foliage was taking on its autumn hue, but flowers were still blooming in the gardens and along the roadside. It looked like productive farmland; however, the tour guides informed us that the soil is quite thin here on the plateau and there was no way they could have made a farming community out of the lovely village on the Cumberland Plateau in east Tennessee.

We ate lunch there in Rugby at the Harrow Road Cafe, a restaurant specializing in British Isles cuisine. It was a fun day browsing in Historic Rugby and a relaxed day for me as I didn't do any of the driving.

In addition to a hectic schedule filled with work, sports, and lots of social activities, the kids were in the process of buying a house up the road from the one they were renting here at the lake. We all referred to the new property as the "Doober" place. The kids were confronted with a major renovation project. Although it was a well-built, large structure, it had not been maintained and would require lots of work. They had taken on this large do-it-yourself project and were approaching it with enthusiasm and a positive attitude. No wonder I love being around these two.

On the 12th, I went into Oak Ridge for a much needed haircut with Lois's stylist. The kids had suggested having dinner with some of their friends at Chay's before we all drove home to the lake. It was good food and good conversation with delightful young people.

At this point, my Mark had decided that he'd buy a chain saw and remove five huge trees at the Doober place. Thank God, the group convinced Mark that tree removal was an art, especially when three of these 100-foot oaks were up against the house. Mark kept grinning as everyone discouraged him from doing such a foolish thing and pointed out that the house needed a new roof anyhow. However, he did heed advice and did not tackle cutting down the trees. We were in hysterics at the thought of Markus up in those trees waving back and forth in the breeze watching pieces fall through the roof of the house. This mother was thankful to the kids for convincing Mark to give up that project.

Friday, the 14th, the kids went camping for the weekend in Tessie. I stayed at the lake with the dogs. I met with a fellow for an estimate on removing those five trees at the Doober place and was happy to do it. The fall foliage was glowing on this weekend. The dogs and I walked and savored all those shades of pink, orange, and red. I sat in a grove of dogwoods and soaked up all this autumn color which had prompted me to take my trip east at this time of year. I just lazed around, knowing this was a delightful place to be.

However, I was beginning to feel I should be on my way. It was much more than three days that this guest had imposed on time that Mark and Lois needed to get organized for their move and renovation. They arrived home Sunday afternoon tired, but happy with their outing and telling me what a gem Tessie was.

The 19th was my last full day with the children. I had gone into town for supplies and the laundromat. We all met at the yacht basin for a picnic lunch. That evening, we drove to Knoxville for an Italian dinner. As we were driving over, I said to them, "I can't tell you how much it means to me to feel so loved and so cared for. You two are so good to me and it has just been great being here with you. But it's time to continue with the journey."

On Thursday morning, we said our good-byes and my kids headed off for work. I slowly and reluctantly got the gypsy caravan ready to roll. It was a bummer. I had been so happy and comfortable here that, for the first time, I wasn't elated about getting back to the open road.

All of us, from time to time, long to have someone else take over, make the decisions, and take care of us. It's not the way life is, however. Ultimately, each of us is responsible for his or her own well-being — no one can do it for you. It had been wonderful being cared for by these two kids of mine. I did shed a few tears as we headed down the lane because I knew how much I would miss those endearments. Yet, I wanted to continue with the journey. On we went, even though I was saddened by leaving such love.

I drove slowly, sniffling away and chiding myself for having the poor me's. In working on my attitude adjustment, I knew this good-bye wasn't as wrenching as the one when the kids left New Mexico for Tennessee. Mark had his Master's and Lois her Bachelor's. Oak Ridge was the magic kingdom for furthering career goals and they made the move. We didn't see each other that often when the kids were at Tech, but I had the comfort of knowing they were only 2 hours away. Tennessee seemed a different planet and I really hated to see them go so far away; however, I survived and it was a wise move for the kids.

It was at this time that Samantha came into my life and filled that void. She and Theo did become my family in Las Cruces. There's always someone or something that comes in when you most need it. I blew my nose, laughed at myself for being such a sentimental fool, and got on with the journey. Ink and I were both subdued that morning driving away from our loving visit. Guess both of us were thinking, We're on our own again. You can't have it all. I put on an upbeat jazz tape, gave Inkus a reassuring pat, and the gypsy caravan was on its way.

Lois had suggested that we drive though Cade's Cove in the Great Smokies since I had stayed long enough for the fall foliage to catch up with us. Although people were saying the colors weren't vivid that year because of the drought, to me they were heavenly. I hadn't seen those colors in many years and I loved them.

The drive through Cade's Cove eased the pain of leaving. Nature does nurture. It's a loop drive with adequate places to pull off and savor those flaming colors. The other viewers were gracious and at each stop there was some kind soul with whom to talk and enjoy the panorama. I stopped often and took enough pictures to last the century. Didn't know when I'd have the opportunity to see all this beauty again. We really dawdled in Cade's Cove. I was satiated with autumn's riotous display of reds, pinks, oranges, and every hue in between. Drove right through the middle of Great Smoky Mountains National Park past clear brooks reflecting this glorious color. Great Smoky is the nation's most heavily visited national park. There were lots of tourists, but it didn't seem crowded. Driving those scenic vistas helped me to put myself back together and recognize why I was on the road again; to see and to savor, to meander and to enjoy.

# XV. Interstate Driving, Major Decisions and Chicken Pickin'

Since I had dawdled all afternoon, we made it only as far as Cherokee, North Carolina, that evening. Pulled into a campground surrounded by foliage-flaming hills and lots of open space. It was getting late and the weather was clouding up. Got ourselves parked up, popped up, and plugged in — still remembered the routine. We had a couple next to us with a young pup named Coffee who came to greet us. Ink was happy to make a new friend and the dogs romped. The couple invited me over to sit by their fire and have a cup of coffee with them. I thought, there's always someone kind and good. We spent a comfortable night. The rain started after we had settled in. It sounded soothing on Tessie's roof. We were easing back into our travel mode.

Woke to rain. The countryside was soggy and socked in, the sky leaden grey and sullen. It looked like an all day rain. The only color in this grey world were the trees on the hills. They seemed to be holding the sun within. I enjoyed that radiant color while I had my coffee. Ink and her buddy had another romp. Rain or no, it didn't bother the dogs. I got myself together — even looked at a map. We left Cherokee early after farewells to the couple next door.

It was raining hard, but the run to Asheville was uneventful. I gritted my teeth and pulled onto Interstate 26 heading southeast. It was a lackluster day; interstate driving, the windshield wipers humming, and traffic whizzing by us. Ink curled up and slept, I drove and missed the kids, but felt so blessed to have had such a great visit with them. Not a very upbeat day. However, on rainy days, it's just as well to be driving and the Interstate was easy going.

A worrisome problem had been gnawing at me since my visit with the Hennings. They had all asked what I planned to do when I returned to Las Cruces. Would I buy a house, or rent, or what? I didn't know what I'd do and it was troubling me. I didn't think I could afford to buy and I didn't want to search for a decent rental. I did know for certain I was not about to unpack those boxes until it was for the last time.

As we were rolling along that rainy morning, the solution bubbled up. I thought, I don't have to stop! I'm not ready to stop! All my affairs are set up for traveling. Why should I stop this carefree life? Had quite a dialog with myself. I decided I would continue traveling, continue this magical journey. I knew it was the right decision for I felt a ton lighter. This was the ideal time to continue seeking my bliss. It was the one bright spot in an otherwise gloomy day.

We skirted Columbia, South Carolina, and continued on Interstate 26 until we got to Interstate 95, then turned right. We wrapped it up that evening in Walterboro. The campground was next to the Interstate. One of those with easy access for all the condos on wheels and appropriately named Green Acres. It was a nice park, but more geared to the tourist trade than I prefer. The sites were large and set amongst tall pines for we had left the mountains behind and were in South Carolina's Low Country. They had a zoo theme at this campground. My God, there were all kinds of birds and fowl roaming everywhere. Geese, peacocks, exotic chickens, and plain chickens strutting every which way. This dog of mine, the spaniel-setter, was ready to get out among those birds and do a little work. I did not let Ink hop out and explore while I parked Tessie up, not here. I had visions of birds flapping frantically for the branches of those tall pines. Ink sat on her lead looking at all the fowl. I could tell by the gleam in her eye that she certainly could not be loose in this park.

The rain had ceased. After I started dinner, I took Ink way to the back of the grounds and she had a good run. I spent my time watching for any stray birds as Ink nosed around checking out all the scents. We ate and settled in early. That was a mistake. All we could hear was the roar of big trucks speeding along the Interstate. It was a noisy, irritating night; however, I had chosen to pull into this accessible campground.

After a horrendous night of fitful sleep listening to those diesels roaring and shifting gears, to top it off, the bird menagerie started greeting the dawn about 5:30 a.m. There was a cacophony of crows, whistles, and cackles joining the roar of the diesels. I hit the floor and turned the coffee on with a strong expletive, saying, "I give up! Inkus, we've got to get out of here." Sat back and had a cup of coffee then started to giggle about all the noises.

I ate, and started securing Tessie so we could leave. I knew Ink had to have a run before we pulled onto the Interstate. I put her on lead, and back to the rear portion of the park we went, away from the zoo. Inkus got her run. The incident of the run is really Ink's story:

Boy, this park Mom pulled us into was some kind of bird heaven. I don't know why all those birds were strutting around. I only know that because they were, I couldn't run loose which made me mad. Then, it was a terrible night. Mom kept swearing each time a truck went by and I could smell those birds all night. When they started crowing at dawn, I thought if Mom would just let me out I could clear those damned birds away from here in no time and we could get some rest. But she wouldn't let me do that. Mom does think of my needs, though, and before we left, she put me on lead and we headed back the lane so I could have my run. I did my duty and nosed around while Mom was walking on down the way.

I was just checking things out when I saw him — this silly looking rooster — black with a big, white topknot — just sitting there on a stump. Well, I looked at him and thought, I'm gonna get you, little guy. Looked around and Mom hadn't seen him yet, so I went for it. Boy, he started flapping and fluttering and jumping straight up. He didn't have a chance. I just leaped straight up and grabbed that little sucker right out of the air.

I headed for the camper with this silly bird cause I really had him. Put him down. You know, I just wanted to take him home. He was mine! About that time, Mom came running up all white and shaking and upset and I couldn't understand why. Lord, she tossed me into the camper and bent over that little, black devil — he wasn't even moving. Then she disappeared for awhile.

I was sitting in Tessie wondering, what did I do wrong? I just grabbed that little sucker and brought him home. Anyhow, Mom came back and put me on my lead, then went over to look at the chicken who was just lying there on the ground in a bunch of feathers. As she bent over him, he bolted up and took off like a bullet for the zoo enclosure. I'll tell you this about that chicken — he wasn't gonna crow for a few mornings, and he sure had lost a lot of tail feathers.

Mom seemed relieved that the dumb chicken was okay. She just didn't understand, but about that time the zoo man came. He was a nice man and he understood. He had an easy, soft voice and he gave me a big pat and said to Mom, "Now, ma'am, you hadn't ought to be mad at this beautiful dog. She's just doin' what she was bred to do. We lose chickens all the time, so don't be upset with this sweet gal."

Mom said, "Well, it wasn't dead, you know. She's got a gentle..." The zoo man interrupted with, "I know this dog has a good mouth. She's a lovely animal." He patted me again and said to me, "Just doin' what you're supposed to do, aren't you, Ink?"

I don't know why Mom was so upset. I only know that little black rooster with his silly white topknot wasn't feeling so cocky now, but I felt a lot better. I got rid of a few frustrations about this noisy place, too.

The man stayed and soothed both Mom and me. I guess maybe she thought I wanted to kill that dumb chicken. I never want to kill a chicken, I just like to take them home. Anyhow, we all were friends, the zoo man, Mom and me. She gave me a pat and a hug, said good-bye and thanks to the man, and we got out of that place. I know this, I could become a pretty good chicken catcher given the chance.........

It did shake me to see my dog running down that lane with head held high and a black chicken flapping in her jaws. This was a side of my girl's personality I hadn't seen before. Thank God, she has a gentle, bird-dog mouth. I could see no blood on the chicken, but I thought he was dead when I looked at him. I went over to the office to let them know that my dog had killed one of their zoo members and to offer to pay for it. They were kind and not at all concerned.

Evidently, Ink wasn't the first dog to grab one of their chickens. When I got back to the camper, the chicken was still lying there motionless. It must have been scary to have that big, black dog jump straight up in the air and grab him. As I bent over to take another look at the rooster, he bounded up and went hell-bent for election across the campground. I was relieved and felt much better. Then, the zoo man did point out that Ink was, after all, living up to her gene inheritance.

We left the campground early in spite of my dreading Interstate driving all day after such a restless night. It was the only way to travel south. We rolled along slowly, not feeling rested, through the southern tip of South Carolina. I read all the advertisements along the Interstate. Most were geared to retired people, a pitch to spend their "golden years" in this area of the country.

The ones for Hilton Head perked me. I had heard that name, besides we'd spent time at Hilton Beach, Ontario, so we took a break from the Interstate and drove over to Hilton Head Island, the home of eleven championship golf courses and demanding construction codes. Houses are built with the preservation of trees and other natural growth in mind. It was a sybaritic setting oozing wealth. Reminded me of Orange County, California — everything neat and done in earth tones with lots of shrubbery. The gypsy caravan did the loop and did not stop, but it was a nice detour. I was still sorting my emotions about my dog's ability to catch chickens and still feeling a bit shook, but it was getting more humorous. I laughed and patted her, knowing we'd never starve to death if Ink could find a chicken.

Back to the Interstate and a short hop into Georgia, the largest state east of the Mississippi. We were skirting the coast and it was clear sailing along Route 95. Didn't have to deal with Savannah, just rolled on south. We stopped, fixed some lunch, and I took a look at the camper guide. I promised Ink we would not stay in a chicken park that evening.

God bless Georgia. There were all kinds of state parks along the coast. This meant a drive east to the sea, but it meant we'd not have traffic noise either. In checking the guide, I read that no dogs were allowed in Florida's state parks. Told Ink I knew we'd spend the night right here in Georgia. It was too early to avail ourselves of Jekyll Island, the spot where all the millionaires' cottages are located, even though it did sound fascinating. Read more and decided we'd head for Crooked River State Park by the town of St. Mary's.

We pulled off the noisy Interstate early and drove across low country with lots of tall pines. It took a bit of searching, but we found Crooked River. It was great, just what we needed after the zoo of the previous night. We went into the park and drove slowly, checking out sites. It was a Saturday, but the park wasn't crowded. The people waved as we drove around and I knew this was a pleasant place.

We chose an isolated site with an upslope for Tessie, a picnic bench surrounded by lots of vegetation. We were in Spanish moss country — it was hanging from many of the trees. Down the road was an open field leading to the river and the restrooms were close. It was a primitive site, but no matter if we didn't plug in. We set up, then headed down toward the river for a relaxing walk. Ink could run and I didn't have to worry about chickens; however, there were lots of native birds here. The water faucet at our site dripped and they all came in to drink, but Ink wasn't interested in them.

We ate early at the picnic table and watched the birds. It was comforting to be back with nature. We took another walk at sunset. The weather was perfect; not too warm, not too cold. The campers were friendly but not intrusive.

Spent a relaxed night at Crooked River. I knew I'd need this time to psych myself up for the trip down to Ft. Lauderdale. We had lived in Florida for two years and it's not my favorite state. I did want to see my Aunt Dora and Uncle Els, so had to confront the Interstate and an area I did not much care for. I was hoping to be in Lauderdale in time for the full moon as Aunt Dora had expressed a desire to sit and watch it rise over the Atlantic.

I had set a time schedule for myself, which I didn't like to do, but thought it would be nice to take this 82 year old, supportive aunt of mine to the beach for the full moon. This peaceful state park was doubly enjoyable because I knew we weren't going to have another like it for a number of days.

I could tell I wasn't anxious to tackle the Interstate that Sunday morning. We doodled, ate outside, and watched the birds. Ink and I took another long walk and visited with some of the campers. We weren't anxious to get going and it was almost noon before we left Crooked River. Rather than go back the way we had come in, we took a road along the inland waterway and through the turn of the century Georgia town of St. Mary's. There were gleaming plantation houses behind white picket fences shaded by huge magnolia trees. Stopped and took some pictures of a white church sitting in the midst of green lawns and big trees. We fooled around but finally got back on that Interstate and drove farther south.

# XVI. No Magic Kingdom
# for Ink and Me

It was a day of Interstate driving, cars and trucks zipping by us, the tape deck turned up to blank out the noise. Not much to do but read billboards enticing the northerners to come and spend their "golden years" here in balmy Florida. It was a day when I sat there and kept driving. Nothing very stimulating except millions of mobile home parks rimmed by sand and stringy pine trees and lots of traffic and billboards.

Florida is to the south what California is to the west. Neither is true to the region. The great influx of people has changed the demographics radically in both states. Since the state parks would not allow dogs, I checked the camper guide. Got off the damned Interstate and headed again to the coast where we found a park at Malabar. The spaces were tight. You didn't dare put your arm out your window or you'd be shaking hands with the next door camper. The sardine effect. There was open space for Ink and there were no chickens, so it was okay. We were on the water and that helped. As it was just an overnight stop, we didn't need anything too fancy.

After dinner, I went for a shower. The restroom was clean and close to our site and the water was hot. Ink chose to stay outside as the weather was warm. I had curled up in Tess and was reading when I heard a man's voice frantically yelling, "Get down! Get away! Stop!" At the same time, I felt Ink tugging on the bumper. It was dark out there and this black dog was invisible.

I opened the door and asked, "What's the problem?" The man's voice jabbered, "There's a big dog jumping on me." I asked rather huffily, "What are you doing in my space?" I heard

no more. I don't know who it was. It could have been someone
cutting across spaces to get to the restrooms. I thought, boy with
Inkus outside and as black as she is, no one can see her. There's
no way anyone could come up to my door surreptitiously in the
middle of the night. I had a good laugh over the incident. Think
Ink scared the man to death. He had no way of knowing she
merely wanted to say hello. It gave me a sense of security to
know that she could scare someone. This seemed a better trait
than retrieving chickens. All was quiet after that. We settled in
for the night, knowing that tomorrow we'd get to Ft.
Lauderdale, God willing.

We left the cramped campground early, heading straight into
the vortex of all those beach cities along the eastern coast of
Florida. It was Interstate driving and hectic, but we got to the
Lauderdale area early afternoon.

I was faced with a dilemma; I did not want to park my Tessie
at Aunt Dora and Uncle Els' house and I knew this would hurt
their feelings. The area in which they had settled many years
before had changed for the worst. It was not safe. I knew I
didn't want to spend the night in the camper parked in their
drive, but I also didn't want to leave Tessie in their drive
unattended.

It saddens me to see this happen to two gentle people in their
eighties. They have been robbed many times. Luckily, these
break-ins have occurred, thus far, while Dora and Els were
away; however, I shudder when I think of what the scenario
might be if they arrive while the hoodlums are still cleaning
them out.

When I flew down to visit during my Christmas stay with
Mark and Lois in 1986, the cab driver asked me, "Are you sure
you have the right address?" I rechecked my address book and
told him it was right.

As he left me off, this cabby warned me not to go out alone
on those streets. Dora and Els moved to Florida after retiring
and bought this nice house on a quiet two-lane street across from
a park. It's all changed now. There's a six-lane highway in front

of the house and the neighborhood is no longer safe.

As they told me when I offered to help them move, "This is our home. We're staying. We're too old and tired to make a move." I do worry about them there and I have to question this golden years image. It's sad and scary.

Since I refused to place myself in a compromising situation, I located a campground close to where Dora and Els live. I went to see about a site there before I checked in with my relatives. It seemed the discreet way to manage this sticky wicket.

We pulled into a campground that looked rather like a fortress; high fences all around it, a security gate. I realized that the entire area was changing for the worse. It was a nice campground and it was accessible to my destination. They had overnight spaces along with permanent mobile homes, great facilities, and a pool all behind sturdy walls. This luxury and security was available for $22.00 per night. It was the highest price I paid for a site on my entire trip. Since I had no alternative, I registered, but did not set up. I called Aunt Dora to let her know I was in town and had made arrangements for staying at the park. Stopped at a bank for a cash advance, then went on to see my aunt and uncle.

Aunt Dora was the youngest child in the Dean family and is now, as she so poignantly puts it, "The last leaf on the tree." When I was a kid, we really weren't close. I lived with Aunt Clara. She had no children, whereas Dora was raising two of her own with whom I spent some summertimes. But we weren't that close. As the years have gone by, we have become much closer. One aid to this close relationship was Dora's life history which I asked her to do with me for a Women's History assignment. I sent her my tape deck along with lists of questions about her life. She sent me reels and reels of information I didn't know about her life and my family. It was meaningful for both of us. In working on that project, we discovered each other.

She's awesome. At the age of eighty-two, she's so with it. She was one of my strongest advocates when I told her of my desire to make this trip. She would write: Do it, Barb! Do it while you're young! Take off and see and do while you can. She's youthful in her approach to life and she's with today's world — watches Yvonne Lindel, follows baseball avidly, and is alert and aware. Dora was a Latin teacher for many years in Pennsylvania. She's a super woman and I feel honored to have her for an aunt.

When I arrived, they let me know they were disappointed that I wasn't staying with them, but they're both mellow and they accepted my decision. When they saw Ink's size, they were relieved that we weren't moving in. I never think of my girl as big, but she is a big, black, sturdy dog. I was worried that she might knock one of these dear people off balance. Ink seems to have a sixth sense about people — knowing when she can be exuberant and bouncy and when she must be more subdued.

Nothing would do but that we stay for dinner and a visit. Never got back to the park until nine. It was dark and muggy as we set up. Ink did not like the heat and humidity. I told her this was Florida and we'd have to make the best of it. We took a walk around the campground, noting that all the campers were inside with the air conditioning and TVs going strong. I flopped into bed as I was tired and, although there was some traffic noise, I was thankful that I was secure behind the sturdy fences rather than in the driveway. Ink stayed outside on her lead and watched the frogs hopping about.

Started the morning slowly. I had said we'd be over once we were squared away. Ink was still outside. I had been in and out and had noticed that my Burks were sticking to the floor. I didn't think much about it until I looked out at Ink while I was sipping my coffee. She looked spotted. I wondered, what is this?

Went out to check and my Ink was covered with sap. The ground was covered with sap, the camper was covered with sap. It was a mess. They had assigned us a space beneath a tree that was literally raining sap. Ink was the sappiest of all. The poor thing must have felt like Tar Baby because each time she moved she got herself into more sap. I walked down to the office and asked what they suggested to get the sap off everything at my site.

Two ladies ran the campground. They were apologetic and upset about this mishap. They moved us to another site, but the damage was done to Ink. They suggested trying nail polish remover to get the sap out of Ink's coat. I stopped and bought two large bottles, then went on to Dora's and Els' with my sappy dog. We all went to the carport and tried to clean Ink. Used one and one-half bottles of nail polish remover on her and she was still sticky. Uncle Els spent a full hour cleaning the sap off my Burks. Ink was beginning to think Florida was not a fit place for dog nor human. She panted and scratched and itched and was generally miserable. Aunt Dora had fixed a beef roast for dinner. A few tidbits of beef put Ink back in better spirits.

After dinner, we took Tessie and headed for the beach to watch the full moon rise out of the Atlantic. Dora is so mentally alert, it amazes me. She directed me, anticipating each turn and leading us flawlessly. We parked up; however, there was a thick cloud bank on the eastern horizon so we didn't get to see the moon rise like thunder out of the bay. Still, we had a warm, loving visit sitting there with Ink up behind us.

Aunt Dora looked over at me and said, "Don't let a man in your life, Barb. You're really attractive, you know, and you could." This was the first time I had ever had Dora tell me she thought I was attractive, and it touched me. I told her, "It's lonely at times, but you can't have it all. I wouldn't give up this freedom for any man. Not at this point in my life. Don't worry, Aunt Dora, I'm not looking for a man. They impose too much on my time. I just don't think I'm interested."

I told her of my decision to continue traveling. She gave me encouragement with, "Don't stop. If you feel like going, just do it. You have everything taken care of. Just go ahead and do it."

Ink was there between us, happy and content in spite of the sap. Dora asked, "Barbie, you'd never have made it through this life without dogs, would you?" I had to answer, "No, I don't think I would have." We sat there for two hours holding hands, having easy conversation, and enjoying each other's company.

I left Dora and Els that night with an invitation to come for dinner at the park the following evening. Aunt Dora accepted with alacrity. She often said, "I've been cooking for over sixty years, and I'm sick of it." She may be sick of it, but she's a superb cook. I knew if I fixed dinner it would be a break for her.

Arrived at the park late again, but had a sapless space. We took our stroll around the grounds. It was warm and humid and Ink chose to sleep under the camper.

After coffee the next morning, I took a long, hard look at Ink. Put her up on the picnic table and cut off all her hair. It was the only way to get rid of the damned sap. Poor dog was a mess and there was no way to loosen all that sap on her. Besides, she'd be cooler without that heavy coat. She didn't think much of the climate, the sap, and especially didn't like all the frogs and chameleons scooting around the trunks of the trees. Try as she might, Inkus couldn't catch the elusive things.

Got her clipped, then went and had a shower. Scooted to market, since I was to cook this evening. On the way back, the radio conked — nothing, it was dead. That was no loss but the tape deck wouldn't operate either. Got to Buglewood and there was a call from Dora saying Els did not want to come for dinner. Please come over and dine with them. Such is life. Although I was disappointed, I went over.

We had another fabulous dinner which Aunt Dora had to prepare. That evening we went through boxes of memorabilia. Dora had my Grandma's last letter, written when she was 79 just before she died in 1947. I had been to visit her from Grier. She wrote — Barb and I had such a nice visit. It was a long and lucid letter. This was a new dimension of my Grandma. I had no idea she wrote such great letters. We looked at photos that Dora had stashed in old Whitman Sampler boxes. She offered me any that I'd like to have and there were some that were precious to me.

We were on the sixth box when Dora said, "You know, I really ought to get these all organized." I suggested softly that she at least write names and dates on the photos. There were some stolid German couples that Dora was not sure about already. When she dies, there will be no one to chronicle this priceless family background.

Next morning, it was down to the office to inquire about a garage where I could have the radio checked and get an oil change for Tessie. The girls directed me to a place not far from the campground. I set up an appointment, then went by for lunch with Dora and Els. I had told them the gypsy caravan was going to hit the road the following morning. Ink stayed with them in the air-conditioned house while I sat in the garage waiting for Tessie. It was a good RV facility with a group of mechanics who kept telling me I should take that Chinook to Alaska. The radio had blown a fuse and they fixed it quickly, then changed the oil and filter and Tessie gal was ready to roll. I was so happy to have my tape deck operable again, I stopped and bought three new jazz tapes. Went back to collect Ink and say wrenching good-byes to those two adorable people. Of course, I had a big piece of Aunt Dora's pumpkin pie.

The farewell was hard. My heart goes out to them. They are no longer young and vigorous and the world has changed. The home which should be their castle has become a scary fortress. Their children live in Pennsylvania. Our kids never live close-by anymore, what with retirement moves and upward mobility. In my mind's eye, I can see them standing there in the drive waving good-bye. Two gentle people coping with stressful changes and finding them overwhelming.

It was a long, tedious trip down the Florida peninsula, but I'm glad I made the effort. Ink and I were back to Buglewood before dark; Ink panting and staring at frogs and chameleons in the trees, I feeling dragged out and concerned about Dora and Els. They need help and they know it.

Aunt Dora hugged me close when we were parting and asked, "Why don't you just stay here with us? You know you're welcome." I had to remind myself that they have two grown children to whom they should turn. But Dora and Els don't want to burden them.

I could understand that. I strive to be self-sufficient and not burden my sons. At times, I question if this is the right approach. We, as parents, worked hard at raising these children and gave it our best shot. Don't they owe us something when we're infirm and no longer able to handle the complexities of a rapidly changing world? In more primitive societies, children care for and revere the older members of their clan. It's a major reason for birthing children — so that you will be cared for in your old age. Not so in this civilized culture of ours. Too many older people are shoved aside and forgotten. It doesn't seem humane to me.

I gathered from the conversations that Dora and Els know they'll manage while both of them are living; however, their underlying fear is what will happen when one of them dies. I fixed a quinine and grabbed Joseph Campbell. I knew I couldn't fix the world and it didn't help to dwell on its inequities. Read *Myths to Live By* until dusk. Then Ink and I took a final round of the park. The gypsy caravan would be rolling tomorrow.

We pulled out about 11 a.m. Wound our way through the metropolitan area and finally found Alligator Alley, now called Everglades Parkway. Headed west across the peninsula through the middle of Big Cypress Swamp. I hadn't been on this route since 1971 when we moved to Florida. It hadn't changed. Monotonously flat land covered with saw grass and supporting some scrawny pines dripping Spanish moss. The birds were numerous and entertaining: egrets, ibises, herons stilting about in the water sloughs. Being a desert rat, this country looked forbidding.

Strange how some topographies seem foreign to us. Had to remind myself that any Floridian would ask, "How can anyone survive out there in that arid desert?" I feel that way about this southern section of Florida. To me, it's more forbidding than the desert. I imagine snakes slithering along under all that grass, and shudder. There were construction projects along the highway and it was slow driving. Ink was on her pillow, happy to be leaving the sap and frogs behind. I patted her with the promise that all would be better and the weather would be cooler once we made it up the peninsula and started west.

I had been unaware that my dog read the road signs until she asked me, "How do they know panthers are going to cross this road for the next six miles?" There had been a number of signs reading: Panther crossing next six miles. I laughed because I had been wondering the same thing.

I replied, "Ink, that's governmental agencies for you. Perhaps they've built a pathway and the panthers aren't allowed to cross anywhere else. I don't understand it either." We tooled along watching the birds and hoping not to see snakes or alligators. We both hoped to see a panther, but didn't. Could only assume the panthers weren't in the mood for crossing that day. We were on the west coast in no time.

Since I was not inclined to pull off the highway in the swamp area, we found a spot near Naples and stopped for lunch and a stretch. Checked the guide and decided to spend the night in Venice. We were heading north and that seemed a good spot for the evening. Pulled onto Interstate 75 for the short run up to Venice, then into a campground on the Myaaka River far from the traffic noise.

As we pulled into the campground, I wondered what had hit it. There were logs and picnic tables scattered around and debris clinging to the trunks of trees. It was chaotic. There was a sign on the office door stating they were open, so I went in to see about a space. The owners explained the chaos. The Myaaka River, which is usually docile and sluggish, had reared up and flooded them out about two months before. It had taken out a large portion of the campground. They apologized that the restrooms were still not operable. That was no problem for us and I registered for the night after The Question. They assigned us a site right on the banks of the river.

Man's attempts to have Mother Nature conform to his whims are always amusing. The drive across Alligator Alley — that ribbon of concrete through swampland where man strives to change the course of rivers that have flowed and sustained this area for years, where panthers are to cross within defined boundaries — is an example of these attempts to control nature. Yet, Mother Nature, when she's in the mood, can still remind us of the forces she can bring to bear. Evidently, the Myaaka River had been in the mood.

I had backed Tessie into the site so that I had a wide view of the river from the back door. I had put Ink on her lead while I was setting up. I glanced out at this sullen, primordial river and there was an alligator floating silently and eyeing my dog with interest. Needless to say, I did not allow Inkus to swim in that river at all. I put dinner into the oven and Ink and I took a long walk. It was a fascinating park — green and jungly, Spanish moss hanging from the trees, the evidence of Nature's force everywhere. I felt we were walking on earth in the age of the dinosaurs.

Had dinner at the picnic table and listened to the mutterings of many birds. I would not allow Ink off lead, but she showed no inclination to go far from me nor to swim in that river. She has an excellent nose. I could tell she smelled the alligators and was uneasy.

We settled early. Ink wanted to be outside, so I left the camper door open. I thought if an alligator came for her, I'd have to beat it off. I did not sleep well, knowing Ink was out. I was up often to check on her. About 2 a.m., the moon had risen above the oaks and was shining into Tessie. I sat there in the doorway marveling over this silvery scene. I was sure we were going to see a dinosaur come down for a drink. It was akin to being on the shore of a Jurassic swamp.

We didn't leave our primordial campground early. I ate outside, looked at that river, and watched the birds. Took Ink for a run and got away about 11 a.m. This area had been home base for a short period in my life. We had lived in a small community south of Sarasota called Coral Cove.

Rather than taking the Interstate, we wound our way up the old Tamiami Trail. Stopped for gas in Nokomis and was amazed at the growth in the area. These had been small towns back in the early 70's and now it was one continuous housing development. I was coming into Sarasota from the south, looking for landmarks, but was hard-pressed to find any. I did, however, spot the entry gate to Coral Cove and decided to do a drive around and see how the area looked.

I was again confronted with the synchronicity of this journey. Here I was, with no planning on my part, driving through Coral Cove on my ex-husband's 58th birthday, October 29.

The move to Florida had been wrenching for the boys and me. Chuck felt he must get out of engineering, so we left New Mexico and moved to Florida to start a business of our own. It was difficult, but we learned that we could manage wherever we lived. If I were to do it again I'd stop saying what I know this man wants to hear and say what I truly feel. We women are very guilty of this. We don't say what is in our hearts, but rather what we know this other wants to hear. It becomes cumulative over the years; it builds and builds resentment. Some of us even walk away from a twenty-eight year marriage. A more stormy marriage, but a more truthful one, would be: say what you feel in your heart, don't say what you know he wants to hear.

We drove through the Cove and it still looked the same. The house we had rented was intact. There were some familiar names on mailboxes, but I wasn't inclined to stop and visit. We drove cross-country from Sarasota and picked up the Interstate, tooling north and hoping for cooler weather. Just north of Tampa, Tessie Toyota clicked off 10,000 miles of journeying. I gave her a fond pat for those trouble-free miles. What a joy this little Chinook was and what an integral part of the gypsy caravan. Except for her oil changes, I had no stops to check out problems with this rig's engine. For a woman traveling alone, that's a real plus.

It was Interstate all day, heading farther north. Sat and drove and thought of many things, since driving the Interstates is so easy it's boring. I find it tires me more than meandering on back country roads. About 5:30 p.m. I was ready to hang it up for the day. Saw a sign for a campground along the road and pulled off.

Drove back a paved lane and pulled in.

It was strange. The hair on the back of my neck stood up. I'm not sure why, but I don't fight that intuitive sense. I made a circle around the grounds and the vibes were not right. Ink was ready to hop out and explore. I patted her and told her no, not here. We went back to the Interstate. I knew I was not to stay in that campground. We drove on to Lake City.

We drove down the main street of Lake City to a campground appropriately named In and Out RV Camppark. They directed us to an open space with big pine trees. I backed in to take advantage of the meadow view behind us. There was a large area at the back of the park where Ink could run. It was more than adequate since it would be in and out for us.

We were settling in; Ink on her lead, I with the door open enjoying the meadow, both of us enjoying the cooler temperatures.

I heard a man's voice calling, "Little lady, hey, little lady." Stuck my head out and there stood a hefty man who asked, "How do you put that top up? I'm really curious. You look so little."

I laughed and said, "Oh, it's a spring load. It's pretty easy and I've had quite a lot of practice."

This gentleman was a truck driver from the Chicago area. He and his wife were parked down the way from us in a Dolphin. They had watched us pull in and set up quickly. He invited me over to meet his wife. We had a lovely chat extolling the joys of our Toyotas.

Didn't tarry too long. Took Ink for a run, then started dinner and did some laundry. Took a shower and turned in early. I knew that just north of Lake City we would be heading west across the Florida panhandle. Gave Tessie one more pat that night and thanked my guides for the 10,000 joyous, trouble-free miles. Told Ink the weather would become more tolerable from here on. We curled up and slept well.

We woke early that Sunday morning, October 30, in Lake City. The birds were singing their hearts out and the sun was shining. Said my good mornings to the Dolphin owners who were heading on south. Got us squared away, then called Mark and Lois before we left. The kids had taken a vacation at Fort Walton Beach and had suggested that I tour that portion of the Gulf. I let them know I was on my way. The kids and I had our usual supportive, loving conversation. They were happy to hear I had survived Florida. Cautioned me to be careful and have fun. I promised to stay in touch and we signed off with love.

It was only a matter of miles north of Lake City to our connection with Interstate 10 heading west. We were heading west. What a joyful feeling! We rolled along the Interstate, jazz blaring, weather sunny, and going in the right direction. We breezed across the panhandle. It's different from southern Florida; gentle, rolling hills, lots of live oaks, great horse farms, and, best of all, cooler and less humid weather. We went through Tallahassee and on to Chattahoochee where we turned south on Route 231 to the beaches and the Gulf for a few days of meandering and escaping the Interstate. We needed some pike-shunning and I knew it.

There was no traffic and no towns. We pulled off the road and had lunch and a walk. The weather was changing. It was getting very cloudy and the wind was rising. I told Ink I thought we were going to have rain. Thank God, I didn't know how much rain.

Just before we got to Panama City, the heavens opened. The deluge was like nothing I had ever experienced. Tessie was leaking from the force of the water, the windshield wipers could not clear the windows, and I couldn't see. I could not see the road. We were crawling along. The highway was under a good two feet of water. I didn't like this at all.

About that time, I saw a Deere tractor store on the right side of the roadway with a big parking lot. I eased into that lot and stopped. We stayed right there. The force of that rain was like having six fire companies' pumping engines directing their hoses at the camper. This wild rain pounded us for almost a half hour, then it rolled on by. The sky lightened up, but I was in no hurry to get back onto the flooded roadway. After a few cars drove by, I pulled back onto Route 231 gingerly.

We eased into Panama City slowly and carefully. It was obvious that this cloudburst had hit the whole area forcefully. At a stop light in downtown Panama City, there was a pickup truck ahead of me. The intersection was a massive river, but when the light turned green, the pickup started across. I'm not sure why I hesitated, but I'm glad I did. That pickup had gone only about 10 feet, when it sank. It sank right before my eyes. I was sitting there laughing and saying out loud, "Oh, my God! I don't believe this!"

Evidently, the whole street had washed out and there was a gaping hole under that water. The light was still green, but I didn't move. No way was I going to have my Tessie sink into that hole. I just sat there. In a few minutes, the police arrived and cordoned off the area. They kindly directed me up around the pickup. The driver wasn't hurt, a little wet, but safe. The pickup, however, was under water.

We drove through soggy Panama City, across Hathaway Bridge which divides North Bay from St. Andrews Bay. Headed down Thomas Drive to a little spit of land bounded by Grand Lagoon on the north and the Gulf on the south. This section had not had the heavy rain. We pulled into a KOA on this lovely spit of land. The Gulf was across the road on the other side of a group of high rise hotels and restaurants. The Florida panhandle is a summer vacation mecca. The campground was devoid of many people. We made arrangements for a space.

There was a store, good, clean restrooms, and a variety of activities for the permanent residents. Ink and I were mainly interested in having some shore time. We parked up, popped up, and plugged in. The clouds had scudded away and we headed over to the beach. We had to go down a path between high-rises and restaurants, most of them closed since the tourist season was over here in Panama City. We had the entire beach to ourselves. There wasn't a soul on the sand. Ink chased birds, took a splash in the Gulf, ran and played and frolicked. There was no one to complain about this dog running free. The weather was refreshing and I felt like a free spirit, too. I ran and skipped in and out of the surf with Ink. It was great. The Gulf is incredibly blue and gentle in this area. The solitary romp replenished both of us.

Got back and fixed dinner. Spent some time drying Tessie out from the deluge. It had been one hell of a storm, but we were safe and only slightly damp — not like the pickup driver. There were scads of mocking birds warbling happily. My heart sang along with them. We had a pleasant, relaxed evening. Felt very in sync with our world again. I thanked my God for bringing us safely once more to a lovely spot.

The next morning was cloudy and misty. I was feeling tired in spite of a good night's sleep. The drive around Florida was taking its toll. I decided to spend another day right here, walking the beach, watching and listening to the mockingbirds, and kicking back. There was no one around. We ambled on the beach and enjoyed the Gulf. I did clean Tess thoroughly, but mostly we relaxed. I read and took a nap. It was a different Halloween. We had no trick-or-treaters here. I thought of the previous year when Sam and Theo arrived at my door and came in for hot tea. I would have loved a cup with my little family that evening; however, we were a long way from Las Cruces. We were heading west, though. We did enjoy this quiet time before getting on with the journey.

We woke to sunshine and raucous singing of the mockingbirds. I felt much better and ready to travel. We left the campground at 10 a.m. Stopped at a local bank for a cash advance. Then we meandered. We took Route 98 skirting the Gulf through Laguna Beach — shades of California — and Ft. Walton Beach. We stopped along a stretch where there were rolling sand dunes, glorious stands of sea oats, yellow flowers in profusion, and that incredibly green-blue Gulf. Ink and I took one last stroll. I took some pictures since there were no high-rises obstructing the view. We continued to Pensacola where we turned inland and caught the Interstate once more.

# XVII. Bayous and Spanish Moss

Although we prefer pike-shunning, the Interstates are the easy way to negotiate big cities and high density areas. Inland, we again watched live oaks and Spanish moss as we breezed along though the deep South. The Interstate carried us easily through Mobile, Alabama. As I drove, I thought back over our travels. The first day of the month was always a marker day: the first of September, we were in Woodstock, New Brunswick; the first of October, we were at Chincoteague; and now, the first of November, we were rolling west on the southern boundaries of the United States.

We stopped at a roadside park for lunch and a stretch. I checked my maps and guide. Read that Gulf Islands National Seashore was just east of Biloxi, Mississippi. It sounded intriguing — off the Interstate and down by the Gulf. Ink was amenable to my suggestion that we try for a night there. We turned and headed south to the Davis Bayou section of Gulf Islands Seashore in Ocean Springs, Mississippi. We found the campground easily; however, it wasn't on the beach, but on a primordial bayou. We were back in alligator country. Their scent makes Ink uncomfortable and I'm not at ease with those creatures either. It was a charming park and the people were so friendly that we decided to stay.

The sign on the office stated that you should choose your site then pay the ranger at the office from 5 p.m. to 8 p.m. We drove carefully around the campground looking for the proper site. It was nice to have all the campers wave a welcome as we were browsing. Found the perfect site and pulled in. There was a picnic table, glorious big trees, a drop-off at the back that was swampy and steamy; however, it afforded us a lot of privacy.

The people in this park were friendly and compatible. There is a great difference in people in different parks. I prefer it where everyone walks and talks and visits. This campground was one of the best. I was setting up when a couple from Massachusetts came by to say hello. The Roches were on their way to California to spend Christmas with their children in Oakland. They also were meandering and we had a pleasant chat. Everyone in this park strolled and spoke. Since I had had a number of solitary nights, I welcomed the companionship.

When I plugged Tessie into the electrical connection, it didn't work. I wasn't getting power. It blew me away for a minute until I remembered that I could take the system apart and check it out just as John LeVert had taught me. Was not in the mood just then, so decided to use the reserve battery and check the system in the morning. I sat in Tessie looking into the heavily forested gully behind us and imagined all kinds of creepy crawlies down in that jungle.

Ink and I took a long walk around the grounds and found a spot where she could take a run and tend to business. This was down by the bayou. There was a dock extending out into the still, murky water. I couldn't get Ink to walk out on that dock at all. Her nose was twitching and I knew there were alligators in that dismal pond. We walked on around the campground which had fifty-one sites, all occupied by friendly campers.

We had dinner at the picnic table at dusk. The bird calls and sounds were straight from a jungle setting. Just before dark, I put Ink on lead and we walked up to pay our fees at the ranger station. Ink put both paws on the counter and greeted the ranger effusively. He patted her and fussed over her and we talked for a time about my travels with this big, black dog. He warned me not to leave any food outside because of the large raccoon population. I told him I worried more about alligators.

He eased my mind by saying that there weren't many around and they did not come into the campsite. He did admonish me to keep Ink on her lead and I assured him that, indeed, I would. By the time we left the ranger station, it was quite dark. I had not brought my flashlight, but it wasn't far to Tessie so Ink and I stumbled along the road listening to all the night sounds in the bayou.

We had just turned into our site. I had left Ink's bowl behind the camper along with her long lead. Quite obviously, a raccoon had found the bowl. I did not see it, but Ink either saw it or smelled it and that big, sturdy dog went for it. She lunged and I was totally unprepared. That 65 pound dog on the other end of the lead knocked me off my feet. I fell hard, really hard. I never let go of the lead nor did I drop my purse. I took the brunt of the fall on my left side; however, my head flew back and hit the tarmac with such force I could feel the grey matter thud against the back of my skull.

I didn't lose consciousness. I just lay there on the ground stunned. Ink was at my side immediately, kissing my face and whining. Saying in her fashion, "Oh, Mom, I forgot all about you being on the other end of that lead when I saw some animal in my bowl." I had to lie there for a few more minutes, but finally eased myself up and into the camper. All parts seemed to be functioning. I was having a horrid chill, however, and suspected that I might have a concussion. I knew I was to stay alert and awake, but I was shaking and chilling so badly that I got Ink inside and crawled into my sleeping bag, clothes and all. I didn't even brush my teeth. I curled up inside my bag and conked. Life does hang by a fragile thread. Had I hit that tarmac on the side of my head, I would have died right there at my campsite in Gulf Islands. As it was, I hit on the thick, bony back portion. Still, my body reacted strongly to the trauma of that thud on the skull. I had no choice but to get my head down, get warm, and sleep.

The sun was shining and the birds were singing when I woke, or thought I must be awake. The first question I asked myself was, "What's your name?" I knew the answer; the synapses were still functioning. My body protested when I tried to move. I was one massive ache, but I did get the kettle on. I sat there drinking a cup of caffeine, looking out at the beautiful scene and listening to the birds. Gave myself a hug and a compliment on still being resilient. I noticed there was a cab-over camper in the space up from mine and decided they had come in after I crawled into the camper. I had not heard anything, as the sleep had been deep and dreamless. I was out of it after that fall.

I didn't blame Ink. She was following her instincts. I sat and sipped coffee and knew that I was not going to attempt to drive that day. My body was too sore. The muscles down both sides of my neck were so stiff, it hurt to move my head. After the thunk I had had, it was no wonder I hurt. However, I could move, I could think, and it was a beautiful morning. Still, I was not going to drive that day.

Moved slow and easy. Had some breakfast and tackled the electrical system. I had just started checking my outside panel when Bob and Lois Roche came by. Bob said, "Now before you tear everything apart, Barb, let's check this circuit breaker here at the site." Sure enough, the circuit breaker was tripped and there was one connection that did not work at all. Bob replugged my line and everything was A-okay. It wasn't Tessie at all.

I told the Roches about my nasty spill and that I was staying for another day. They were spending another day, too, and offered their help if I should need it. There's always someone who comes in when you need them. That previous evening had been a real downer; the electrical system and that horrendous fall. It was the low point of the trip thus far. I had learned to give it twenty-four hours. No matter how low I had been, things always looked brighter after twenty-four hours. This morning, I was alive, a little stiff and sore, but moving.

Scary experiences like that fall make me contemplative. I sat at the picnic table mulling over the mystery of this tenuous thread we all hang by and call life. I looked with more appreciation at the bounty this planet offers. The singing of the birds was more mellow, the dank smell of the bayou more sweet.

I thought about how uncertain this time we have on earth is and how little control we have over when it might end. We'd all be better served if we looked at life knowing it might end at any moment. We all might ask more often, "Why am I getting all uptight over this trivia? These frets and strains I create for myself? If I were to die tomorrow, would any of these petty annoyances matter? What difference would it make?" Thinking on those lines always makes me step back, take time to smell the roses, and count my blessings. I did just that that morning in spite of aching all over.

I needed to keep moving so I wouldn't stiffen up. I pulled the cushions out of Tess, put them on the picnic table and mended all the seams. Enjoyed the bird calls. Visited with people as they strolled by. Kept moving, albeit gingerly and slowly. The camper next to us was inhabited by a solitary male. The handsome stranger had arrived at last. He was quite friendly and he wanted to visit more than I cared to that day. He informed me he was *en route* from North Carolina back to Nevada where he had a wife waiting. He was traveling alone and didn't seem to enjoy his own company much.

I wasn't willing to hold Macho Man's hand that morning and went about my chores. I cleaned Tess well, had lunch, then went for a shower and shampoo. I examined my battered body. Had an ugly bruise on my left hip and another on my left thigh. It could have been worse. The hot water felt great on my sore neck muscles and I stood a long time in the stall. I went back to Tessie and stretched out, feeling much better.

It was a perfect park for healing my sore body. The people were friendly and supportive. There was an interesting couple down the way. They had two VW Westphalias parked in their space. Each traveled alone in his own van, but they did park in the same space. Guess they preferred having their own bedrooms.

The man's name was Bob. He was gregarious and visited with everyone. His wife talked with no one; just rode around the campground on her bike. Bob walked up and asked me how I liked my Chinook. I told him about my trouble-free journey in this little rig. It seems we had been traveling the same route.

When I mentioned my trip around Cape Breton, Bob told me they had taken the same circle and his Westphalia had broken down in the highlands. He had paid $1300 to have it towed back to Nova Scotia and repaired. He asked me if I was interested in selling my Chinook. Although I think I had a ready and willing buyer, I smiled and said, "No way."

The Roches walked past while I was chatting with Bob, saying they were going to buy a newspaper. As they put it, "We don't know what's happening in the real world." I asked, "Are you sure this isn't the real world?"

Macho Man came by and gave me the details of his physical fitness program. I worked at being appropriately impressed. Was going in to start dinner when Bob and Lois came back by saying, "We didn't buy a paper. We decided you're right. This is the real world. Who needs all that bad news?" Amen! We sat at the picnic table and talked some more. Lois teased me about the lonesome stranger with, "You know there's a single man next to you?"

"Oh, yes, I know. He informed me he was all alone. But, you know, I'm not interested in romance on the road. I prefer my dog's company. It's less stressful." They were lovely people and very kind to me. They went back to their camper to fix dinner and I was on my way into Tessie to do the same.

Macho Man came over and invited me for a drink. I told him I didn't drink. The oven was operable that evening and I put a potato and pork chop in, then took Inkus for one last run before dark. No way was I going to walk my dog in the dark. Had dinner out at the picnic table feeling so much better and so thankful for such a lovely day of puttering and putting myself back together. In spite of my fall, this park had to be one of the nicest places I had camped. It was because of all the lovely people.

Ink ate under the picnic table that evening and I then put her bowl in the camper. I was having a cup of tea, enjoying the golden glow of the sunset and the raucous settling of the birds. My neighbor gave it one more try. "Won't you come over and see my rig?" I accepted, since I could see no excuse for not going. And, of course, heard all the merits of his camper and all the stories of how great he was. I was congratulating myself on my restraint. Reminding myself how vital all this posturing is for the male ego, until he asked, "Why don't you find a boyfriend and have some fun?"

Damn! Those are fighting words for me and I did get a little testy. I asked coolly and quietly, "What makes you think I'm not having fun?" I didn't pursue this discussion, but I do wonder what it is that makes men unable to fathom that some women are self-sufficient and perfectly content without a man in their life. I could have lectured him on the merits of solitary living, but had to consider the source. Just chalked it up to Neanderthal thinking. Said good-night and went home to Tessie and my own company, which I prefer to his concepts.

Ink and I snuggled in. I read a bit and looked back at the healing 24 hours I had had. Thanked my God for having no injuries other than bruises and a stiff neck. Rolled over and had a good night's sleep at Davis Bayou.

I was puttering around next morning when Bob and Lois pulled up in their camper, ready to leave. They told me they were going down to New Orleans. Didn't I want to join them? I did not think New Orleans was the place for this woman and her dog. Told them I was going to head on west. We all exchanged hugs and fond wishes for safe journeying. I thanked them again for their support and help. Lois asked me about my bruises. I laughed as I told her, "Boy, they're getting really colorful. No one who saw my body would believe I was traveling and living alone." I was feeling better and was ready to meander on west. There was no breeze at Davis Bayou that morning and the bugs were buzzing and biting with a vengeance. We waved our good-byes to the Roches, then Ink and I took a fast walk.

I was ready to leave when Macho Man arrived once again. I suppose I should have been flattered that he found me attractive, but by this time he was becoming a nuisance. He walked over with all his maps, asking me where I planned to go that day. I flipped out, "I'm heading west."

I think Macho Man was hoping we could set up a mutual camping spot that evening. I didn't want to be bothered. I knew I'd heard all he had to say. I didn't rise to his coy bait. Told him I wished him a safe journey home to his wife, it was nice to have met him, and good-bye.

It was 11 a.m. before we left that pleasant park. Drove over to Biloxi, then inland to the Interstate. We were whizzing along; carefree, trouble-free, boring driving. I was tired of live oaks, Spanish moss, bayous, and alligators; however, we were in the deep South.

West of Baton Rouge, we climbed a high bridge spanning the Mississippi River. I must say, that little tad in Minnesota had grown a whole lot by the time it reached this area. I don't think Ink and I could have made it across the river here, even in a boat. We chugged over it feeling we had come another full circle. We were west of the Mississippi. Yahoo!

My neck muscles were still stiff so I was happy to be driving on the unchallenging Interstate. We stopped for the night at a KOA campground in Lafayette, Louisiana, the heart of the Cajun country. Back with the Acadians. More circles. The campground had a grocery store combined with the office. There was an ad for frozen Cajun food on the freezer. I bought a brown-and-serve package of Cajun shrimp to celebrate being back with the Acadians.

We had a very narrow site, the sardine effect. But there was no one close to us. Put the Cajun shrimp into the oven, and Ink and I took a long walk. There was a lake and the grounds were well-kept. We could hear freeway noise, but this was a quickie stop for the night. It was cloudy so we ate inside. I missed the group at Davis Bayou. This park wasn't friendly at all. No one spoke. We didn't fight it, just settled in early.

Thought of the Acadians and the religious intolerance in the world. It will never be overcome as long as each religion is convinced that theirs in the only way. I agree with the Buddha who says there is no way. Each of us must spend time and energy on our own soul work in our own way. If each of us did that, the world just might become a better place. Turned off the lights, patted Inkus, and slept well — hoping my soul work was progressing and I was in tune with my God.

# XVIII. Highs and Lows in the Lone Star State

That Friday morning, we left Lafayette at 10 a.m. No visits from friendly people here to delay getting on the road. It was Interstate 10 on across Louisiana past Lake Charles and into Texas. I was happy to be in Texas, although this eastern portion is not much different from the Bayou country. Texas is New Mexico's next door neighbor. It's vast and we were a long way from Las Cruces, but we were getting closer.

We stopped at a Texas Tourist Bureau just over the border. They were so accommodating; loaded me up with maps, state park information, and genuine Texas hospitality. It was a good place to be parked. Ink took a run on lead and I had a little lunch before we went on to Houston.

I congratulated myself on my poor timing. We got into the Houston area about 4:30 on a Friday afternoon. The commuter traffic was the same as California's. The ubiquitous orange barrels narrowed six lanes of traffic to two in many sections of the freeway. Typical technology — six lanes of traffic moving and spewing out fumes as we all crawled along this marvel of engineering at 10 miles per hour. From what I could see, they were using the standard solutions to alleviate the problem; throwing more concrete at it. There were half-completed bridges and ramps on each side of the existing freeway. I used the time to study the Houston skyline as we all crept along.

On the eastern outskirts, we took Route 59 heading southwest. I pulled over and checked the state park brochure I had gotten at the information stop. Brazos Bend State Park was off the beaten path, down the road a bit, and sounded interesting. We meandered cross-country past tidy farms and fields of cows. It was flat land — not even a small hill on the horizon, but there were lots of trees and the road was good. Texas claims it has no dirt county roads in the entire state. I didn't check them all, but I think Texas has a superb highway system. There were no cars and it was nice to be off the Interstate and rid of the commuter traffic of Houston.

We arrived at Brazos Bend about 6 p.m. and were greeted with, "Sorry. We have no space." That was a low blow. It didn't sit well at all until the Ranger handed me a brochure for Brazos Bend. There was a map on one side; alligator etiquette on the other. We pulled into the parking lot. I took a look at this blurb which started in caps: Please stop and read this before leaving your vehicle. Brazos State Park is one of the best places in Texas to see alligators in their natural setting.

Ink and I didn't care for those alligators, but I dreaded the trek back across country. The choice was clear, however. There was no place to park here, so it was back to highway 59. There was a lingering sunset, but I was uneasy about driving in the dark on unknown roads. I had checked the guide before we left the state park. Had not let Ink out of the camper, not with all those alligators around. One other statement from the brochure: Alligators are remarkable links with the past. They are fascinating creatures who have lived on the earth since the age of dinosaurs. They've survived when many other animals have become extinct. Indeed, those ugly critters are adaptable. I didn't feel badly about taking my dog away from their habitat and searching for another campground.

We wended our way across the fields of east Texas in the dark heading for a USA campground in Richmond, Texas, on Route 59. It meant backtracking, but it was the closest park. It was stressful driving in the dark in this unknown country, but we took it slow and easy. Ink was ready for her dinner and I was ready to pull off the road. We finally got to Route 59 and turned back toward Houston.

I saw the USA Park on the right side of the highway. We pulled onto the access road. On the first pass, I missed the entrance. Drove right by it and in less than half a mile was back on Route 59. Luckily, Texas has these wonderful turn-arounds. We pulled onto another access road and drove under 59 and were ready for another attempt. I slowed down when we got back to the park and did find the entrance. It was almost 8 p.m. and very dark when I went into the office.

There was a cute young gal at the desk named Vicky. I asked, "Do you have space for one tired traveler and her dog?" I know I looked as stressed and tired as I felt. She answered, "Sorry. We're all filled up." I just stood there. She eyed me and asked, "Wait a minute, what kind of rig do you have?" I told her and pointed to Tessie parked out front. Then it was, "You're traveling all alone?" I gave my usual replies half-heartedly.

"We don't have a real space but I think we can find room for you and that small rig. Come on. Let's see if you can't park up in front of the shed. It's not much, but it's better than being on the highway." My sentiments exactly. She led the way through the park to the shed. There was plenty of room for Tessie. I gave Vicky a warm hug and pulled in.

Took Inkus for a quick turn around a field close by. She was about to burst a kidney. Fed that patient dog an extra portion, fixed myself a bowl of soup, then headed over to the restroom for a hot, soothing shower. There was one other woman using the facilities and she was a delight. She and her husband were Ontarians going to Florida for the winter. We chatted as we showered, both of us exclaiming over the good, hot water. This warm woman put her arms around me as we were leaving, gave me a big hug and said, "God be with you."

After my harrowing experience driving for hours in the dark, that sweet woman's kind words were more needed than she knew. I was ready for sleep. Ink and I snuggled in there in Tessie parked in front of the shed. God was with us and we were safe and snug once more.

We woke early. It was a sunny day and the park was bustling. I felt tired and decided to do laundry and household chores that morning. Took a couple of loads to the laundry and got them started. Had breakfast inside, since the shed space did not come with a picnic table. Called through to Samantha to let her know I was coming down the homestretch. This was the first I had mentioned to anyone in Las Cruces that I did not think I would be staying, that I planned to continue traveling. Since I loved it and my possessions were packed up, it seemed the perfect time to continue with this wonderfully free lifestyle.

Sam was encouraging and, at the same time, unhappy that I wouldn't be settling down. She missed me, but she could understand my desire to continue journeying. She asked, "You are coming to Las Cruces, aren't you?" I told her I planned to touch base and probably spend the holidays there, then head on west. Sam extended an invitation to park up in back of her adobe and stay in her yard. I accepted with pleasure and told her I'd be there sometime after Thanksgiving.

Finished the laundry, saw Vicky and thanked her again for her kindness. We left the campground about 11 a.m. This was a day for pike-shunning. We drove south on Route 59 to Victoria, then it was back to the sea again. Took a county road across to Route 53 and meandered along the Gulf. Our destination was Goose Island Recreational Area on Aransas Bay. It was not far and we arrived about 3:30 p.m. It was a Saturday. I didn't even think of it until we were pulling into the park.

I still had not learned that one should not take chances with finding accommodations on the week-end; however, the park was not filled. There was a helpful lady at the desk. She told me there were spaces available, then gave me a choice of parking amongst the live oaks by the office or going over the bridge to sites right along the bay. I chose the bay and registered.

Ink and I found our way through the extensive grounds, crossed a wooden bridge, and pulled into space #34. It overlooked Aransas Bay and was complete with a shelter that shaded the picnic table. Had no one parked close and there were birds everywhere. St. Charles Bay was behind us as we were on a narrow spit of land between the two bodies of water. The bays were like mirrors as it was still with no wind. I was setting up and Ink was out on her lead. All of a sudden, she ran full tilt into the camper. With no breeze, the bitey bugs were out in force and they had been dining on poor Ink. A gentle breeze came up and ended that problem before I had gotten settled. Ink and I walked down to the shore. She had a swim while I looked for shells.

We ate dinner at our sheltered table watching fish jumping in the bay. Listened to a multitude of birds whistling, calling and cackling. It was good to be connected with nature once again in such a pleasurable place. A few of the campers were fishing and talking. It was warm and lugubrious. Ink was stretched out under the picnic table and we both loafed until dark. It was a beautiful sunset with that golden disk sinking into Aransás Bay. Sounds were muffled, the whole world seemed at peace. I had such a sense of well-being.

As I was looking at it, one of the shells I had collected and put on the table started moving. That gave me a start. I took a look and discovered a critter inside the shell. I put it down on the ground so he wouldn't fall and break his house. Ink and I fell asleep to the lapping of the waves.

The next morning was clear and warm. I wasn't ready to leave this lovely spot. Walked over to headquarters and signed up for another night in space #34. Ink had a run by the rec building. It was a graceful structure done in mission style, but didn't look like it had been used for months. Called Pam from the pay phones at headquarters and told her of my decision to keep gypsying. Pam, too, was encouraging and offered to keep the mail flowing. I suggested Del Rio, Texas, as the next pickup sometime around the 19th of November, since I had decided to go to Big Bend.

We walked down to the beach and waded. Got the binoculars and spent hours watching all the shore birds and was able to identify some. The little devils would always fly before I made positive identification. The highlight of the session was seeing a scissor-tailed flycatcher. With their long, long tails, there's no mistaking them. We talked with the people who were fishing.

They told me the smily, jumping fish were mullet. I found purple seaweed on the beach, really purple. It was a lazy day of marveling over the bounty of nature.

That evening, a family pulled into the space next to ours. The son had a VW van like one Mark had owned. His name was Chris and his parents were Fred and Anne. They were friendly, but not intrusive. I had just finished dinner when they all walked over with some steak tidbits for Ink. She wiggled and thanked them profusely. We sat at my picnic table and visited. Fred and Anne had a camper mounted on a Toyota pickup body. They told me they had wanted to buy a Chinook, but couldn't find one. I urged them to keep looking and told them how great I thought my Tessie was. We all put the sun to bed and then turned in after a great day. I asked myself if the desert rat was becoming a sea-faring gypsy. Much as I loved the tranquility of the water, I longed to see some jagged mesas and cactus.

Monday, we did more loafing, visiting, wading, and bird watching. Was still not in the mood to leave this serendipitous setting. Felt so blessed that I could stay and drink my fill.

Tuesday morning I knew we must leave. We were low on supplies and Ink and I cannot abide fasting. I looked at the maps and thought Padre Island National Seashore sounded interesting. We were still in the mood for more Gulf time. The lady at the office had reminded me that the long Veteran's Day week-end was coming up. She suggested we find a spot and stay off the highways. Ink and I took one last walk, one last look at the mullet jumping in the bay, and headed out.

I stopped at headquarters to thank the lady for a delightful stay and get some information on Padre Island. She informed me that it was a first-come-first-serve arrangement and I'd just have to take my chances. We did go by and see "The Big Tree," an ancient, gnarled oak of immense proportions, before we left Goose Island. We didn't tarry long as the bitey bugs were out in force that morning.

We drove south on Route 35. It was humid and warm along the Gulf; hard to believe it was November. At Rockport, I spied a supermarket and pulled in to stock up. Apologized to Ink for leaving her in the warm camper, but she said she'd be fine, just remember to get her food. It was a friendly place, well stocked and good for browsing. I marvel at how well I am led and, also, at what a slow learner I am. In this market, I finally purchased a whisk broom. I had been using a small vacuum that plugged into the lighter. John had included it when I bought Tessie, but it didn't do a good job. I passed the display of cleaning utensils and decided I needed a whisk broom. I had also been wrestling with dish cloths and the problem of keeping them white. Using Clorox to bleach them out and spending needless energy. It dawned on me, after three plus months on the road, that Handy Wipes would be infinitely simpler. I bought a package of them too. I left the market with heaps of food plus Handy Wipes and a whisk broom. It was a fun marketing. Tess was loaded when I unpacked the cart.

We rolled on south on Route 35. Caught a free ferry boat across Aransas Pass to Mustang Island, thereby avoiding Corpus Christi. Mustang was open sand dunes and not much development. The road led us right on to Padre Island. We could look across JFK causeway to the Corpus Christi skyline, but didn't have to deal with the city. We went on south, hoping we'd find space to park up.

We drove along this chain of barrier reef islands which protected the mainland from the violent battering of tropical storms and hurricanes. It was a fascinating environment of beaches, dunes, grasslands, and tidal flats: a natural world of variety and richness.

Came to the ranger station and checked about accommodations. They told me there was a host at Malaquite Beach and suggested I drive down and check on sites. I thanked them, picked up some literature, and away we went. Pulled into the camping area about 3 p.m. and was relieved to see there was all kinds of space. I understood why immediately. The campsite was a long strip of tarmac running parallel to the Gulf. There was no electricity, no shade, cold water showers under the open sky, and lots of fine, white blowing sand. The incredible beauty of the Gulf and the setting far outweighed the lack of amenities as far as Ink and I were concerned. Eased Tessie into a space partially covered with drifted sand. We had this great expanse of the Gulf to the east, sand dunes covered in wildflowers to the west, and a picnic table. Who could ask for more? I popped the top and put foodstuff away. The breakers were rolling and Ink and I went down to the beach. We romped and walked for hours. She jumped waves, chased birds, and frisked about. I felt so energized that I found myself singing and skipping. There was no one around to catch the zany antics of some crazy woman and her big, black dog. There were blue, bubble-like Portuguese men-of-war littering the beach; however, Ink seemed to recognize that they were not to be bothered. I found them beautiful in a sinister sort of way.

A couple from UC-Santa Cruz strolled by and stopped to chat while I was sitting on the picnic table. They mentioned that this Tuesday, November 8, had been election day. I knew I'd be on the road at election time and I had never missed exercising my franchise since I turned 21. I had thought about applying for an absentee ballot before I left Las Cruces. In thinking over all those elections, I realized that not once in almost 40 years had there been a candidate for whom I was gung ho. My vote had always been cast for what I hoped would be the lesser of two evils. So I sat out the election of 1988 and didn't bother to make a choice. Surely our nation can offer something better to the electorate.

I'd like to see the ballot for national elections have a voting square reading: None of the above. It might increase voter turn-out and, at least, let those who do not like the choices have a voice. Election day was a non-event for me nor did anyone at this glorious spot seem to give a damn.

The wind was up and the fine, white sand was sifting into the camper. I thanked my guides for the whisk broom and gave it a good work out. Ink insisted on being outside. Her eyes and nose were rimmed in fine, white sand. She was intrigued by the crabs here. They were colorful; yellow with gleaming black eyes. She couldn't intimidate those little fellows one bit. They would rear up, extend a pincher, and dare her to mess with them. There was a great blue heron wandering up and down the beach grabbing tidbits from the fishermen.

We took another walk at sunset. The whole world was pink and lavender. I looked at the open-air showers and decided I wasn't strong enough for a cold water spray that evening. We settled in with Tessie rocking in the breeze and the sound of the surf lulling us to sleep. Since there was no electricity, the heavens were brilliant with billions and billions of stars.

Wednesday morning, I had my coffee and watched the sun rise up out of the Gulf. Ink and I ambled down the beach before breakfast. I was eating when the young couple came by and told me that George Bush was president. Ho hum. It seemed unimportant here on this magnificent barrier reef. I sat and watched a blue heron wading along the shore fishing. He got one. The gulls descended en masse on the great blue hoping for a free handout, but the heron did not share. Watched the yellow sand crabs scurrying to and fro. In spite of all the beauty we had seen on this journey, I still marveled over the grandeur and force of nature. It was an ever changing scene which filled me with awe and wonder.

I stretched out in Tessie and finished Joseph Campbell's *Myths to Live By.* Ink and I took a little snooze, then headed down to the sea again. We walked north along the shore for miles. There were no people, no buildings, just sea and sky and a few shore birds. It was early evening when we got back to the campsite. I put Ink on her lead and went into the shower enclosure. I tried the water and, my God, it was cold. I did rinse my feet and legs, but no more. We had a quiet dinner, made sure all the stars turned on, and hopped into bed.

Thursday morning, I was awake before sunrise. There were clouds on the eastern horizon. Clouds that looked like a huge Chinese dragon gobbling up the rising sun. I hopped out of Tessie and stood on the picnic table to take a series of pictures of this cloud formation. What a nice way to start the day. While I sipped my coffee, I decided this was the place to be over the long Veteran's Day week-end. It was perfect. We'd just stay here and enjoy. I put the table up that day. The whisk broom worked well. How nice that I was led to buy a whisk broom just before I had a crying need for one. With the constantly blowing fine sand, it was getting much use. I cleaned a bit, sat at the table and started work on a sweater sleeve while I sat there looking at the Gulf pounding away.

I walked up to the campground host's trailer and paid my fees through Sunday night. They were a delightful couple. They had a closed box outside the trailer door with a sign on it which read: baby rattlers. I gave it wide berth as I went into the trailer. I'm not much on snakes or alligators. The host asked me, "Don't you wanta see the rattlers? I found them right out here." I nodded with, "No, thanks."

He kept pressing and pressing. "Come on take a look. They can't get out." His wife was standing there smiling broadly. Finally, I said, "Well, okay."

I sidled over and looked cautiously into the box. There were four plastic baby rattles with ribbons on them down in the box. I laughed with relief. The host laughed heartily at the joke he had played on a woman who didn't like snakes.

That evening was very windy. Since I had the table set up, I ate inside in style with a place mat and candle. The winds were gusting at 40 miles per hour, but my little womb Tessie was cozy and snug. Except for the winds, the weather was ideal. Nice warm days filled with sunshine and surf. Nights cool enough to sleep comfortably. After dinner, I knew I had to scrub myself. I still hadn't been able to face a cold shower. I took my first bath in a bucket. It can be done. I worked bit by bit from my grimy face on down. Found that I could get both feet into the bucket for the grand finale. Probably not squeaky clean, but it was an improvement over the dirty body I had had. I learned yet another lesson. One can bathe in a bucket. It was rather pleasing, especially by candlelight. Had good hot water and sat on a towel as I scrubbed away. I even gave Ink a face wash that evening. She looked so silly with those white sand rings around her eyes and nose. Tess rocked violently that night as strong winds buffeted her, but not even that sand storm made me regret that we had come to this paradisiacal spot.

I phoned through to both my sons from Padre. It was heady to walk up to the phone booth after dark with all those stars above and the surf humming in the background. In order to dial this phone, I had to use my flashlight to see the numbers. I said to the kids, "This is paradise." It felt that way to me. I felt so connected with nature and so much a part of all that is.

I sat on the beach one day and thought about housing. About the fact that I wasn't ready to trap myself with a house. In their way, houses are traps. You're tied down. You can't hop into a camper and meander. It seems to be a cultural requirement: You've got to buy a house and settle down. I had felt that way for many years. Now I knew if I wanted to meander, I couldn't burden myself with a house. Yet another reason to continue the pilgrimage now — while I was not encumbered with a cozy nest. Tessie had become home, she was all I felt I needed. She was the only security blanket necessary. It certainly does free one up. The Hermit Crab is wiser than we humans.

I did not keep my journal up to date. Found it too hard to write each day after driving. I did mark maps and kept a record of my stops. Here at Padre, however, I found time to write. The following are excerpts from my journal, dated November 12:

"I did my bath in a bucket routine again. Will always remember Padre Island as: bathing in a bucket, phoning by flashlight, watching billions of stars, and whisk brooming billions of grains of sand. Tonight it's calm. There's only the sound of the surf. The new moon is setting behind the sand dunes. Ink's already settled, sand and all. I'm so glad we came to this place late in the journey. Would not have been as inclined to stay early on. It amazes me that after all the glorious areas I've seen, I'm still overwhelmed by the incredible beauty of our planet."

In the course of my stay, there was a diverse group of campers coming and going on the tarmac. Most of them friendly, outgoing people. The students from Santa Cruz, a lady visiting the hosts, a cute couple from England, an older couple from San Antonio who were gregarious.

Then there were two couples in mobile homes — the big, status symbol kind — with New Mexico license plates. They were there when I arrived and still there when I left. However, they were a closed club. It was apparent that these four people did not want to talk with anyone or have anyone talk with them. I don't know where this exclusivity comes from, but, as is always the case with campers, no one imposed on them. You miss so much when you refuse to interact with the people at a campsite, as I see it.

I watched the two women — always together — and not talking with anyone. I was sure that they had that Neanderthal outlook about me — she has to be looking for a man. It would not have been their spouses had I even been looking. They were two good old boys who wound up the generators on the motorhomes each evening so they could catch the news.

I thought perhaps I was being unduly critical until Doris and Lou, the couple from San Antonio, stopped Sunday morning to say good-bye. They had to leave, but wanted to wish me well on my travels and chat a bit more. They asked me, "Why is it that you're from New Mexico and so friendly, but those other people won't talk to anyone?"

I didn't know how to answer their query other than to tell this nice couple that those fellow New Mexicans didn't talk to me either. When I had pulled into the campsite, those New Mexico plates were the first I had seen since Quebec. I went bouncing over to say hello and met with a cold rebuff. So be it. But I was embarrassed for my fellow New Mexicans and their aloof ways.

Ink and I spent Sunday walking, wading, and shelling. I found myself looking even more closely at all this beauty, knowing it was our last day in paradise. It had been a delightful interlude; one of great beauty, one of connectedness.

We took one last solitary walk along the shoreline Tuesday morning and said our good-byes to that magical beach. Got back to the camper and packed things up. Talked with a few people; did not say good-bye to the New Mexicans — didn't want to disturb them.

We left Padre about 11 a.m. going back north on the reef. Took JFK Causeway across the channel and grabbed Interstate 37 which led us through Corpus Christi. It's a sprawling town, but we skirted it on the Interstate. I knew I didn't want to drive very far. I was gritty and grimy. My hair was stiff and standing on end from sand and surf. I desperately needed a hot shower and shampoo, laundry facilities, and all those amenities.

We were heading northwest. Once we got out of the metropolitan area, there wasn't much traffic. There was a KOA listed in my guide just outside Mathis, close to Lake Corpus Christi and off the highway. It was early, but I had a crying need to get scrubbed up and to clear all the sand away. I love the back to nature life. After a while, however, I need a good scrub and today was one of those days.

We turned off the Interstate and followed a country road through rolling hills and mesquite trees. Pulled into KOA, registered with the pleasant staff, and answered the usual questions. They gave me a lovely spot under some mesquites, not far from the laundry and restooms.

I had popped up and plugged in. Was gathering up all the dirty clothes, stripping the covers from Tessie and getting ready to make an assault on the laundromat. Ink was outside on her long lead enjoying the shade and cool, sandless ground when I heard her give a cry and fuss. I went out and here came a whole flock of wild turkeys. They were a unique greeting committee, gobbling, looking, and posturing at the new arrivals.

You can imagine how Ink reacted to the group of birds. She was pulling on her lead as if to say, "Boy, I've gotta get one of those big birds." The turkeys knew just how far she could reach and stayed out of range, gobbling and teasing. By this time, some of the other campers had come up saying, "Let that dog get one of those pesky things." I could tell they enjoyed the turkeys and was not about to let Ink off that lead.

It unsettled Ink, but she was aware that she was outnumbered as there were a full dozen turkeys milling around. She retreated under the camper and watched them apprehensively. We were getting over the turkey greeting when a graceful fawn came to check us out.

Fran, the camper across the site from us, came over and introduced herself. She was there for the winter, as were many of the campers. She told us the story of the fawn: "Lucky Buck" had lost his mother and they took him in here at the campground. This KOA is unique. They have 47 acres and it is a wildlife preserve, hence the unique greeting committees. Lucky Buck was tame and not at all shy. He came over to our camper and he and Ink touched noses and decided to be friends.

I got all the laundry together and went up and loaded three washers full. I knew I couldn't walk Ink in the campground with all the wildlife, so we hiked down a country lane leading to the lake. It was more humid and hot inland without that sea breeze and Ink wasn't interested in going far. When we got back, I cleaned Tessie then brushed Ink and fed her, put my dinner into the oven and said, "Now, it's my turn. I'm going for one wonderful scrub." There was no one in the ladies room, so I spread out and fully enjoyed that shower. Stood and let the water run over me. No one came into the restroom the whole time I was there. I had noticed this before and wondered if I were the only woman who used these great facilities. Had my dinner watching the turkeys and listening to the birds. Fran came over and we talked. Just after dark, we called it a day. Went to bed in a clean camper with a clean dog and a clean body feeling quite civilized once again.

When we awoke, Ink wanted out immediately to look for those big birds. There was no sign of them anywhere, but I put Ink on lead. I was sitting and drinking my coffee, looking out on this green setting, when Lucky Buck came across the grounds.

He seemed to like Ink. The two of them had some kind of affinity. She was wiggling but not jumping in her usual greeting fashion. He eased up to her and they sniffed each other. This young buck wasn't much bigger that my black dog. They nosed each other fondly. I wondered if Ink thought this was some kind of new dog. It amazed me that she was quiet and gentle with Lucky Buck for, after all, she'd pounce on a bird if she got the chance. I sat and watched the two animals seeming to talk over the morning.

Lucky Buck was a wild thing and he'd start and retreat from time to time, but come back to talk some more with Ink. It was beautiful to watch them. Finally, the buck wandered off for greener pastures. I took Ink and we headed down the country road for a run. I had not seen the turkeys, but didn't want to press my luck. When we got back, Fran was out and said, "You know we ladies have a meeting this morning. We're always scheduling all these activities. Barb, would you be kind enough to attend and just talk with us briefly about your travels and your experiences?"

"My goodness. How nice of you. Of course, I'll talk to the ladies with pleasure."

Fran suggested that I be at the office about 9:30 a.m. Lucky Buck had ambled back to see what was happening. I got some photos of this young buck with Ink and Fran.

I did some chores, then went up to the meeting. This was a group of supportive women. No Neanderthals here. They were amazed that I had traveled so far with just my dog and asked lots of questions. The crux of my talk with them was that campgrounds are the best kept secret in the United States. I told them a woman alone feels secure and at ease. The campers are helpful and friendly. I reiterated that we still have good, kind people in this country which, unfortunately, never makes the headlines. My feeling is that the news media dwells on the negative and it's making us a nation of paranoiacs.

One lady came up to me after the meeting and said, "You've got to write a book about your travels."

"I've thought of it. I don't know how else I could share all these experiences without writing, but we shall see."

She patted my hand and said, "Do it!" It was a great encounter with wonderful, vital women. I made arrangements for having the propane tank filled, then after lots of hugs and good wishes, left this hospitable group and headed up the highway. It was nurturing, encouraging people like these who made my travels so meaningful and affirmed my faith in the human species. I had a number of ladies tell me they couldn't head out on their own as I had done. I reminded them there was no reason why they should. This trip was something that I wanted to do. It's not what most women would consider seeking their bliss, but for me it was just that. I assured them I wasn't crusading for women to head out in campers and discover America. However, any woman can and I knew it was right for me.

I had checked the map and saw that Interstate 37 would lead us directly into San Antonio, which I didn't want. At Three Rivers, just north of Mathis, we headed directly west on Route 72 past Choke Canyon Lake and through wide open country for more pike-shunning. This was cattle country. The entry gates to some of the ranches were fabulous: solid pillars on each side of a lane, a cross-bar decorated with steer horns and the name of the spread or whatever they chose to proclaim that this was their land. Some were quite ostentatious, but it was fun to view these monuments to success.

There was no traffic, just green, open country. We rolled along, waiting to see what the next entry gate would look like. Route 72 ended at Route 97, so we hung a left. I chuckled when we passed through Los Angeles. Thought I should stop and take a picture, but I blinked my eyes and we were through Los Angeles, Texas.

We arrived at Cotulla which was just a cross-roads, about 12:30 p.m. I was planning to drive north on Interstate 35, then again cross-country to Uvalde. We ran directly into 35 and turned right. I noticed a store which I thought was a food market and pulled into the parking lot, since we needed a few supplies.

When I entered, I realized it was a variety store, so got out of there. I didn't want to keep Ink waiting as it was hot and humid.

I hopped into Tessie, ready to leave Cotulla, Texas, and she wouldn't start. I got her running and started to pull out of the parking lot when she died. I could get the engine to turn over, but it seemed it was not getting gasoline. I managed to get back into the lot and coasted over to the side where there was a spot of shade. Thought to myself, well, my little rig has let me down at last. It was an unsettling feeling. At least, we were in a parking lot; not stranded beside the highway out in the middle of nowhere. I checked under the hood. Couldn't see anything amiss as far as my limited knowledge could determine. Jiggled a few wires and talked to Tessie. She was not running properly and I knew we could not attempt driving.

I saw two matronly women coming out of the variety store. Walked over and asked, "Are you ladies from Cotulla?"

"Yes, ma'am, we sure are."

"I'm having trouble with my camper. She won't run. Do you know a mechanic in town?"

"Well, you know, there aren't many, but my husband has been takin' our car to Roy. He's just learnin' mechanic'n, but we've been real pleased with him."

"Do you think Roy would come out and look at the camper?"

"Why, of course, he will, dear. Don't you worry. We'll stop by the station and tell Roy where you are and he'll be right out here to help you."

I did need a helping hand about now. I went back and sat down, tried to comfort Ink, who was panting heavily. I sat there in Tessie feeling totally helpless and hot. The thought did cross my mind that the ladies might not send Roy out, but I pushed it aside and thought, of course, they'll send someone. They're two good Christian ladies and they'll send help.

In about twenty minutes, Roy pulled up beside us in a blue Ford pickup. He stepped out and came over. Roy was about thirty, not tall, but heavily built, wearing blue jeans and a blue work shirt which his eyes matched perfectly. He had on a straw

Stetson.

"Havin' some trouble, ma'am?"

I filled Roy in, saying it seemed like she wasn't getting gas. He tried to start Tessie and had no more luck than I had. He checked under the hood, then tried again to get Tessie running. I asked him, "Do you think it could be a fuse?" He pulled the panel and couldn't see a problem. He tinkered a bit more. She'd start but wouldn't keep running. She wasn't getting gasoline. Roy wasn't into small talk. He tinkered, climbed in and out, and would shake his head occasionally.

I stood there helplessly and sweated. By this time, Roy was sweating, too, and I noticed he kept a big plug of tobacco in his mouth. He looked at me with those clear, blue eyes and said, "Well, ma'am, I think it might be the fuel pump. We need to get down to the station."

Roy gave me instructions on turning the ignition key to get a little gas to the carburetor, assuring me he'd stay close and we could get her to the station. I had noticed the Mobil station on the corner when I turned onto Interstate 35. I followed Roy's instructions and we limped into the station. It was about 1:30 and beastly hot. I got out and sat on the curb in the oil and the sun. Ink came out to join me, but opted for curling up in Tessie away from the pesky, biting flies.

Roy proceeded to work on Tessie. I must say, this young man gave it his all. He'd work a bit, chew his tobacco a bit, go back into the station and read a bit, then come back and work some more. I was sitting there on the curb in the grease feeling really defeated, depressed, and lost. Anyone who has never relied totally on a rig can't imagine what a sinking feeling it is to be inoperable.

I had not had lunch, but didn't feel hungry. Went into the station and bought a Dr. Pepper. Sat back down on the curb and swatted at flies while I drank it. I thought I'd like to cry but knew if I did, it would unsettle Roy even more. So I didn't. Just sat there with my heart in my throat feeling very, very alone. Roy kept working, chewing his tobacco, checking his book, and sweating. He had shed his Stetson, and his jeans and shirt were grimy. It was hot and he was doing all he knew to do.

He finally said, "You know, I think it has to be the fuel pump and I don't know anything about that." Another fellow came by and the two of them climbed over and under Tess while I sat on the curb swatting flies and drinking Dr. Pepper. What are you going to do? About 4:30 p.m. Roy, looking as haggard as I felt, shook his head in disgust and said, "Ma'am, you know I'm just learnin' mechanic'n and I don't know what's wrong with this machine, but I can't fix it." With that, he walked into the station. I just sat there on the greasy curb feeling panicky.

I gave myself a pep talk, collected my thoughts, and followed Roy into the station. I asked, "Roy, do you think there's a mechanic in town who might know what's wrong?"

"No, ma'am, I don't think so. There's the Lucero brothers up the way, but, you know, ma'am, we all mostly work on Fords and Chevys here in Cotulla."

So there I was, past nowhere and beyond somewhere. At this point I asked, "Well, Roy, what do you think I should do?"

"Well, ma'am, I think you're gonna have to have it towed. The closest towns with Toyota dealers are Laredo or San Antonio. I'm just really sorry but I don't know what's wrong."

"It's too late today to get towed, isn't it?"

"Yes, ma'am. Most everyone goes home about five."

"Well, is there a place to spend the night?"

"Oh, yes, ma'am, the Cotulla Motel is just across the street."

I walked back out to Tessie and Ink. They were my security blankets. I sat down and lit a cigarette, thinking, this is a helluva mess. I sat there feeling forlorn and sorry for myself. Ink put her head on my lap and the unasked question in her eyes was when are we getting out of this hot, buggy place? I patted her and told her it would be okay, but I really wasn't sure it would.

Just then Roy came over to the door all grinning and washed up, saying, "Ma'am, I called over to the motel — my wife works there — and they'll just be happy to give you and your dog a room for the night. You can stay there and in the morning

we'll see about a tow. I'm really sorry I couldn't fix it, Ma'am."
Roy started back toward the station. I said, "Roy, I owe you
some money."

"Well, no, I didn't fix it, Ma'am."

"But, Roy, you've spent over three hours trying to fix it and
I've got to pay you for your time. It's not your fault you
couldn't fix it."

"Well, ma'am, would twenty dollars be all right?"
I smiled and told him that would be just fine.

The station manager came up and assured me the camper
would be safe there at the station with, "Don't you worry, little
gal. Your camper will be just fine right here. There's no crime
in Cotulla, Texas. You just go over and have a good night's
rest."

These kind people were so helpful and I was feeling more at
ease. I threw some clothes, my toothbrush, and Ink's bowls and
food into some plastic bags. Put Ink on her lead and over to the
Cotulla Motel we went.

Roy's wife was there to greet us and check us in. John, the
owner, was behind the desk. In the office were two miniature
Schnauzers named Pepper and Sweet Pea. They greeted Ink and
she wiggled all over, thinking what a great new adventure. I
knew she was as thankful as I to be out of the oil, the heat, and
the pesky flies. John was not a Texan. His accent was more
northeastern United States. He asked, "I hear you broke down?"

"Evidently. She won't run and Roy can't find the problem."

"It's too late tonight to do anything, but tomorrow morning
we'll call Elmo. He's the only reliable tow service in this town.
Just come by for your coffee in the morning and we'll get Elmo
to tow you up to San Antonio."

"John, do you think there's any mechanic in Cotulla who
might be able to fix my Toyota? I'm really scared to have her
towed."

"No. You're not going to find anyone in this town. Better to
take it to San Antonio."

I registered and visited with these accommodating people. Did think to ask about a restaurant. They told me the Cattlemen's Cafe was just a short walk up the street. Ink and I went to our room and found it very nice. We had a huge king-sized bed, TV, air conditioning, and a big, clean bathroom. We both bounced around in all these creature comforts. It was the first time on the entire journey that we had stayed in a motel room. Ink sprawled out on the floor and soaked up the cool air. I washed my face and hands in the big, private bathroom.

I took Ink for a turn around the grounds. Pepper and Sweet Pea joined us. Then I fed her and walked up the main street of Cotulla to the Cattlemen's Cafe for my dinner. The sun was low in the western sky and it was cooler. It was a pleasant town and the walk unwound me. I discovered I was famished. I had a great Mexican meal which made me feel better. Thought how fortuitous that Tessie broke down in such a quiet, lovely town.

I ate and gave thanks for a good meal with friendly people. Was on my way back to the motel before dark. There was a market on the corner. I went in and bought myself a book, deciding I might as well read something light and easy this evening in a motel room. They had an excellent selection of paperbacks. I purchased Margaret Truman's *Murder in the CIA*. I had never read any of her novels.

Ink and I took another short walk when I got back. She was happy with the large, cool room. We were returning to our room when the two ladies who had sent Roy to help me came out of another motel room. They asked me about my car troubles and I told them I'd have to be towed since Roy could not find the problem, but I did thank them for being so kind and helpful.

The ladies then invited me to a Baptist revival meeting they were having that evening at the church across the street from the motel. They asked, "Why don't you just come on over and join us. We'd love to have you." I begged off, but thanked them. They were, indeed, good kind Christian ladies.

I closed the door and looked at this large room. With no windows open to the world, it seemed confining. However, I hopped into the bathroom and had a shower in total privacy.

Stood under that hot stream of water and knew all would be right. I had this feeling that the problem with Tess was minor, but there wasn't anyone in Cotulla who could rectify it. I was apprehensive about having her towed. I didn't like any part of it, but, as I stood there under the soothing water, I recognized that I had no choice, so I might as well accept it. Dried and roamed around the room. Turned on the TV, but after five minutes, turned it off. Stretched out on the king-sized bed and read my Truman murder mystery.

I thought about calling someone. Misery loves company. Here I was down and out in Cotulla, Texas, and not liking it one bit. I reconsidered, knowing there was nothing anyone could do. Why bother, why bother anyone? Ink had hopped onto the large bed and was stretched full length. I eased down and hugged my faithful dog and said, "Let's give it twenty-four hours, my gal." *Murder in the CIA* was a good read. It took my mind off what tomorrow might bring. Read for a while then slept very well in the Cotulla Motel.

I woke quite early and for a moment wondered where in the world I was. Jumped out of bed and padded into the private bath. I had a lot on my mind and was fretting about having Tessie towed. I knew I didn't have a choice. Ink was still lounging on the bed just reveling in all that space. I got dressed and went over to the office. The coffee was on and I drank a cup while John called Elmo. Elmo told John that he could tow me, he had hauled many cars up the highway, and he knew where the Toyota agency was in San Antonio. This was a 95 mile tow job and Elmo's fee was two dollars per mile. John grimaced a little at that. Elmo said he'd be over and look at the camper and meet with me. I had another cup of coffee and went back to the room. Ink and I took a walk. We were passing the office when a wiry little man with piercing blue eyes came out the door. He looked at me and asked, "You Miz Thacker?"

"Yes, I am."

"I'm Elmo. Just took a look at your little rig. No trouble. Now let the dog ride in the camper. You can ride up with me, but I don't allow smoking in my truck. I've had triple bypass surgery and can't stand the smoke. If you can be ready at nine, I'll take you up to the Toyota dealer in San Antonio and I'm sure they can help you out."

"Very good, Elmo. We'll be ready and meet you at the Mobil station." Thought, my God, if this man who has had triple bypass is the competent tower in town, I'd hate to see the incompetent ones.

I took Ink back to the room, hiked up to the Cattlemen's Cafe for a hearty breakfast, then back to the room where I packed our few items into the plastic bags. Stopped at the office and paid my bill and thanked John for his help. I was getting Ink settled in the camper and explaining to her about the towing process, when Elmo arrived with his big wrecker.

Elmo looked the situation over with a practiced eye and proceeded to hook Tessie up to the winch. I could tell he knew what he was doing. Thanked Roy and the station manager once more for all their kindness. By that time, Tessie was hooked up, hanging there and looking helpless. We were off at 9 a.m. heading north on Route 35 for the 95 mile trip to San Antonio and Red McComb's Toyota Agency.

I climbed into the wrecker and noticed that Elmo kept his Stetson hung from the roof of his cab. He smiled and said, "Hate to make you leave so early, Ma'am, but I need to be back here by one o'clock this afternoon. This is our 50th wedding anniversary. Our kids are coming and we're gonna celebrate."

On the way out of town, Elmo pulled into his shop. His wife came out to say good-bye. It was touching to see the love and consideration between these two people. She was a quiet woman and didn't say much, but wished me well on having the camper fixed. Then we were underway.

I noticed that Elmo drove confidently and checked often to see that all was well behind us. He knew what he was doing. I sat and enjoyed the scenery and the freedom of not having to drive myself. We talked easily from time to time. My fate was out of my hands at this point, so I relaxed and listened to Elmo's vignettes. He was alert, astute, and a kind, gentle Texas man who had lived and worked for 71 years in this part of Texas. He and his wife had four children.

Elmo told me that he and his wife disagreed on house temperatures. It seems she prefers to have the temperature in summer at about 60 degrees and Elmo freezes. He told me he had to wear sheepskin slippers in the house during the summer while his wife ran around in her bare feet. He glanced over at me with those clear, blue eyes and asked, "How do ya suppose we ever have managed to get along for fifty years?" Some couples have the capacity to work out differences, thank God.

He told me another story that kept me in stitches. It seems that Elmo was losing his hearing. His wife was complaining bitterly that he didn't hear a thing she said. Elmo decided that he should get himself a hearing aid. He thought if one would help, why not try two. So, he went to the doctor without telling his wife a thing and was fitted with two hearing aids. He grinned and said, "Law, that woman is the noisiest thing in the kitchen I've ever heard! I know she stands clear across the room and just throws those dishes at the sink." He admitted the world was too noisy with those hearing aids. He doesn't bother with them anymore.

It was a comfortable ride. Tessie wasn't giving Elmo any trouble. Ink seemed happy enough looking at us from the camper. The trip passed more quickly than I had imagined. We were in greater San Antonio and the traffic was heavy. Elmo told me he knew where he was going and wheeled along confidently. He looked over and said, "You know, Ma'am, you aren't a back seat driver at all."

"No, Elmo. You've got it under control. I don't have to tell you what to do. You're the pro here."

He smiled and retorted, "Sure appreciate that, Ma'am. I get a little testy when people try to tell me how to do this job I've been doing for fifty years."

We were on a busy thoroughfare by now. Elmo told me we only had two blocks to go. He suggested pulling in and leaving

Tess hooked up until we found out what they would want to do. Red McComb's was a big agency and the service department was humming. I stood there watching people scurrying and answering phones. A nice looking man finally came up and asked if he could help me.

I explained my plight to Grover and told him the camper was outside on the back of a wrecker. Grover and Elmo were old friends who had mutual relatives in Cotulla. They had a visit while I fretted and Tess hung there in the air. In time, Grover asked me to explain what happened. I said, "I could get her to start, but she acted like she wasn't getting any gasoline. The mechanic in Cotulla thinks it's probably the fuel pump."

Grover's eyes lit up, he grinned and asked, "Ya see that '78 long-bed Toyota over there, the red one? It's mine and it's just what you have here. Hold on a minute." Grover reached into Tessie, removed the fuse box, replaced the heater fuse and Tessie was fixed. Shazam! She was all fixed.

As Grover explained, the fuse had a hair-line crack in it which was difficult to see. The fuel pump is tied to the heater fuse and it was bad, so she wasn't getting gas. That's all there was to it. Was I relieved! I had looked at this huge garage when we pulled in, thinking if Tessie had to be kept here, where in the world would Ink and I stay in San Antonio? We all laughed. I counted my blessings. Grover didn't even charge me for the fuse.

Elmo had requested that I pay him for the towing before he left San Antonio as he had a payroll to meet. I owed him $180 and needed to get to a bank. Grover gave us directions. Off we went back up the street we had come down, except that now I was driving Tessie and feeling elated. Elmo was following me in all the city traffic. I lost him for a few minutes, but he knew where we were going. It fleetingly crossed my mind that I wouldn't want that wonderful man to think I was trying to skip out without paying him. I pulled into the bank lot and Elmo soon arrived. Got the money and paid him. We hugged and Elmo told me, "It's been a real pleasure, Ma'am. If you're ever back this way, do stop in and say hello."

"Elmo, I certainly will. My memories of Cotulla will always be fond, in spite of being scared to death about my camper."

"You have a safe journey, now, and be careful."

"Don't worry, Elmo. You have a glorious anniversary celebration."

In less than twenty-four hours, all was under control. There was nothing seriously wrong with my Tessie. It renewed my faith and I felt fifty pounds lighter. By noon, we were on our way. The gypsy caravan was operable again.

I decided to drive to Del Rio that afternoon. I should have mail there. It was easy driving and I was thankful that Tess's problem was minor. It's a scary feeling when your rig fails you. All was well now and we rolled along. Passed through Uvalde and I was sure it couldn't compare to the hospitality and kindness of Cotulla. It wasn't a long drive and we were in Del Rio about 4 p.m. I saw the Post Office sign as we were coming into town. As I parked in the lot, I noticed the zip code on the building and thought, they must have more than one office in town. That's not the zip I sent to Pamie. I went on in and, no, they didn't have mail for me. I asked if there was another office in Del Rio and was again told, no. I checked when I got back to Tessie. I had given Pam the right city but the wrong zip code. I'd screwed up again.

Went back into the post office and told the clerks what I had done. They laughed and told me the mail would show up, but they wouldn't hazard a guess as to just when.

Del Rio seemed a nice town and I was glad. It looked like we might be here for a few days waiting for mail. We drove out Route 90 and found a campground at Amistad. There were big shade trees, lots of room for Ink to romp, and far in the distance, I could see some rugged buttes. It was beginning to look more like home. It was wonderful to be able to see for vast distances and have a clear azure sky above. Behind the park was an open area where Ink and I walked and watched the sunset in this spacious Texas sky. Did the dinner round and turned in early. It had been a momentous day. I was grateful that my little Toyota hadn't let us down. Chastized myself for not looking more closely at the fuses; however, it was a good learning experience. Twenty-four hours can make a world of difference, if you don't get too discouraged. Gave extra thanks to my God for our good fortune.

We woke feeling no urgency about anything. I needed to stay and see if the mail would catch up with us. It was a great area in which to have to wait. The Amistad Recreation Area outside Del Rio is an international recreational area on the border of Mexico and the United States with lots and lots of water. The dam was constructed jointly by the US and Mexico and is operated jointly by the International Boundary and Water Commission. The dam impounds water from the Rio Grande plus the Pecos and Devil's Rivers. It was built in 1967. The storing of the water started on the last day of May, 1968. The dam was dedicated by Presidents Richard Nixon and Diaz Ordaz on September 8, 1969. The primary functions of Amistad Dam are flood control and water conservation. These make possible many water-oriented recreational opportunities. The dam consists of a 254 foot high gravity concrete section in the Rio Grande channel with flanking earth embankments at each end. The whole structure is approximately six miles long.

Ink and I had a full day to squander. We puttered around during the morning at the campsite. Early afternoon, I said, "Well, dog, we'd better go into town." Decided I should do a thorough marketing since I was going to Big Bend National for Thanksgiving. We took Tess down and secured everything. Stopped at the office and let them know we'd be spending another night. Planned to give the mail until Friday. If it didn't arrive by then, so be it. We drove up to Rough Canyon Marina. Meandered around this remarkable recreational area. It was high plateau country, chapparal country. I was overjoyed to see creosote, sotol, yucca, and mesquite. It was my kind of country with the bonus of all that water stretching for miles.

On the outskirts of Del Rio, just before the turn for the post office, was a gigantic supermarket with a big parking lot. It was cool, so I left Ink to guard the house. I went into this warehouse type market and had a grand time stocking up. Picked up a canned ham, canned cranberries, sweet potatoes, and lima beans for my Thanksgiving feast. Much more canned food than I prefer; however, it was the essence of a Thanksgiving meal for primitive camping. Spent a lot of time in the market. I liked the feel of Del Rio. The people were friendly, it was a slow pace — not much hustle and bustle — and browsing this market was fun.

When I got to the Post Office, the clerks remembered me and greeted me with, "No, Ma'am, it's not here yet." I told them I'd check back tomorrow. They suggested coming in anytime after noon since they got no mail later in the day. Inkus and I went back to the campground. I stashed all the supplies while she loafed in the shade of a big tree. I had become a master at arranging the refrigerator and congratulated myself on how much I could pack into that tiny Dometic. Tessie seemed to expand to accommodate all my buying whims. When I got this round of foodstuffs put up, I felt sure we could survive for a month in the wilderness, if we had to. Ink and I took a long walk through the fields, then had dinner. I went over and had a shower. It had been a good day. I had talked with a few people at the campground, but there weren't many here. I wasn't feeling that sociable anyhow. It seemed nicer to wander around the countryside.

Friday morning, November 18, I loafed around, sat and drank coffee while I looked out at glorious sunshine in a vast, clear, sky. Ink and I walked for miles up a dirt road behind the park. The land smelled like desert, the sun was hot, and the air was dry. I made a call to my auto insurer, USAA, and filed a claim for towing. The USAA headquarters are in San Antonio.

When I told the clerk I had broken down in Cotulla, she exclaimed, "You broke down in Cotulla? That's the middle of nowhere!" We both laughed and I gave her all the information plus my fond views of Cotulla and its good citizens. The claims clerk assured me that the check for towing would be in Las

Cruces before I got there.

I secured Tessie and we returned to Del Rio to see if my screw-up had been rectified by the United States Postal Service. One should double-check zip numbers. Arrived at the post office a little past noon, not feeling optimistic at all. Lo, and behold, the mail packet had arrived. I was amazed and delighted. I thanked the clerks who showed me that the packet had gone first to at town named Mexia in Texas. That was the zip I had mistakenly given Pam. Someone in Mexia was on the ball and sent it along to Del Rio. I had had good luck with my mail all over the country. Only that one packet which got caught up in Canada's mail strike was returned to Pam.

By 12:30, we were leaving Del Rio, heading west on Route 90. We came to a turn off that led to the Dam and thought we should look at this cooperative venture in water conservation. Drove a couple of miles down the road to the dam. Could have driven across to Acuna, Mexico, but did not bother. On the Texas side was an inviting picnic area with shaded tables, portable johns, great water views over marshy land, and lots of green grass. Ink and I parked up. I fixed a sandwich and she roamed and explored. We had the park all to ourselves, so we enjoyed the solitude and had a break before we really started.

Wandered back to Route 90 and turned left. Drove across a large causeway spanning all the water, then through high mesa country. I had checked the map and noted with interest Seminole Historic State Park at Seminole Canyon which is the site of some fine pictographs. It was only 3 p.m. and we were only 45 miles from Del Rio when I drove into Seminole Canyon Headquarters and Visitor's Center. It was cool so I didn't mind leaving Ink. It was a great visitor center with a life-sized diorama depicting the lifestyle of early man who had been cave dwellers in the region.

A woman at the desk told me I was in time for the tour down to Fate Bell Shelter to view the pictographs. Sounded good to me. I hiked back to Tessie, grabbed my camera, and asked Ink to be patient. Only seven people were hiking down with the

Ranger, so we had good conversation and input.

The cave was on the west side of the canyon and in shade. The pictographs were difficult to see; however, they were interesting and similar to the great body of rock art done by these early peoples. I tried to get a photo of one of the shaman figures and found I was out of film. Damn. I never learn. It was a great hike and an interesting tour, in spite of not getting photos. I preferred the siting of the rock art here to the rock art along Lake Superior. No need to rappel over cold water to see these.

Fate Bell Shelter contains some of North America's oldest pictographs, believed to have been painted as long as 8,000 years ago. The distribution of this distinct style is limited to a district which includes a portion of the Rio Grande, Pecos, and Devil's Rivers. More than forty pictograph sites are known to contain examples of this style of rock art, ranging from single paintings to caves containing panels of art hundreds of feet long. Although numerous figures or motifs are repeated in different locations, the exact meaning of the painting is buried with the people who painted them. The name Seminole is attributed to the Seminole Indian scouts who were stationed nearby back in the 1870's.

When the group got back to the visitor's center, I asked about camping facilities and found there was a campground over on the mesa. Decided to spend the night, and registered. We drove over a paved road to a neat campsite. There were only 31 spaces on this heavenly mesa, and each had a shade shelter, picnic table, cooking grill, and fire ring. There were clean, tiled restrooms with showers. Up on this knoll, the buttes were even closer. I sat at the picnic table and read through my mail packet, then fixed dinner which I ate outside.

Ink and I took a long walk and were back at our site in time to watch a lingering golden sunset light up a distant mountain range. It was great to be able to see for sixty miles. There was no electricity and the stars were brilliant. Just before I dozed off, I heard coyotes yipping in the distance. There were some winds, but we were in windy country. It was feeling more like home.

Ink and I curled up and slept well.

We woke early in this high mesa campground at Seminole Canyon. Took a walk, ate at the picnic table, and greeted the few people strolling by. November is not a peak tourist season. Those high bluffs and mountains on to the west were calling me and we were on the road about 10 a.m. This was dry, high, plateau country. There weren't many towns or much of anything but sparse vegetation, and the thin ribbon of highway that was Route 90 stretching though this vast area so close to the Mexican border.

We came to the town of Sanderson about noon. The railroad track ran parallel to the highway. Possibly, there were some cattle ranches in the area, although it would have been sparse grazing for cattle. There were a few wooden front buildings along the road. I noticed an inviting cafe with a parking area across the street. I was sick of my own sandwiches, so pulled into the lot and went over to the cafe for lunch. Leaving Ink was no problem, the weather was ideal for November. We were away from the warming influence of the Gulf and there was a zip in the air.

The cafe was busy. Think all of Sanderson was there for lunch that Saturday. Big, raw-boned Texas men in cowboy hats and boots. It was a friendly atmosphere and a nice change of pace. Got back to Tessie and headed west to Marathon.

# XIX. Thanks Giving at Big Bend

Big Bend National Park sweeps so far south that it really is not on the way to anywhere. An automobile is the best and only easy way to visit this remote region. It's an area of vast uninhabited land. At Marathon, we turned south on Route 385. After almost 40 miles of solitary travel, we arrived at the entrance to Big Bend at Persimmon Gap.

I stopped and availed myself of the restrooms and talked with the rangers. They told me we'd have to drive farther south to the Visitor's Center to check on campground availability. On we went. I was enthralled with the rugged cliffs, the wide open desert country and felt I was in my native land.

About 25 miles below Persimmon, there was a sign touting the fossil bone exhibit, so, of course, we had to take a look at it. This was north of Tornillo Creek bridge.

This exhibit shows an extinct mammal whose remains were found in sandstone deposits about 50 million years old. Tornillo Creek is one of the largest drainages in the Park. We pulled into a parking area with a path leading up to a covered shelter. It housed a display of the earth's geologic past, landmarks of the past, and the fossils. These particular fossil finds were between the Mesozoic and Cenozoic periods after the age of the dinosaurs. They represent roughly 20 million years of geologic history.

There wasn't a soul around, so Ink roamed while I read all the fascinating information. These fossil beds were at the beginning of the age of mammals. They've found remains of 29 species of early, extinct forest dwelling mammals near the fossil bone exhibit site on Tornillo Flat.

The same flat plain later accommodated a hippo-like plant

269

eater, a browsing collie-sized mammal, a panther-like cat, and the little ancestral horse, *Eohippus,* no bigger than a fox terrier. *Eohippus* had not yet developed the typical horse hoof and still had four toes on his front feet and three on his hind. He browsed among low forest plants, because nature had not yet invented grass.

We hiked up to the top of the hill. Could see the Chisos Mountains which rise like an island out of the desert floor. I felt so small and insignificant in the vastness of this land that has been relatively untouched by man. The Tornillo plateau at one time had been part of a great inland sea and the digs were revealing much of the geologic history of the area. We wandered around the fossil beds, savoring the deserty country with stark exposed mountains off in the distance. Such a fascinating planet is Mother Earth.

We finally arrived at the Visitor's Center at Panther Junction. This was the park headquarters — a long way from anywhere. Went in and found that some of the literature I had been reading was not accurate. There was supposed to be a campground with full hookups at Rio Grande Village; however, this was only for those rigs which were fully self-contained. Tessie did not have a holding tank nor cumbersome hose to empty, so we weren't allowed to stay there. The ranger told me there was another site with water and toilet facilities and the showers, laundry, and gasoline facilities were close by. I said it sounded good to me. She said, "Just another twenty miles south, another twenty miles south to Rio Grande Village." I thanked her and we kept driving farther and farther south.

We kept chugging south on a two lane road devoid of traffic. The Chisos Mountains were fading in the background. If you make the effort to get to this remote area, you really want to be here. We were driving along slowly, looking at the scenery when, up on the driver's side of the camper, flapped a big old crow. I looked up at him and he gave me a loud caw and looked down at our gypsy caravan. He flew along beside the camper looking at us and cawing as much as to say, "Welcome to Big

Bend country." The crow followed along beside us for at least ten miles, kind of meeting and greeting us. It seemed a good omen for our stay here.

We arrived at yet another visitor's center. At this one, I was able to register for the campground and get more information about Rio Grande Village. It was a large park on the banks of the river with cottonwoods everywhere and spacious sites. It had bathroom facilities and water, but you had to hike about a half mile over to the store for the shower and laundry facilities. The campground was divided into sections for those rigs with generators and those without. As it was, we weren't far enough away from the generator section to escape the noise those pesky things make when they're running. Luckily, they may not run after 10 p.m. Still, the campground was lovely and green here on the banks of the Rio Grande. There was a magnificent sandstone cliff on the other side of the river that glowed orange in the sunlight.

I got set up, as I intended to stay in this lovely setting for a few days. Ink was outside on her lead checking the population. It was a large site, there was no one close to us. It is one of the best features of the state and national parks, you have space — no sardine effect. I had gone out to draw water from the faucet when I heard someone yelling, "Barb!" Thought, Oh, oh, I'm losing it. Heard "Barb" again and looked across the grounds toward the restrooms. There were Bob and Lois Roche, the wonderful people I had met and enjoyed so much at Davis Bayou in Mississippi waving and yelling at me.

I ran across the grounds and we hugged and greeted each other like long lost pilgrims. We marveled at the odds of being in the same place at the same time, but were happy to re-establish ties and exchange tidbits of our travels. The Roches had gone on to New Orleans and were at Big Bend for the night as they were pressing on to California. It was a great visit with great friends in this small world.

When I got back to Tessie, Ink was bursting a kidney. The rangers had stressed being alert and careful with the dog as there were many coyotes and lots of wildlife here by the river. I didn't bother to tell them that this dog would do nothing when she was on lead and had to be free to take care of business.

Hooked Ink up and we walked through the park. There were many birds flitting around. Water, water is the sustaining force in any desert environment. The river was flowing and clear here, the trees were huge, and the animal life populous near this source of water. Down at the end of the campground there was a narrow, paved road which led back to the group facility. It was removed from the campers and I could let Ink free to do her thing.

We hiked way down this deserted road. That sandstone cliff glowing in the afternoon sun was majestic. It was a lovely walk with the birds chirping and singing all around us and that cliff glowing over us. You could smell the green here by the river.

Took a turn by the Roches when we got back to the campground and Ink said her hellos. Had a short visit, then went over for dinner at the picnic table. Watched the sunset, talked with a few strollers, listened to the birds settling in, then we did the same. I was happy we had made the drive to this remote region and knew we'd enjoy Thanksgiving here. It was another world.

Sunday morning, the sun was shining through the green cottonwoods, the birds were singing, and my sense of well being was complete. It was a day for rest and reading — had a book on the national park that I wanted to study. Decided that I'd take a hike, relax, and not do much else on this warm, sunny Sunday.

The Roches stopped by. They were leaving early as it was a long way out of the park. They asked me about my plans. I told them I was going to stay at Big Bend for Thanksgiving, then go to Las Cruces for Christmas. After which, I planned to head on west. We all laughed and proposed running into each other somewhere in California. We had our hugs and fond goodbyes. They were beautiful people, but then I met so many beautiful people on my travels.

I ate breakfast, then Ink and I took a walk. Put her on lead and she was content lying there in the shade of the cottonwoods, so I hiked over to the general store and inspected the facilities. Glad I did that; the showers were metered. You had to pay 75 cents for a five minute shower here at Big Bend. There were a number of washers and dryers. The store had a mix of this and that. I did buy some post cards, then hiked back to Tessie and Ink.

I stretched out and read about this marvelous park: Big Bend National Park came into being in 1944. Today, it sprawls across 1,106 square miles inside the southernmost tip of the Bend. Even with Interstate highways, park headquarters is a long distance. It's 410 miles from San Antonio to Panther Junction, 323 miles from El Paso, 108 from Alpine, and 68 miles from the last community of Marathon. The journey is well worth the effort as this park preserves some of the nation's most dramatic land forms and rare life forms.

The main body of the park is a great forty mile wide trough or "sunken block" that began to subside millions of years ago when Mesa de Anguila and Sierra del Carmen cracked off and slowly tilted up to the west and east. The Rio Grande defines the park's southern boundary, slicing through three mountain ranges to form Santa Elena, Mariscal, and Boquillas Canyons. In the middle of the sunken block, rising higher than all the other mountains, the Chisos hang above the desert like a blue mirage.

What makes a desert, of course, is scanty precipitation. Because of the great range in altitude — from 1800 feet along the river to 7800 feet atop the Chisos — there is a wide variation in available moisture and in temperature throughout the park. This has produced an exceptional diversity in plant and animal habitats. Almost half the park is scrub desert, receiving less than ten inches of rainfall a year. This plant community begins right next to the river and runs up to about 3500 feet. Another forty-nine percent of the park is desert grassland, somewhat less dry, that you encounter on mesa tops and foothills to about 5500 feet. The Chisos receive about eighteen inches of rain per year and are considerably cooler than the desert. These mountains sustain typical southwestern woodlands with piñons, junipers, and oak trees. A lush green jumble grows in a narrow belt along each bank of the Rio Grande and pushes out across the desert along creeks and arroyos.

Big Bend National Park is home to more than 70 species of mammals, almost as many species of reptiles and amphibians, a score or more fishes and a fascinating host of insects. The wide choice of habitats makes Big Bend a paradise for birds. It offers more different resident and migrant birds than any other US National Park. Its location marks the southernmost reach of some United States plant and animal species, and the northernmost reach of some Mexican species. Some plants and animals found here occur nowhere else in the world.

I read and relaxed. Early in the evening, I took the nature trail hike just down the road from the campground. It was a study in contrasts. Where there was water, there were green marshes, lush growth, and multitudinous birds, but a climb up to the overlook is through typical desert country — many cacti and lots of sand. I climbed to the top and looked at the river. A mature Rio Grande here as compared to the frolicking mountain stream I had seen in Colorado. This river had changed the contour of the earth, carved canyons of great depth, and sustained an otherwise barren environment. It flowed, at this time of year, tranquilly and majestically, reflecting the azure sky and the rugged cliffs of the Sierra del Carmen. I sat up on the desert knoll watching the river below flow around a bend and through the canyons it had chiseled for millions of years. Looked off in the distance to mountain ranges within Mexico and marveled once again at the bounty of nature. There was a fine overview of the campground area looking lush and green way down below me. It was a timeless setting, this river and the mountains that had been here for eons.

Pulled myself back to the present. Went back to the park and civilization — or what we term civilization. The big news was the killing on the river. People were upset and, as is always the case, bad news travels fast. The story I heard was that a couple along with a male companion were rafting the river. A sniper on the Mexican side started shooting at them as they floated along like sitting ducks down in a narrow canyon. There's no easy way to get out of those canyons and definitely no place to hide. The rafters yelled up to the sniper begging him not to shoot, offering money or anything. But the "crazy" shot the husband and killed him and wounded the wife in her thigh. He left them down there in the canyon miles from help. A senseless act of inhumanity. The male companion was not hurt. He left the woman and her dead husband on a sand spit while he attempted to hike out for help. This woman spent the night down in the canyon with the body of her dead husband lying there beside her. The next day a rescue team reached them and got them out. People were unsettled. The rangers were nervous. No one had a clue as to who had done the sniping. A sad incident. Far removed from today's violent society, one would think, floating lazily down the river. Yet some "crazy" takes a shot and ends a life. It surely is a tenuous thread. All the more reason to savor each day as it comes.

Ink and I lounged outside, had dinner at the picnic table. Visited with a nice, and rather subdued, group of people who were sobered to think murder could happen even here in the Big Bend. The other topic of conversation was that half of Texas descends on this campground for Thanksgiving. I began to think I didn't want to participate in that event. It was no evening for decision making, however. Ink and I walked down our road at sunset. That crimson mountain in the last rays of the sun just blew me away. We lingered to watch it shade from crimson to pink, to violet, to lavender, to deep purple. Hiked quickly back to Tess before all the night beasties came out. Settled in as the coyotes started to howl.

After my day of loafing, I woke Monday morning knowing I had to tackle overdue chores. It was a day of mundane work laced with hikes and visiting. More and more vans, campers and rigs of all types were pouring into the park. I checked under Tessie's hood: the oil, water, batteries, brake fluid, and belts. Ever since my Cotulla experience, the gas gauge was not

.

working properly but I couldn't determine what was wrong with it. I washed windows, did dishes, cleaned the tape deck and paid fees for one more night at Rio Grande Village when the ranger stopped to chat. Got some postcards written. By late afternoon, all was sparkling except me. Ink had been brushed and her ears cleaned. I was cruddy, so I headed over for a shower and shampoo with seventy-five cents in my pocket and a change of clothes in a plastic bag.

The shower room was wall-to-wall women. I don't know where all these people were staying in the park, but it was dense here. I waited and finally had my turn in a shower stall. Communal showers leave a bit to be desired — there's never room to move, never enough space to place all your items. However, you grate your teeth and work it out. I felt intimidated by the fact that the water only lasted for five minutes. Had visions of being all lathered up when it stopped. Took my shower quickly and hated the stress. The water was not hot, it wasn't even tepid. In fact, it was cold. That did help me hurry. But to Big Bend National, I grant the "shitty shower award." It was the worst, most unsatisfying shower I had on the entire trip. I realize that the facilities had been used heavily; however, I'm sure this was not the first time a multitude of women and girls had descended on the shower room. Our government should plan ahead.

I warmed up walking back to the campground in the sun. Found I had a new neighbor across the road in a tent. This was only the second woman I had met on the entire trip who was also solo. Joan was from Austin and the two of us had a warm visit. After dinner, we sat by her fire and had a cup of tea together. The generators were really humming that evening. The campground was beginning to take on a carnival atmosphere. Joan and I visited until dark. When we settled, I told Ink we were going to look for a more quiet spot tomorrow. The moon was almost full. I lay in Tess and looked out at it and the cottonwoods and listened to the coyotes. I knew we'd find the perfect spot for Thanksgiving.

We woke next morning and got started. It was the day to move on and seek a less-peopled area. We had our hike, said good-bye to Joan, and went to the village. Filled the tank with gasoline, posted mail, and did a necessary load of wash. The laundry was as full of people as the shower room had been. There was a crowd of Mexicans who came over the border to use the facilities. They had heaps of clothing scattered over the floor and the tables. Looked like they made the trip only once a month. I had to wait, but it was fun to watch the hustle and bustle. I eventually got a washer and threw everything into it. There was a shady deck outside and I sat down to wait. Visited with others who were also waiting. Campers from Texas and all over the nation were pouring into the area.

I was talking with a woman who had lived in Truth or Consequences and was telling her that my son had gone to New Mexico Tech in Socorro, when a handsome man — lean and tan — interrupted with, "Did you say Saqqara?" I looked at him, at that tan and the shorts, and knew he was a Californian. Explained that I had said Socorro, New Mexico. He sat down and told all of us about his trip across northern Africa in a Land Rover and his travels in Egypt where he had visited the Old Kingdom city of Saqqara. He was an interesting man who had had some fascinating tours. He drove a van, nothing ostentatious, just a sturdy van. We chatted and exchanged stories of our travels. My laundry was finally dry and we got away from the village area before noon.

Outside the village and above the visitor's center, there's a road leading to the right which takes you to Boquillas Canyon. We had to take a look. As we were turning, standing alongside the road was a big coyote. They'd been serenading us each night. I waved my hello to Brother Coyote and thanked him for the night time songs.

We drove slowly along the road to Boquillas Canyon. Pulled into an area on top of the mesa at Boquillas Canyon Overlook. Boquillas is the largest of the three canyons in the park. It juts through the massive limestone of Sierra del Carmen. You look at these canyons carved by the river over eons and think, what force, what patience. The overlook was deserted. The American public tends to stay on the main roads always.

At the end of the parking site was one of those sturdy wooden signs erected by the park service with some information on this canyon. Sitting on top of the sign was a roadrunner. I grabbed the camera and took his picture sitting there atop the sign with the Sierra del Carmens behind him. I had just seated myself in Tessie when — almost as if he had materialized from the earth — a Mexican man appeared at my door. He was standing there by the open door.

I don't know why I wasn't startled by his sudden appearance, but I wasn't. Possibly it was the friendly smile and his gentle brown eyes. He was the stereotypical Mexican peasant: liquid brown eyes, white hair, wearing a loose white shirt and white trousers and a straw hat. He greeted me with, "Buenos dias."

I returned his greeting with a smile and lapsed easily into the little Spanish I knew. We spoke, as best we could, and I gathered that he was selling crystals. He held up two of them. Crystals from Mexico, he told me. One was a lavender color, but the other was a large piece of calcite. (My geologist son, Mark, tells me it's a rhombohedron.) I asked him how much he wanted for the large crystal, knowing that I didn't need another object cluttering up what little space I had. I thought, how enterprising of this man. He's not asking for a handout, he's selling a product. I bought the calcite. We talked and he told me his name was Pablo.

He invited me to come and see the other crystals he had. I walked back to a rock on which he had them spread. We discussed the beauty of this wild country and many things. He was a beautiful man. Before I left, I asked Pablo if he would stand by the wooden sign and I'd take his picture holding my crystal. He was delighted. I shook his hand and told him we must be on our way. Put my crystal on the floor up front and waved good-bye to this lovely person.

We drove on down to the end of the road and looked at the

canyon one more time. Then we headed back to the main road for more exploring. As I was driving, I thought, I suppose I should have been afraid when that man came up to the camper. I didn't know who this Mexican man was. It didn't occur to me to be leery or question what in the world Pablo was doing out there in the middle of nowhere. Obviously, I'm not a fearful person. It was an easy, comfortable encounter. But with the killing on the river, I probably should have used more discretion; however, I knew this lovely man was a friend. Pablo and I bonded and had a great visit and I had a beautiful crystal.

We drove through the desert country towards Panther Junction watching the Chisos loom larger and larger ahead of us. Passed Panther Junction and came to the road which led up into the Chisos. Ink and I agreed we should take a trip up into the mountains since it was only six miles to the Basin. Away we went to look at the mountains in the middle of the desert. The road to the basin isn't recommended for large rigs because of the sharp curves and steep grades so there was little traffic.

As soon as we turned onto Basin Drive, we started climbing and we climbed and climbed. Tess did her thing, slow but steady. We weren't in a hurry and it was fascinating to watch the change from dry, rainless desert, to a few scrub oaks, then juniper and pinyon. The higher we climbed, the more lush the countryside became. We were almost to the Basin when we were lucky enough to see a Sierra del Carmen whitetail deer standing beside the road. This little deer lives only in the Chisos and across the river in the Sierra del Carmen.

They're tiny and have smaller ears than the usual muledeer of the Southwest and are more grey in color. It was browsing at the roadside — a young buck in velvet — I snapped a picture from the driver's seat. I was elated to have seen one of these rare subspecies found nowhere else in the world.

We kept climbing and it was delightfully cool and green. Came to the Basin which is a tourist mecca with shops and cars. There were great granite outcroppings and it was wildly beautiful. We drove through the campground which was full. Was glad we couldn't stay 'cause I would have frozen my buns.

This point in the Basin Campground was 5400 feet with peaks rising to almost 8000 feet. The peaks that ring the Basin all came into being when molten rock squeezed up from deep within the earth. Some of the lava cooled so quickly that it cracked in long vertical fissures. Then, as the ages passed, joints toppled and square-faced peaks, buttresses, and free-standing spires emerged. Eons passed and the softer surface rocks wore away, exposing the dome-shaped peaks which now rim the Basin to the north and west.

This high country supports a great diversity of wildlife; bobcats, panthers, golden eagles, peregrine falcons, and an abundance of small animals and birds. We were in the Chisos too late in the season to see the Park's most famous bird, the Colima Warbler. It arrives in early April from southwest Mexico and leaves in mid-September. In all of the United States, it nests only here in the Chisos Mountains.

We meandered and looked. Then it was back down the road, back down to warmer country. At the junction, we headed to the left past Government Spring, Croton Spring to Santa Elena Junction where we turned south on the Ross Maxwell Scenic Drive. We were trying for Castellon and Cottonwood Campground. Stopped and took pictures of sotol growing thick as a forest on one slope. Kept glimpsing the Mule Ears Peaks as we rounded curves and ambled up and down hills. They rise 3800 feet and contain a spring which can be reached by a hiking trail. There wasn't traffic in this region of the park, in spite of the big holiday coming up. We were getting away from the great horde of tourists. Meandered and gawked in this remote region.

We were losing altitude as we drove this road. When we got to Castellon, we saw a sign giving the elevation as 2100 feet. Castellon is an historic town, but we didn't stop that afternoon. Drove on by and pulled into a primitive campground called Cottonwood, close to the river. When we pulled in, I knew we had found the spot. This was the place to be for Thanksgiving. The park had only portable outhouses, no electricity, and not many campers. Down the center of the grounds was a magnificent stand of cottonwoods starting to turn golden. At the far end of the grounds was a huge butte rearing its head above everything. I drove slowly and checked out the facilities. Chose a site over from the cottonwoods, but close to the johns, with a lovely mesquite shading the picnic table. It was level and sandy and there was a water faucet close by. Ink and I staked out our space. I was setting up when the Ranger came driving by. They come and register campers at this site. He was still shaken by the events on the river. He cautioned me not to leave the camper unlocked if I went away. Pointed to a barbed wire fence saying, "That's Mexico right over there. Be careful." I assured him that Ink and I were going to relax and stay put. This lad would have flipped had he seen me walking around a barren parking site with Pablo. We signed up for our space through November 25 and got that out of the way.

We walked the grounds and discovered a large herd of javelina. They stink. Ink had no inclination to bother with them, thank God. The birds were soaring and singing. The few campers were friendly and pleasant. It was a great place to be. We had dinner at the picnic table, gazing at the butte in the setting sun and feeling at peace with our world. I was happy we'd be here for a few days. Once again, I had been led wisely and well. The coyotes sang a lullaby intermingled with the chirps of crickets and little critters. The chorus lulled us to sleep.

The next day was one in which I sat and looked, just looked. It's very heady looking closely at nature and all her wonders. I had never taken time to sit and look before this trip, at least, not in this fashion. I reflected on the journey and the people I had met along the way. I had learned much — much about myself, much about my camper. I knew with a certainty that I had been right about seeking my bliss. I acknowledged that I was a self-sufficient person, a damned optimist who refused to take life or myself too seriously. I even learned that I liked my own company. I knew there were still kind, decent, helpful people in our country.

Ink was studying the trunk of the mesquite tree intently and I went to see what she was looking at. It was a bright green walking stick making its way slowly up the bark. We both watched it for a while. I hugged my dog and said, "Ink, I don't care who they might be, I doubt that two people could have traveled so far and had so many adventures and still have ended up loving each other the way we do. You're the world's best travel companion, my gal."

This phase of the journey was coming to an end. I knew I was not ready to stop and didn't intend to. It was comforting to know I'd be in Las Cruces with friends for the holidays, however. In spite of the pilgrimage being so filled with joy, it was nice to park up in a snug harbor from time to time and not have to find my way. I had been guided surely and well and was grateful. I sat there looking and thinking. Gave my thanks one day before the nation did.

Toward dusk, I saw a van pull in and thought that it looked vaguely familiar. It parked in a space down the way from us and behind Michael and Michelle, the students from Austin. Up the road came the pleasant California man I had chatted with at the Village on Monday.

Henry greeted me with, "Aha, I see you found this place, too." Ink was stretched out, I was knitting and we looked as ensconced as two old gypsies could be. Asked Henry to sit down. We both agreed this was the perfect spot. The weather was super, warm, brilliant days, cool, crisp nights. It was full moon that Wednesday and it rose directly over the great butte. Some hooty owls joined the chorus of coyotes and crickets for the night-time seranade. We were lulled to sleep quickly and slept well.

We awoke that Thanksgiving morning of 1988 in Cottonwood Campground at Big Bend to another incredible, perfect day. The sun was beaming, the cottonwoods were shimmering, the birds were singing, and there were muffled sounds of other campers round and about. I drank my coffee feeling very thankful indeed. Ink and I took a turn around the grounds and she took care of business.

As we were walking back to the camper, we passed Henry's van and he stepped out to say good morning. I spontaneously asked, "Henry, why don't you join us for Thanksgiving dinner?" I explained that it was canned ham and not quite the usual fare, but that we had lots of food and would love to share it. I suggested we eat about four-thirty at the picnic table. Henry accepted with alacrity, asking what he could bring. I smiled and suggested he bake a pumpkin pie, then we both laughed.

Ink and I went back and had breakfast, and, again, sat and looked. Michael and Michelle came by to ask me to keep watch over their camper while they hiked. I told them I planned to be at my site all day, not to fear. About noon, Henry drove down and invited me to join him for a trek across the river to the small Mexican village of Santa Elena. I declined, but said we'd see him for dinner. This thoughtful man asked, "Do you need anything?" I asked him to bring me a pack of cigarettes.

Preparation of this Thanksgiving meal was the easiest I'd ever experienced. When one has only a saucepot and two skillets, one keeps it simple. My biggest problem was how to cook everything in my meager utensils. Ended up doing the sweet potatoes in with the ham. That left the saucepot for the lima beans.

Henry walked up about four-thirty. The picnic table was set and the weather was cooperating. Ink frolicked with our guest and Henry patted her and gave her some attention. We ate and the dinner was passable: ham, sweet potatoes, lima beans, cranberry sauce, and rolls. Henry brought a can of peaches in lieu of pumpkin pie. It was cookies and peaches for dessert, with a cup of hot tea. He had also remembered my cigarettes.

We sat there under the mesquite tree amidst all that beauty and it was a bountiful feast. I was glad I had made the gesture and glad it had been Henry I had invited. This man was not into male-female posturing and neither was I. We spoke as two people who had discovered the joy and freedom of this lifestyle. He told me tales of his trip through North Africa. I told him of my journey. He asked, "Gosh, Barb, do you wake with the sun shining in and have this wonderful sense of well-being?"

"Oh, yes, many times. I've seen so much beauty but I still sit and look and am overjoyed with it."

It was a sharing of our feelings and views. None of the coy posturing. Henry was no Neanderthal man. He was a delightful person who viewed this free manner of living as I did. We sat and ate and talked until dusk. Henry had sold his house in Oakland, California, and had bought a piece of land in the Baja. He told me I should see that peninsula, and planted a seed. He very kindly urged me to write the story of my travels. I had to say I knew of no other way I could share my joyous experiences with the world; however, I always asked myself who would care what this old broad did. Henry took his leave and I took Inkus for a turn around the grounds. Just got back when Michelle and Michael came over with steak bones and goodies for Ink, saying she should have something special for Thanksgiving.

We closed up early. I had a hot bucket bath by candlelight. It was cozy sitting in my little womb scrubbing and listening to hooty owls and coyotes. Read for a short time then slept well after a memorable Thanksgiving at Big Bend National Park.

Friday, the winds came up and it was dusty. Not a day to sit at the picnic table, so I read and loafed in Tessie. Henry came by late in the morning to say good-bye. He was *en route* to Florida to spend the holidays with his brother. He was going east and I was going west. He thanked me again for the meal and I told him I had enjoyed his company. We both agreed that we didn't like to write. We didn't like the obligation imposed by exchanging addresses and saying you'd stay in touch, so we didn't do that. We shook hands and the last thing Henry said was, "Write that book, Barb." I still remember fondly that nice man who didn't play the male-female game, but was a fellow pilgrim and traveler.

There wasn't much activity in the campground with the wind blowing lustily. The church group played ball and games. Ink curled up under the camper, content to watch. I read and ate and loafed. The weather was finally taking on a winter tint.

I was ready to get to Las Cruces and the shelter of friends. It was the final phase of this journey. I was pleased with this trip and felt secure with my decision to continue after the holidays. When Ink and I woke, the church group was packing up and getting ready to leave. The wind had subsided and the sun was shining. The birds were calling raucously to one another in the cottonwoods. It was cold, but the kettle boiling and the sun's warm rays heated Tessie quickly. I sipped my coffee and knew that we, too, must be on our way. I had to grapple with the concept that I must get back to the real world when, for me, this world seemed more real. However, it was time to move on. The gypsy caravan was going to head out.

We packed it up and pulled out about 10 a.m. Went back to Castellon. It's an historic site that I wanted to see. In the early part of the century, Castellon had been a farming community. They grew crops and cotton in this riparian settlement. The profit motive helped with exploitation of even this formidable country. There were mining operations of mercury and cinnabar all around the region. Where there was water, a few settlements grew up. The settlers cut down all the trees to feed the mining furnaces and build houses. They cleared the land of its protective ground cover and turned this fragile ecosystem into a wasteland.

Man always wants to control nature. With the cutting of the trees, the land became more and more arid and farming was not feasible. It was only after the Park was established that the cottonwoods re-established themselves here on the flood plain at Castellon.

There were a number of small, quaint buildings and an old general store. I stopped at the ranger station to inquire about Old Maverick Road, which I had noticed on the Park map. As I saw it, the distance from Castellon to the entrance at Maverick, via the paved road, was 35 miles, whereas if I drove on out to Sierra Elena Canyon and then took Old Maverick Road cross-country, it was only 14 miles up to Maverick. I went into the station and asked the ranger about it. He said, "Well, it's pretty rough road, Ma'am, but you can make it. Doesn't look like we're gonna have any rain, so it should be passable." Seemed a good idea to me.

We looked a bit more at this settlement a million miles from anywhere. Then left Castellon and drove out the road to Santa Elena Canyon. This road winds along a bench that varies between fifty and a hundred feet high and gives you an idea of what water means to this arid land. We were atop the bench looking down on a vertical green line of cottonwoods, mesquite, and the ever-invasive tamarisk. It was lush and green where the river ran off to our left as we drove towards Santa Elena.

That canyon is proof of the force of this great river. The canyon mouth was in shadow, but the limestone cliffs rise forbiddingly in mute testimony to the power that cut through it over eons of time. The Rio Grande ranks with a few of the other rivers of the world that traverse desert country and leave it still alive: the Nile, the Indus, the Tigris and Euphrates, and the Colorado. The rollicking mountain stream I remembered so well in the mountains of Colorado had become an aged veteran here in the canyons of Big Bend.

Took my last look at the canyon and the river and we were on our way. The sign was up — Old Maverick Road — and I thought why not? It was quite an adventure. This was the most god-awful washboard road the gypsy caravan had been on in the whole trip. It stretched across the bleak Chihuahuan desert. Anyone with a modicum of sense would have turned around and retreated to paved highway, but I forged ahead, laughing and telling Tessie and Ink that we could make it.

It was slow going. Tessie was rattling and shaking, letting me know she did not like this road one bit. The closet door kept popping open and eventually the shelf came loose and fell down. I'd stop and fix everything, but in another two miles, the door would be swinging back and forth madly.

Ink had come up front. She sat in the passenger seat looking at me reproachfully. I knew she was thinking what in hell are we doing? We kept jolting along. In spite of my fellow travelers being unsettled and angry, I found it exhilarating and fun. I kept telling Ink and Tess we'd make it just fine as we jounced over a landscape that looked like the moon. It was a bad road, but magnificent country. There were wide arroyos which could wipe you out during a sudden rain. No moisture problems this day. However, the beds of those arroyos were sandy and I knew we had to keep going or we could bog down and never get out.

Just as I thought there's no one in the whole world out here, a big white Cadillac with Texas plates went around us speeding over this washboard road as if it was a freeway. I laughed and said, "See, girls, someone else is as crazy as I am." It was comforting to know an occasional car did take this by-pass. We were in the back country. As it was, this 14 mile "shortcut" took over an hour of hard driving. We crossed a cattle guard and were on paved road and shortly arrived at a restroom facility. Here we were.

I pulled in and stopped. Let Ink out to run. She was still looking at me quizzically. I walked around and swung my aching arms. Went to the middle of the road and took a shot down it so that I'd always remember Old Maverick Road. There was a good stand of lechuguilla here. This plant is the definitive species for the Chihuahuan Desert. It's a fiber plant with a bloom stalk that shoots up like an asparagus spear sometimes as high as 15 feet. The Indians used the fibers for matting and household items. It can reproduce both by seed and rhizomes. It flowers from the bottom up in close-packed purplish or yellowish blooms. It perishes by degrees. The blades dry while the bloom stalk can still be moist and green, but eventually it too turns into a dry wooden stalk. It's not an especially handsome plant, but is well adapted for this desert. It grows nowhere else in the world.

We walked and took a little break. I ate lunch standing beside Tessie where I could see for miles in all directions. Not a house, not another human being. Nothing moving. Big Bend looked as timeless and permanent as the planet itself and as beautiful and barren as the moon.

Got Ink back into the camper and assured the girls the road was smooth and paved from here on.

At Maverick, we caught Route 118 heading straight north. It was driving on a cloud after Old Maverick Road and everyone was happier. Arrived in Alpine, Texas, about 4:30 p.m. I decided to spend the night. Found a quiet campground on the outskirts of town and knew we'd not be bothered by traffic noises here. Pulled in and went into the office. Answered the same questions I had answered on the whole trip.

"You're all alone?"

"No. I have my dog."

"Aren't you afraid?"

"Of what?"

This older Texas man looked at me oddly, but directed me to a site. There was a distinct chill in the air. Winter was coming. Walked up a country road and let Ink do some exploring. Went to the laundry and did a load of wash which I folded while I fixed dinner. The warmth of the stove was welcome. Ink hopped in and I went for a shower and shampoo. The restrooms were warm and the water was hot. No one in the facilities, so I sang as I scrubbed. Bucket baths work, but a good, hot shower is better. Snuggled in early. It was cold that night in Alpine and I was thankful for the heat from Ink's furry body.

The camper was frigid Sunday morning when we woke. If there's one thing that depresses me, it's being cold. I hate to be cold. The kettle eased the chill. The sun rose higher and that helped, too. But it was cold. Ink didn't want to go outside. I sat there huddled up in my sleeping bag and knew I wanted to get to Las Cruces. It had been a glorious trip, but it was time to head for the warmth of good friends. It was time to take a respite from gypsying and the open road.

I ate breakfast, layered a bunch of clothes and went over to the phone booth. I called Sam and asked, "How would you like a guest?" Her response warmed my heart and my cold body. "Oh, Barbie, we thought you'd never get here. We've been waiting for you. When will you be here?"

"If you can put up with the gypsy caravan, we'll be in this evening."

"Great! We'll be looking for you."

We left Alpine about 10:30 a.m. We took Route 90 through scenic high country. There were canyons, juniper and pinyon stands, a few live oaks. Past Marfa, a Chinook coming toward us blinked lights and the driver waved. I hoped his rig carried him as safely as mine had carried me. Stopped in Van Horn and ate a restaurant lunch. It was too cold to picnic. Pulled onto Interstate 10 and it was clear sailing through El Paso and on north. We arrived in Las Cruces that Sunday evening, November 27, 1988, about five.

It was a warm and loving welcome, lots of hugs and joyful giggles. It was wonderful to be with Samantha and Theo. There were two new puppies to greet Ink. We both felt at home as we plugged in and popped up. We ate dinner together in Sam's cozy kitchen just like the old days. Sam had classes Monday. I was letting down and felt weary, so we didn't talk late that evening. We had time enough for that. We said our goodnight and Ink and I climbed into Tessie.

I lay there feeling grateful for the safety of a journey that had encompassed 12,000 miles, grateful for wonderful friends, and as safe and snug as when I was with Mark and Lois.

It had been an outward and inward journey for me. I knew who I was. There was a quiet assurance and satisfaction from having found my way and handling whatever came up. I did it. You can do anything you really want to do. I had wanted to make this pilgrimage. I was thankful to be back, thankful for a safe, joyful, loving journey and thankful to my God for leading me so well. We slept peacefully and soundly.

Footnote: When I had film developed in Las Cruces, I had photos of Boquillas Canyon, but nothing of Pablo. I had taken two shots of him by the sign, but they weren't there. Had the frame of the roadrunner, but no Pablo. Checked the negatives and the two shots of Pablo were black. It was an eerie sensation. I wonder to this day who I met at that deserted overlook. I still have my beautiful crystal and consider it quite a gift.

**INKWELL PRESS**
**P. O. Box 44817**
**Rio Rancho, NM  87174-4817**

**ORDER BLANK**

**HOW CAN I BE LOST?**

# of copies _____ @ $14.00_____

Shipping [$2.50]                _____

        **Total, enclosed**   _____


**Send to:**

    **Name**_____

    **Address**_____

    **City, State, Zip**_____